Your All-in-One Resource

On the CD that accompanies this book, you'll find a fully searchable version of this *Step by Step* book as well as additional resources to extend your learning. The reference library includes the following eBooks and reference materials:

- *Microsoft Computer Dictionary, Fifth Edition*
- Sample chapters and poster from *Look Both Ways: Help Protect Your Family on the Internet* by Linda Criddle
- *Windows Vista Product Guide*

The CD interface has a new look. You can use the tabs for an assortment of tasks:

- Check for book updates (if you have Internet access)
- Install the book's practice file
- Go online for product support or CD support
- Send us feedback

The following screen shot gives you a glimpse of the new interface.

Microsoft

Microsoft® Office Access® 2007 Step by Step

*Steve Lambert,
M. Dow Lambert III, and
Joan Preppernau*

PUBLISHED BY
Microsoft Press
A Division of Microsoft Corporation
One Microsoft Way
Redmond, Washington 98052-6399

Library of Congress Control Number: 2006937014

Printed and bound in the United States of America.

7 8 9 10 11 12 13 14 WCT 2 1 0

Distributed in Canada by H.B. Fenn and Company Ltd.

A CIP catalogue record for this book is available from the British Library.

Microsoft Press books are available through booksellers and distributors worldwide. For further information about international editions, contact your local Microsoft Corporation office or contact Microsoft Press International directly at fax (425) 936-7329. Visit our Web site at www.microsoft.com/mspress. Send comments to mspinput@microsoft.com.

Acquisitions Editor: Juliana Aldous Atkinson
Project Editor: Sandra Haynes

Body Part No. X12-48783

Contents

What do you think of this book? We want to hear from you!

Microsoft is interested in hearing your feedback so we can continually improve our books and learning resources for you. To participate in a brief online survey, please visit:

microsoft.com/learning/booksurvey

4   Sharing and Reusing Information   79

5   Simplifying Data Entry by Using Forms   103

What do you think of this book? We want to hear from you!

Microsoft is interested in hearing your feedback so we can continually improve our books and learning resources for you. To participate in a brief online survey, please visit:

microsoft.com/learning/booksurvey

About the Authors

Steve Lambert

Steve has written 18 books, most of which are about Microsoft applications. As President of Online Publishing and Programming Solutions, Inc. (OP²S), he has managed the development of many tools for creating and viewing training material. Steve takes advantage of the Internet and computer technology to work from home—a ten-acre horse ranch on the Olympic Peninsula. When not working on technology products, he and his wife Gale spend their time working on the property, training and riding horses, and picking up horse poop.

M. Dow Lambert III

During 20 years in academia, Dow authored or co-authored 19 social science research publications, developed curriculum and training programs for social services professionals, and managed longitudinal studies of human behavior. In 1995, he moved from academia to the private sector, where he worked for a small company that developed and maintained reservation systems for the travel industry. Here he learned the difference between writing research reports for scientific journals, writing technical specifications for programmers, and writing user guides for the people who actually needed to understand and use the software that his company produced. In his spare time, Dow and his wife Marlene enjoy birding and bird photography.

Joan Lambert Preppernau

Joan has worked in the training and certification industry for 12 years. As President of Online Training Solutions, Inc. (OTSI), Joan is responsible for guiding the translation of technical information and requirements into useful, relevant, and measurable training, learning, and certification deliverables. Joan is a Microsoft Certified Technology Specialist, a Microsoft Certified Applications Specialist (MCAS) Instructor, and the author of more than two dozen books about Windows and Office (for Windows and Mac). Joan lives in America's Finest City—San Diego, California—with her husband Barry, daughter Trinity, and stepson Charles.

The Team

Without the support of the hard-working members of the OTSI publishing team, this book would not exist. Susie Bayers and Marlene Lambert guided the editorial process, and Robert (RJ) Cadranell guided the production process. Lisa Van Every laid out the book using Adobe InDesign, and Jeanne Craver processed the graphics. Jaime Odell proofread the book, and Jan Bednarczuk created its index. Another important member of our team, Microsoft Press Series Editor Sandra Haynes, provided invaluable support throughout the writing and production processes.

Online Training Solutions, Inc. (OTSI)

OTSI specializes in the design, creation, and production of Office and Windows training products for information workers and home computer users. For more information about OTSI, visit

www.otsi.com

Introducing Access 2007

Microsoft Office Access 2007 is a powerful relational database application that includes hundreds of tools that allow you to quickly start tracking, sharing, and reporting information, even if you are new to database development. Users have access to a large library of professionally designed application templates, wizards that automatically create tables, forms, queries, and reports, and extensive local and online help resources.

Access supports sharing data with other sources, including other programs in the 2007 Microsoft Office system, Microsoft SQL Server, Microsoft SharePoint Products and Services, and documents in XML, HTML, XPS, and PDF formats. Advanced features allow you to create sophisticated executable database applications for use by employees and customers to gather and view data without their needing to know anything at all about database design or development.

This book gives you straightforward instructions for using Access to create databases. It takes you from knowing little or nothing about Access—or, for that matter, about databases—to a level of expertise that will enable you to create complex databases for use by one person or by many people.

New Features

There's no question that Microsoft Office Access has been extensively reworked and improved with this version. The new Microsoft Office Fluent user interface, designed to make the features you need easily available when you need them, is an obvious indicator. But beyond the appearance and navigation, Access 2007 also has a lot of new and improved features that really do make this a superior program to its predecessors. Because there are so many changes in this version, we don't identify new features with a special margin icon (as we did in previous versions of this book). We do, however, list them here. Throughout this book, we include complete coverage of features that are new in Access 2007, including the benefits of the feature, how to use it, and any potential problems you might encounter.

If you're upgrading to Access 2007 from a previous version, you're probably more interested in the differences between the old and new versions and how they will affect you than you are in the basic functionality of Access. To help you identify the entire scope of change from the version of Access you're familiar with, we've listed here the new features introduced in Access 2002 and Access 2003, as well as in Access 2007.

If You Are Upgrading from Access 2003

Access 2007 has a long list of new and improved features that make it easier than ever to create databases to track, share, manage, and audit information. To locate information about a specific feature, see the index at the back of this book:

- **The Ribbon.** This feature of the Office Fluent user interface organizes the most common commands for any database object into tabs and groups so that the appropriate commands are immediately accessible for the current object.

- **Quick Access Toolbar.** You can customize a portion of this toolbar, displayed above or below the Ribbon, to include commands you regularly use, regardless of which Ribbon tab or database object is currently active.

- **Navigation Pane.** The customizable Navigation Pane replaces the Database window from Access 2003. You can display or hide all tables, queries, forms, reports, macros, and modules, or create a custom group to display only the objects that you select. You can hide the Navigation Pane to make more room on the screen for your database object.

- **View toolbar.** This context-sensitive toolbar located in the lower-right corner of the program window provides single-click switching among supported views of the current database object, including Datasheet view, Design view, PivotTable view, PivotChart view, Form view, and Layout view.

- **Database object display options.** Choose from Tabbed Documents, in which you can quickly switch between multiple database objects by clicking tabs at the top of the database window, and Overlapping windows that you can arrange individually on the screen.

- **Template library.** Quickly locate and download professionally designed templates for common database projects.

- **Improved sorting and filtering.** Easily sort all records in a table based on one or more fields, or filter a table or form to display or not display records matching multiple criteria.

- **Layout view.** Redesign a form or report while viewing it.

- **Stacked and Tabular layouts.** Group controls in a form or report layout so you can easily manipulate the entire group as one unit.

- **Automatic calendar.** The date/time data type includes an optional calendar control. Click the calendar, and select the date you want.

- **Rich Text.** Memo fields now support most common formatting options, including fonts, color, and character formatting. The formatting is stored with the database.

- **Create tab.** Quickly create a new table, form, query, report, macro, SharePoint list, or other Access object.

- **Totals function.** Add a totals row to a query, and select from a list of formulas to automatically calculate aggregate values for forms and reports.

- **Field List pane.** Drag and drop fields from one or more related or unrelated tables onto your active table.

- **Attachment data type.** Attach photos and other files to a database record.

- **Embedded macros.** Macros embedded in a form or report offer a higher level of security in database applications.

- **Microsoft Access Help system.** Easily search built-in and online end-user and developer support content from within Access.

- **Share information.** Easily import and export data between Access and other Microsoft Office applications, or XML, HTML, PDF, and dBase files; collect information through e-mail surveys in Microsoft Office Outlook and automatically update your database with the responses; create or link a database with a SharePoint list; publish your database to a SharePoint library and allow users to update and extract information.

- **Improved report design.** Quickly create a professional-looking report, complete with logo, header, and footer. Use Report view, combined with filters, to browse only selected records in the report.

- **Group, Sort, and Total pane.** This feature makes it much easier to group and sort data in reports, and add totals from a drop-down list.

- **Enhanced security.** Adding password protection to a database now causes Access to automatically encrypt the database when it closes, and decrypt it when it opens.

If You Are Upgrading from Access 2002

In addition to the features listed in the previous section, if you're upgrading from Access 2002 (part of the Microsoft Office XP program suite), you'll find the following:

- **Smart Tags.** Track types of data, such as dates, names, and addresses, which can be used in multiple ways.

- **Transform.** Transform script to data when you import or export it.

- **Support for Windows Theming.** Change your display theme.

- **Property Update Options.** Quickly update input mask options.

- **Automatic Error Checking.** Identify and correct errors in forms and reports.

- **Back Up Database.** Quickly back up your database with the click of a button.

If You Are Upgrading from Access 2000

In addition to the features listed in the previous sections, if you're upgrading from Access 2000, you'll find the following:

- **Speech recognition.** Give commands and dictate text.
- **Data Access Page Designer.** Efficiently design data access pages.
- **Save as data access pages.** Save existing forms and reports as pages that can be viewed over the Web.
- **Conversion error logging.** Log errors when converting Access 95, Access 97, and Access 2000 databases to Access 2002 file format.
- **Multiple undo and redo.** Undo or redo several actions instead of just the last one.
- **PivotTables and PivotCharts.** Analyze data by creating dynamic views of data.
- **XML input and output.** Import XML data and publish Access data to the Web by exporting it in XML format.
- **Stored Procedure Designer.** Create simple SQL Server stored procedures.
- **Batch updating.** Save updates to records on a local computer, and send them to the server all at once.
- **Script language support.** Set preferences for complex script languages, including the reading direction.

Let's Get Started!

There are so many new and improved features to this already feature-rich program that there are bound to be some exciting discoveries for even the most advanced users. If you are new to Access, you will find many automated features that let you painlessly create databases and add queries, forms, and professional-looking reports to track and share your data. We look forward to showing you around Microsoft Office Access 2007.

Information for Readers Running Windows XP

The graphics and the operating system–related instructions in this book reflect the Windows Vista user interface. However, Windows Vista is not required; you can also use a computer running Windows XP.

Most of the differences you will encounter when working through the exercises in this book on a computer running Windows XP center around appearance rather than functionality. For example, the Windows Vista Start button is round rather than rectangular and is labeled with the Windows Vista logo rather than the word *Start*; window frames and window-management buttons look different; and if your system supports Windows Aero, the window frames might be transparent.

In this section, we provide steps for navigating to or through menus and dialog boxes in Windows XP that differ from those provided in the exercises in this book. For the most part, these differences are small enough that you will have no difficulty in completing the exercises.

Managing the Practice Files

The instructions given in the "Using the Companion CD" section are specific to Windows Vista. The only differences when installing, using, uninstalling, and removing the practice files supplied on the companion CD are the default installation location and the uninstall process.

On a computer running Windows Vista, the default installation location of the practice files is *Documents\Microsoft Press\Access2007SBS*. On a computer running Windows XP, the default installation location is *My Documents\Microsoft Press\Access2007SBS*. If your computer is running Windows XP, whenever an exercise tells you to navigate to your *Documents* folder, you should instead go to your *My Documents* folder.

To uninstall the practice files from a computer running Windows XP:

1. On the Windows taskbar, click the **Start** button, and then click **Control Panel**.
2. In **Control Panel**, click (or in Classic view, double-click) **Add or Remove Programs**.

3. In the **Add or Remove Programs** window, click **Microsoft Office Access 2007 Step by Step**, and then click **Remove**.

4. In the **Add or Remove Programs** message box asking you to confirm the deletion, click **Yes**.

> **Important** If you need help installing or uninstalling the practice files, please see the "Getting Help" section later in this book. Microsoft Product Support Services does not provide support for this book or its companion CD.

Using the Start Menu

To start Access 2007 on a computer running Windows XP:

→ Click the **Start** button, point to **All Programs**, click **Microsoft Office**, and then click **Microsoft Office Access 2007**.

Folders on the Windows Vista Start menu expand vertically. Folders on the Windows XP Start menu expand horizontally. You will notice this variation between the images shown in this book and your Start menu.

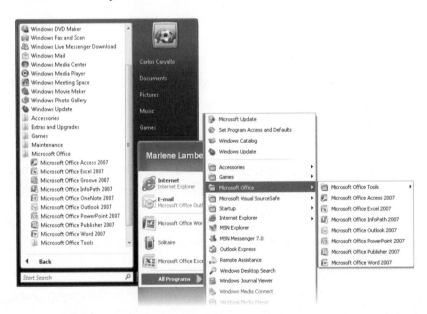

Navigating Dialog Boxes

On a computer running Windows XP, some of the dialog boxes you will work with in the exercises not only look different from the graphics shown in this book but also work differently. These dialog boxes are primarily those that act as an interface between Access and the operating system, including any dialog box in which you navigate to a specific location. For example, here are the Open dialog boxes from Access 2007 running on Windows Vista and Windows XP and some examples of ways to navigate in them.

Windows XP version   Windows Vista version

To navigate to the *Exploring* folder in Windows Vista:

→ In the **Favorite Links** pane, click **Documents**. Then in the folder content pane, double-click *Microsoft Press*, *Access2007SBS*, and then *Exploring*.

To move back to the *Access2007SBS* folder in Windows Vista:

Back

→ In the upper-left corner of the dialog box, click the **Back** button.

To navigate to the *Exploring* folder in Windows XP:

→ On the **Places** bar, click **My Documents**. Then in the folder content pane, double-click *Microsoft Press*, *Access2007SBS*, and then *Exploring*.

To move back to the *Access2007SBS* folder in Windows XP:

Up One Level

→ On the toolbar, click the **Up One Level** button.

The Microsoft Business Certification Program

Desktop computing proficiency is becoming increasingly important in today's business world. As a result, when screening, hiring, and training employees, more employers are relying on the objectivity and consistency of technology certification to ensure the competence of their workforce. As an employee or job seeker, you can use technology certification to prove that you already have the skills you need to succeed, saving current and future employers the trouble and expense of training you.

The Microsoft Business Certification program is designed to assist employees in validating their Windows Vista skills and 2007 Microsoft Office program skills. There are two paths to certification:

- A Microsoft Certified Application Specialist (MCAS) is an individual who has demonstrated worldwide skill standards for Windows Vista or the 2007 Microsoft Office suite through a certification exam in Windows Vista or in one or more of the 2007 Microsoft Office programs, including Microsoft Office Word 2007, Microsoft Office Excel 2007, Microsoft Office PowerPoint 2007, Microsoft Office Outlook 2007, and Microsoft Office Access 2007.

- A Microsoft Certified Application Professional (MCAP) is an individual who has taken his or her knowledge of the 2007 Microsoft Office suite and of Microsoft SharePoint products and technologies to the next level and has demonstrated through a certification exam that he or she can use the collaborative power of the Office suite to accomplish job functions such as Budget Analysis and Forecasting, or Content Management and Collaboration.

After attaining certification, you can include the MCAS or MCAP logo with the appropriate certification designator on your business cards and other personal promotional materials. This logo attests to the fact that you are proficient in the applications or cross-application skills necessary to achieve the certification.

Selecting a Certification Path

When selecting the Microsoft Business Certification path that you would like to pursue, you should assess the following:

- The program and program version(s) with which you are familiar
- The length of time you have used the program
- Whether you have had formal or informal training in the use of that program

Candidates for MCAS-level certification are expected to successfully complete a wide range of standard business tasks, such as formatting a document or spreadsheet. Successful candidates generally have six or more months of experience with Windows Vista or the specific Office program, including either formal, instructor-led training or self-study using MCAS-approved books, guides, or interactive computer-based materials.

Candidates for MCAP-level certification are expected to successfully complete more complex, business-oriented tasks utilizing advanced functionality with the combined 2007 Microsoft Office suite of products. Successful candidates generally have between six months and one or more years of experience with the programs, including formal, instructor-led training or self-study using MCAP-approved materials.

Becoming a Microsoft Certified Application Specialist—Microsoft Office Access 2007

Every MCAS and MCAP certification exam is developed from a set of exam skill standards that are derived from studies of how Windows Vista and the 2007 Office programs are used in the workplace. Because these skill standards dictate the scope of each exam, they provide you with critical information on how to prepare for certification.

To become certified as a Microsoft Certified Application Specialist for Microsoft Office Access 2007, you must demonstrate proficiency in these six areas:

- **Structuring a database.** You must demonstrate the ability to define the appropriate tables, fields, and data types for a database; create, modify, and print table relationships; set, change, and remove primary keys; and split a database.
- **Creating and formatting database elements.** You must demonstrate the ability to create a database from scratch and from a template; create, modify, rename, summarize, and delete tables; create and modify fields and field properties; create and modify various types of forms and reports.

- **Entering and modifying data.** You must demonstrate the ability to enter, edit, delete, and move among records; find and replace data; attach documents to records; and import data or link to external data.

- **Creating and modifying queries.** You must demonstrate the ability to create various types of queries based on one table or multiple tables; add tables to and remove tables from queries; add criteria, joins, calculated fields, and aliases; and create sum, average, min, max, and count queries.

- **Presenting and sharing data.** You must demonstrate the ability to sort and filter data in tables, queries, reports, and forms; create and modify charts; export data from tables and queries; save database objects as other file types; and print database objects.

- **Managing and maintaining databases.** You must demonstrate the ability to back up, compact, and repair a database; encrypt a database by using a password; set database options and properties; identify object dependencies; print database information; and reset or refresh table links.

Taking a Microsoft Business Certification Exam

The MCAS and MCAP certification exams for Windows Vista and the 2007 Office programs are performance-based and require you to complete business-related tasks by using an interactive simulation (a digital model) of the Windows Vista operating system of one or more of the programs in the Office suite.

Test-Taking Tips

- Follow all instructions provided in each question completely and accurately.

- Enter requested information as it appears in the instructions, but without duplicating the formatting unless you are specifically instructed to do otherwise. For example, the text and values you are asked to enter might appear in the instructions in bold and underlined (for example, **text**), but you should enter the information without applying these formats.

- Close all dialog boxes before proceeding to the next exam question, unless you are specifically instructed to do otherwise.

- Don't close task panes before proceeding to the next exam question unless, you are specifically instructed to do otherwise.

- If you are asked to print a document, spreadsheet, chart, report, or slide, perform the task, but be aware that nothing will actually be printed.

- Don't worry about extra keystrokes or mouse clicks. Your work is scored based on its result, not on the method you use to achieve that result (unless a specific method is indicated in the instructions), and not on the time you take to complete the question.

- If your computer becomes unstable during the exam (for example, if the exam does not respond or the mouse no longer functions) or if a power outage occurs, contact a testing center administrator immediately. The administrator will restart the computer and return the exam to the point where the interruption occurred with your score intact.

Certification

At the conclusion of the exam, you will receive a score report, which you can print with the assistance of the testing center administrator. If your score meets or exceeds the passing standard (the minimum required score), you will be mailed a printed certificate within approximately 14 days.

More Information

To learn more about the Microsoft Certified Application Specialist exams and courseware, visit

www.microsoft.com/learning/mcp/mcas/

To learn more about the Microsoft Certified Application Professional exams and courseware, visit

www.microsoft.com/learning/mcp/mcap/

Features and Conventions of This Book

This book has been designed to lead you step by step through all the tasks you are most likely to want to perform in Microsoft Office Access 2007. If you start at the beginning and work your way through all the exercises, you will gain enough proficiency to be able to manage complex databases through Access. However, each topic is self contained. If you have worked with a previous version of Access, or if you completed all the exercises and later need help remembering how to perform a procedure, the following features of this book will help you locate specific information:

- **Detailed table of contents.** A listing of the topics and sidebars within each chapter.

- **Chapter thumb tabs.** Easily locate the beginning of the chapter you want.

- **Topic-specific running heads.** Within a chapter, quickly locate the topic you want by looking at the running head of odd-numbered pages.

- **Quick Reference.** General instructions for each procedure covered in specific detail elsewhere in the book. Refresh your memory about a task while working with your own documents.

- **Detailed index.** Look up specific tasks and features and general concepts in the index, which has been carefully crafted with the reader in mind.

- **Companion CD.** Contains the practice files needed for the step-by-step exercises, as well as a fully searchable electronic version of this book and other useful resources.

In addition, we provide a glossary of terms for those times when you need to look up the meaning of a word or the definition of a concept.

You can save time when you use this book by understanding how the *Step by Step* series shows special instructions, keys to press, buttons to click, and so on.

Convention	Meaning
(CD icon)	This icon at the end of a chapter introduction indicates information about the practice files provided on the companion CD for use in the chapter.
USE	This paragraph preceding a step-by-step exercise indicates the practice files that you will use when working through the exercise.
BE SURE TO	This paragraph preceding or following an exercise indicates any requirements you should attend to before beginning the exercise or actions you should take to restore your system after completing the exercise.
OPEN	This paragraph preceding a step-by-step exercise indicates files that you should open before beginning the exercise.
CLOSE	This paragraph following a step-by-step exercise provides instructions for closing open files or programs before moving on to another topic.
1 2	Blue numbered steps guide you through step-by-step exercises and Quick Reference versions of procedures.
1 2	Black numbered steps guide you through procedures in sidebars and expository text.
→	An arrow indicates a procedure that has only one step.
See Also	These paragraphs direct you to more information about a given topic in this book or elsewhere.
Troubleshooting	These paragraphs explain how to fix a common problem that might prevent you from continuing with an exercise.
Tip	These paragraphs provide a helpful hint or shortcut that makes working through a task easier, or information about other available options.
Important	These paragraphs point out information that you need to know to complete a procedure.
(Save icon) Save	The first time you are told to click a button in an exercise, a picture of the button appears in the left margin. If the name of the button does not appear on the button itself, the name appears under the picture.
Enter	In step-by-step exercises, keys you must press appear as they would on a keyboard.
Ctrl + Home	A plus sign (+) between two key names means that you must hold down the first key while you press the second key. For example, "press Ctrl + Home" means "hold down the Ctrl key while you press the Home key."
Program interface elements	In steps, the names of program elements, such as buttons, commands, and dialog boxes, are shown in black bold characters.
User input	Anything you are supposed to type appears in blue bold characters.
Glossary terms	Terms that are explained in the glossary at the end of the book are shown in blue italic characters.

Using the Companion CD

The companion CD included with this book contains the practice files you'll use as you work through the book's exercises, as well as other electronic resources that will help you learn how to use Microsoft Office Access 2007.

What's on the CD?

The following table lists the practice files supplied on the companion CD.

Chapter	Files
Chapter 1: Exploring Access 2007	*Exploring/Working.accdb* *Exploring/Opening.accdb* *Exploring/Tables.accdb* *Exploring/Queries.accdb* *Exploring/Forms.accdb* *Exploring/Reports.accdb* *Exploring/Print.accdb*
Chapter 2: Creating a Database	*Creating/TableTemplate.accdb* *Creating/Manipulating.accdb*
Chapter 3: Populating a Database	*Populating/ImportAccess.accdb* *Populating/Products.accdb* *Populating/Customers.xlsx* *Populating/ImportExcel.accdb* *Populating/Employees.txt* *Populating/ImportText.accdb* *Populating/ImportXML.accdb* *Populating/OrderDetails.xml* *Populating/OrderDetails.xsd* *Populating/Orders.xml* *Populating/ImportHTML.accdb* *Populating/NewCust.html* *Populating/ImportDbase.accdb* *Populating/Ship.dbf*

Chapter	Files
Chapter 4: Sharing and Reusing Information	*Sharing/ExportAccess.accdb* *Sharing/Exported.accdb* *Sharing/ExportExcel.accdb* *Sharing/ExportWord.accdb* *Sharing/ExportText.accdb* *Sharing/ExportXML.accdb* *Sharing/ExportHTML.accdb* *Sharing/CopyOffice.accdb*
Chapter 5: Simplifying Data Entry by Using Forms	*Simplifying/CreateFormTool.accdb* *Simplifying/RefineProperties.accdb* *Simplifying/RefineLayout.accdb* *Simplifying/AddControls.accdb* *Simplifying/CustomersFormLogo.jpg* *Simplifying/VBA.accdb* *Simplifying/AftUpdate.txt* *Simplifying/CreateWizard.accdb* *Simplifying/AddSubform.accdb*
Chapter 6: Locating Specific Information	*Locating/SortTable.accdb* *Locating/FilterTable.accdb* *Locating/FilterForm.accdb* *Locating/MultipleCriteria.accdb* *Locating/QueryDesign.accdb* *Locating/QueryWizard.accdb* *Locating/Calculate.accdb*
Chapter 7: Keeping Your Information Accurate	*Accuracy/FieldTest.accdb* *Accuracy/Size.accdb* *Accuracy/Accurate.accdb* *Accuracy/Validate.accdb* *Accuracy/SimpleLookup.accdb* *Accuracy/MulticolumnLookup.accdb* *Accuracy/Update.accdb* *Accuracy/Delete.accdb* *Accuracy/Prevent.accdb*

Chapter	Files
Chapter 8: Working with Reports	*Reports/Wizard.accdb* *Reports/ModifyDesign.accdb* *Reports/Manually.accdb* *Reports/ModifyContent.accdb* *Reports/AddSubreport.accdb* *Reports/Printing.accdb*
Chapter 9: Making Your Database Easy to Use	*Easy/Switchboard.accdb* *Easy/CustomCategory.accdb* *Easy/Features.accdb* *Easy/Icon.ico*
Chapter 10: Securing and Sharing Information	*Securing/Password.accdb* *Securing/Prevent.accdb* *Securing/Distribute.accdb*

In addition to the practice files, the CD contains some exciting resources that will really enhance your ability to get the most out of using this book and Access 2007, including the following:

- *Microsoft Office Access 2007 Step by Step* in eBook format

- *Microsoft Computer Dictionary, Fifth Edition*

- Sample chapter and poster from *Look Both Ways: Help Protect Your Family on the Internet* (Linda Criddle, 2007)

> **Important** The companion CD for this book does not contain the Access 2007 software. You should purchase and install that program before using this book.

Minimum System Requirements

2007 Microsoft Office System

The 2007 Microsoft Office system includes the following programs:

- Microsoft Office Access 2007
- Microsoft Office Communicator 2007
- Microsoft Office Excel 2007
- Microsoft Office Groove 2007
- Microsoft Office InfoPath 2007
- Microsoft Office OneNote 2007
- Microsoft Office Outlook 2007
- Microsoft Office Outlook 2007 with Business Contact Manager
- Microsoft Office PowerPoint 2007
- Microsoft Office Publisher 2007
- Microsoft Office Word 2007

No single edition of the 2007 Office system installs all of the above programs. Specialty programs available separately include Microsoft Office Project 2007, Microsoft Office SharePoint Designer 2007, and Microsoft Office Visio 2007.

To install and run these programs, your computer needs to meet the following minimum requirements:

- 500 megahertz (MHz) processor
- 256 megabytes (MB) RAM
- CD or DVD drive
- 2 gigabytes (GB) available hard disk space; a portion of this disk space will be freed if you select the option to delete the installation files

> **Tip** Hard disk requirements will vary depending on configuration; custom installation choices might require more or less hard disk space.

- Monitor with 800×600 screen resolution; 1024×768 or higher recommended
- Keyboard and mouse or compatible pointing device

- Internet connection, 128 kilobits per second (Kbps) or greater, for download and activation of products, accessing Microsoft Office Online and online Help topics, and any other Internet-dependent processes

- Windows Vista with Service Pack 1 (SP1) or later, Microsoft Windows XP with Service Pack 2 (SP2), or Microsoft Windows Server 2003 or later

- Windows Internet Explorer 7 or Microsoft Internet Explorer 6 with service packs

The 2007 Microsoft Office suites, including Office Basic 2007, Office Home & Student 2007, Office Standard 2007, Office Small Business 2007, Office Professional 2007, Office Ultimate 2007, Office Professional Plus 2007, and Office Enterprise 2007, all have similar requirements.

Step-by-Step Exercises

In addition to the hardware, software, and connections required to run the 2007 Microsoft Office system, you will need the following to successfully complete the exercises in this book:

- Access 2007, Excel 2007, and Outlook 2007

- Access to a printer

- 52 MB of available hard disk space for the practice files

Installing the Practice Files

You need to install the practice files in the correct location on your hard disk drive before you can use them in the exercises. Follow these steps:

1. Remove the companion CD from the envelope at the back of the book, and insert it into the CD drive of your computer. If the **AutoPlay** window opens, click **Run startcd.exe**.

   The Microsoft Software License Terms appear. To use the practice files, you must accept the terms of the license agreement.

2. Click **I accept the agreement**, and then click **Next**.

   After you accept the license agreement, the CD interface appears.

> **Important** If the menu screen does not appear, click the Start button, and then click Computer. Display the Folders list in the Navigation Pane, click the icon for your CD drive, and then in the right pane, double-click the StartCD executable file.

3. Click **Install Practice Files**. If the **File Download** and/or **Internet Explorer Security** dialog boxes open, click **Run**.

4. On the **Welcome** page of the InstallShield Wizard, click **Next**. On the **License Agreement** page, click **I accept the terms in the license agreement**, and then click **Next**. Click **Next** on the first screen, and then click **Next** to accept the terms of the license agreement on the next screen.

5. If you want to install the practice files to a location other than the default folder (*Documents\Microsoft Press\Access2007SBS*), click the **Change** button, select the new drive and path, and then click **OK**.

> **Important** If you install the practice files to a location other than the default, you will need to substitute that path within the exercises.

6. On the **Custom Setup** page, click **Next**, and then on the **Ready to Install the Program** screen, click **Install**.

7. After the practice files have been installed, click **Finish**.

8. Close the **Step by Step Companion CD** window.

9. Remove the companion CD from the CD drive, and return it to the envelope at the back of the book.

Adding the Practice File Folder to the Trusted Locations List

The databases provided as practice files for this book contain macros. You can enable the macros in all the practice databases by adding the practice file folder to the list of Trusted Locations for Access 2007.

Follow these steps:

1. Click the **Microsoft Office Button**, and then click **Access Options**.

2. On the **Trust Center** page of the **Access Options** dialog box, click **Trust Center Settings**.

3. On the **Trusted Locations** page of the **Trust Center** dialog box, click **Add new location**.

4. In the **Microsoft Office Trusted Location** dialog box, click **Browse**.

5. In the **Browse** dialog box, browse to your *Documents\Microsoft Press\ Access2007SBS* folder, and then click **OK**.

6. In the **Microsoft Office Trusted Location** dialog box, select the **Subfolders of this location are also trusted** check box, and then click **OK** in each of the open dialog boxes.

If you prefer to not do this, you can enable macros in an individual database by clicking Options in the Security Warning area that appears at the top of the content pane. In the Microsoft Office Security Options dialog box, selecting the Enable This Content option, and then clicking OK.

See Also For more information about the Access 2007 Trust Center macro settings, see the sidebar "Enabling Macros and Other Database Content" in Chapter 1, "Exploring Access 2007."

Using the Practice Files

When you install the practice files from the companion CD that accompanies this book, the files are stored on your hard disk in chapter-specific subfolders under *Documents\ Microsoft Press\Access2007SBS*. Each exercise is preceded by a paragraph that lists the files needed for that exercise and explains any preparations needed before you start working through the exercise. Here are examples:

USE the *Opening* database. This practice file is located in the *Microsoft Press\Access2007SBS\ Exploring* folder.

BE SURE TO start your computer, but don't start Access before starting this exercise.

You can browse to the practice files in Windows Explorer by following these steps:

Start

1. On the Windows taskbar, click the **Start** button, and then click **Documents**.

2. In your *Documents* folder, double-click *Microsoft Press*, double-click *Access2007SBS*, and then double-click a specific chapter folder.

You can browse to the practice files from an Access 2007 dialog box by following these steps:

1. On the **Favorite Links** pane in the dialog box, click **Documents**.

2. In your *Documents* folder, double-click *Microsoft Press*, double-click *Access2007SBS*, and then double-click the specified chapter folder.

Removing and Uninstalling the Practice Files

After you finish working through this book, delete the practice messages, appointments, contacts, and other Outlook items you created while working through the exercises, and then uninstall the practice files that were installed from the companion CD. Follow these steps:

Start

1. On the Windows taskbar, click the **Start** button, and then click **Control Panel**.

2. In **Control Panel**, under **Programs**, click the **Uninstall a program** task.

3. In the **Programs and Features** window, click **Microsoft Office Access 2007 Step by Step**, and then on the toolbar at the top of the window, click the **Uninstall** button.

4. If the **Programs and Features** message box asking you to confirm the deletion appears, click **Yes**.

See Also If you need additional help installing or uninstalling the practice files, see "Getting Help" later in this book.

> **Important** Microsoft Product Support Services does not provide support for this book or its companion CD.

> Digital Content for Digital Book Readers: If you bought a digital-only edition of this book, you can enjoy select content from the print edition's companion CD.
>
> Visit *go.microsoft.com/fwlink/?LinkId=91292* to get your downloadable content. This content is always up-to-date and available to all readers.

Getting Help

Every effort has been made to ensure the accuracy of this book and the contents of its companion CD. If you do run into problems, please contact the sources listed below for assistance.

Getting Help with This Book and Its Companion CD

If your question or issue concerns the content of this book or its companion CD, please first search the online Microsoft Press Knowledge Base, which provides support information for known errors in or corrections to this book, at the following Web site:

www.microsoft.com/mspress/support/search.asp

If you do not find your answer at the online Knowledge Base, send your comments or questions to Microsoft Press Technical Support at:

mspinput@microsoft.com

Getting Help with Access 2007

If your question is about Microsoft Office Access 2007, and not about the content of this Microsoft Press book, your first recourse is the Access Help system. This system is a combination of tools and files stored on your computer when you installed the 2007 Microsoft Office system and, if your computer is connected to the Internet, information available from Microsoft Office Online. There are several ways to find general or specific Help information:

- To find out about an item on the screen, you can display a *ScreenTip*. For example, to display a ScreenTip for a button, point to the button without clicking it. The ScreenTip gives the button's name, the associated keyboard shortcut if there is one, and unless you specify otherwise, a description of what the button does when you click it.

- In the Access program window, you can click the Microsoft Office Access Help button (a question mark in a blue circle) at the right end of the Ribbon to display the Access Help window.

● After opening a dialog box, you can click the Help button (also a question mark) at the right end of the dialog box title bar to display the Access Help window with topics related to the functions of that dialog box already identified.

To practice getting help, you can work through the following exercise.

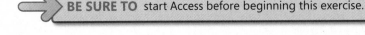

BE SURE TO start Access before beginning this exercise.

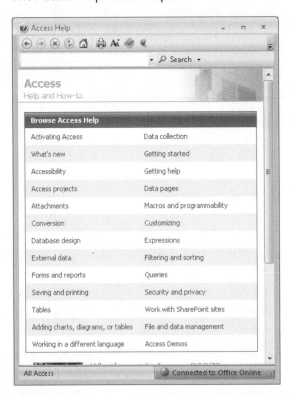

Microsoft Office
Access Help

1. At the right end of the Ribbon, click the **Microsoft Office Access Help** button.

The Access Help window opens.

2. In the list of topics in the **Access Help** window, click **Activating Access**.

Access Help displays a list of topics related to activating Microsoft Office system programs. You can click any topic to display the corresponding information.

Show Table of
Contents

3. On the toolbar, click the **Show Table of Contents** button.

The Table Of Contents appears in the left pane, organized by category, like the table of contents in a book.

Clicking any category (represented by a book icon) displays that category's topics (represented by help icons).

Category   Topic

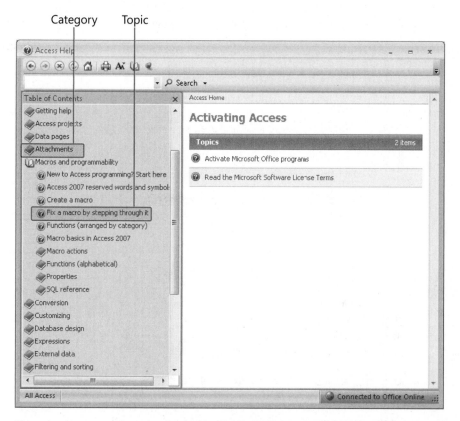

If you're connected to the Internet, Access displays categories, topics, and training available from the Office Online Web site as well as those stored on your computer.

Back   Forward

4. In the **Table of Contents**, click a few categories and topics, then click the **Back** and **Forward** buttons to move among the topics you have already viewed.

Close

5. At the right end of the **Table of Contents** title bar, click the **Close** button.

6. At the top of the **Access Help** window, click the **Type word to search for** box, type Help window, and then press the `Enter` key.

The Access Help window displays topics related to the words you typed.

7. In the results list, click **Print a Help topic**.

The selected topic appears in the Access Help window, explaining that you can click the Print button on the toolbar to print any topic.

8. Below the title at the top of the topic, click **Show All**.

Access displays any hidden auxiliary information available in the topic and changes the Show All button to Hide All. You can display or hide an individual item by clicking it. When you click the Print button, Access will print all displayed information.

 CLOSE the Access Help window.

More Information

If your question is about Microsoft Office Access 2007 or another Microsoft software product and you cannot find the answer in the product's Help system, please search the appropriate product solution center or the Microsoft Knowledge Base at:

support.microsoft.com

In the United States, Microsoft software product support issues not covered by the Microsoft Knowledge Base are addressed by Microsoft Product Support Services. Location-specific software support options are available from:

support.microsoft.com/gp/selfoverview/

Quick Reference

1   Exploring Access 2007

To open a table

→ In the **Navigation Pane**, expand the **Tables** category, and then double-click the table you want to open.

To access additional datasheet formatting options

→ In Datasheet view, on the **Home** tab, click the **Font** Dialog Box Launcher.

To hide the Ribbon

→ Double-click the active tab.

To display the Ribbon when it is hidden

→ Click any tab.

To unhide the Ribbon

→ Double-click the active tab.

To enable macros in the current database

1. In the **Security Warning** area, click **Options**.
2. In the **Microsoft Office Security Options** dialog box, select the **Enable this content** option, and then click **OK**.

To add the publisher of a digitally signed database to the Trusted Publishers list

1. In the **Security Warning** area, click **Options**.
2. In the **Microsoft Office Security Options** dialog box, select the **Trust all documents from this publisher** option, and then click **OK**.

To add the location of this database to the Trusted Locations list

1. In the **Microsoft Office Security Options** dialog box, click **Open the Trust Center**.
2. In the page list in the left pane of the **Trust Center**, click **Trusted Locations**.
3. On the **Trusted Locations** page, click **Add new location**.
4. In the **Microsoft Office Trusted Location** dialog box, click **Browse**.
5. In the **Browse** dialog box, browse to the folder containing the current database, and then click **OK**.

6. In the **Microsoft Office Trusted Location** dialog box, select the **Subfolders of this location are also trusted** check box if you want to do so, and then click **OK** in each of the open dialog boxes.

To change the way Access handles macros in all databases

1. Click the **Microsoft Office Button**, and then click **Access Options**.

2. On the **Trust Center** page of the **Access Options** dialog box, click **Trust Center Settings**.

3. On the **Macro Settings** page of the **Trust Center**, select the option for the way you want Access to handle macros:

   ● **Disable all macros without notification**. If a database contains macros, Access disables them and doesn't display the security warning to give you the option of enabling them.

   ● **Disable all macros with notification**. Access disables all macros and displays the security warning.

   ● **Disable all macros except digitally signed macros**. Access automatically enables digitally signed macros.

   ● **Enable all macros**. Access enables all macros.

4. Click **OK** in the **Trust Center** and in the **Access Options** dialog box.

To open an existing database

1. On the **Start** menu, point to **All Programs**, click **Microsoft Office**, and then click **Microsoft Office Access 2007**.

2. In the **Open Recent Database** list, click **More**, navigate to the folder in which the database is stored, and then double-click the database.

To close a database

→ Click the **Microsoft Office Button**, and then click **Close Database**.

To view records in a table subdatasheet

→ Click the **Expand** button at the left end of the record.

To hide records in a subdatasheet

→ Click the **Collapse** button at the left end of the record.

To close a document window

→ Click the **Close Window** button at the right end of the document tab.

To move through a table one record at a time

→ On the record navigation bar, click the **Next Record** button.

To move to a specific record on a datasheet

→ On the record navigation bar, select the current record number, type the number of the record you want, and then press Enter .

To switch from Datasheet View to Design View

→ On the **View** toolbar, click the **Design View** button.

To view the properties of a query

→ In the **Navigation Pane**, right-click the query, and then click **Object Properties**.

To process (or run) a query

→ In the **Navigation Pane**, right-click the query name, and then click **Open**.

To move through records in a form

→ On the record navigation bar, click the **Next Record** to move forward and the **Previous Record** button to move backward.

To view a form in Design view when you are currently in Form view

→ On the **Home** tab, in the **Views** group, click the **View** button.

To preview a report

1. In the **Navigation Pane**, right-click the report, and then click **Print Preview**.
2. Click the report to display a larger view.

To view a table in Print Preview

→ Click the **Microsoft Office Button**, point to **Print**, and then click **Print Preview**.

To change the page orientation of a table before printing

→ On the **Print Preview** tab, in the **Page Layout** group, click the **Portrait** button or the **Landscape** button.

To close Print Preview

→ On the **Print Preview** tab, click the **Close Print Preview** button.

2   Creating a Database

To open a template and save it as a new database

1. On the **Getting Started with Microsoft Office Access** page, in the **Template Categories** list, click a category.
2. Click the template icon for the template you want to open.
3. In the **File Name** box, type a new name for the database, and note the default path.
4. Click the **Create** button.

To open a new blank database

1. Start Access. On the **Getting Started** page, click **Blank Database**.

2. In the **File Name** box, type the name for the database.

3. Click the **Browse for a location** button, browse to the folder where you want to save the database, click **OK**, and then click **Create**.

To enter information in a database

→ Click in an empty cell, type your text, and then press `Tab` to move to the next cell.

To change a field name

→ Double-click the field name, and then type the new name.

To change the data type of a field

→ In Design view, click in the data type cell you want to change, click the arrow that is displayed, and then click the data type you want to use.

To change the size of a field

1. In Design view, click the field name.

2. In the **Field Properties** area, select the current field size, and then enter the new field size.

To close and save a table or other database object

→ Click the **Close** button to close the table, and then click **Yes** to save changes.

To rename a table or other database object

1. Close the table. In the Navigation Pane, right-click the table, and then click **Rename**.

2. Type a new name for the table, and then press **Enter**.

To delete a table or other database object

1. Close the table. In the Navigation Pane, right-click the table, and then click **Delete**.

2. In the confirmation dialog box that appears, click **Yes**.

To create a table by using a template

→ On the **Create** tab, in the **Tables** group, click the **Table Templates** button, and then click the type of template you want to create.

To copy a table structure to a new table

1. Right-click the existing table in the Navigation Pane, and then click **Copy**.

2. On the **Home** tab, in the **Clipboard** group, click the **Paste** button.

3. In the **Paste Table As** dialog box, supply a unique name for the table, click **Structure Only**, and then click **OK**.

To add a new field name to a table and assign it a data type

1. Click in the first blank **Field** Name cell below the existing field names, type the field name, and then press ⎋Tab⎋.

2. Click the **Data Type** arrow for the new field, and then click the data type that you want assigned to the field.

To delete a table row while in Design view

→ Right-click in the row you want to delete, and then click **Delete Rows**.

To edit a field name

→ Select the part of the field name you want to edit, and then type the new information.

To change the size of a table column

1. With the table in **Datasheet View**, drag the vertical bar at the right edge of a column header to the left or right until the column is the size you want.

2. To size a column to the minimum width that will display all the text in that field in all records, point to the vertical bar on the right of the column header, and when the pointer changes to a double-headed arrow, double-click.

To change the height of all rows in a table

→ With the table in **Datasheet View**, on the left side of the datasheet, drag the horizontal bar between any two record selectors up or down until the rows are the height you want.

To reset all rows in a table to standard height

1. With the table in **Datasheet View**, on the **Home** tab, in the **Records** group, click **More**, and then click **Row Height** to display the **Row Height** dialog box.

2. In the **Row Height** dialog box, select the **Standard Height** check box or type in the height you want in the **Row Height** box, and then click **OK**.

To hide and unhide columns

1. Click anywhere in the column you want to hide, and in the **Records** group, click **More**. Then click **Hide Columns**.

2. To restore the hidden column, click **More** again, and then click **Unhide Columns** to display the **Unhide Columns** dialog box.

3. In the **Unhide Columns** dialog box, select the check box of the column you want to unhide, and then click **Close**.

To freeze and unfreeze columns

1. Drag through the column header of the column or columns you want to freeze.

2. With the columns selected, click the **More** button, and then click **Freeze**.

3. To restore the columns to their normal condition, click **More**, and then click **Unfreeze**.

3   Populating a Database

To import tables from one Access database into another

1. Open the database that you want to import to.

2. On the **External Data** tab, in the **Import** group, click the **Access** button to open the **Get External Data** wizard, and then on the **Select the source and destination of the data** page, click **Browse**.

3. In the **File Open** dialog box, navigate to the database you want to use, click it, and then click **Open**.

4. On the **Select the source and destination of the data** page, with the **Import tables, queries, forms, reports, macros, and modules into the current database** option selected, click **OK**.

5. In the **Import Objects** dialog box, on the **Tables** tab, click **Select All** to select all the tables, or select only the tables you want to import, and then click **OK** to import any tables you selected.

To migrate a database from an earlier version of Access

1. Open the database, click the **Microsoft Office Button**, point to the **Save As** arrow, and then click **Access 2007 Database**.

2. In the **Save As** dialog box specify a name and location for the database, and click **Save**.

To import information from an Excel worksheet into an existing table in an Access database

1. On the **External Data** tab, in the **Import** group, click the **Excel** button.

2. In the **Get External Data** wizard, on the **Select the source and destination of the data** page, click **Browse**.

3. In the **File Open** dialog box, navigate to the workbook you want to use, and then click **Open**.

4. On the **Select the source and destination of the data** page, select the **Append a copy of the records to the table** option, click the arrow and select the table you want to use in the list, and then click **OK**.

5. In the **Import Spreadsheet** wizard, ensure your worksheet or range is selected, and then click **Next**.

6. If appropriate, select the **First Row Contains Column Headings** check box, click **Next**, and then click **Finish** to import the file.

To import a SharePoint list from a collaboration site

1. Locate the SharePoint site that contains the list you want to import, and make a note of the site address.

2. On the SharePoint site, identify the lists you want to copy to the database, and then decide whether you want the entire list or just a particular view.

3. Review the columns in the source list or view, and identify the database into which you want to import the lists.

4. On the **External Data** tab, in the **Import** group, click the **SharePoint List** button.

5. On the **Select the source and destination of the data** page, under **Specify a SharePoint site**, click the address of the site you want to connect to, or type it in the box.

6. Select the **Import the source data** or **Link to the data source** option, and click **Next**. Then, if prompted to do so, enter your site credentials.

7. In the **Import** column, select the check box of each list you want to import into the database.

8. In the **Items to Import** column, for each of the selected lists, select the view that you want to import into the database.

9. With the **Import display values instead of IDS for fields that look up values stored in another list** check box selected, click **OK**.

10. If you want to save the import parameters for reuse, select the **Save Import Steps** check box. On the **Save Import Steps** page, enter a name and description for the specification, and then click **Save Import**.

To create an e-mail survey form, and then send the e-mail survey

1. Create a database table containing the fields you want to include in your survey. Position the insertion point in the first empty record.

2. On the **External Data** tab, in the **Collect Data** group, click the **Create E-mail** button.

3. Follow the steps in the **Collect Data Through E-mail Messages** wizard to create the form, add and reorder the fields from the table, change field labels, specify the Outlook folder to which the survey results will be delivered, elect to have Outlook automatically add replies to the original Access database table, and specify the survey recipients.

4. Customize the text of the e-mail message that will be created, and then on the **Create the e-mail message** page, click **Create**. Make any changes you want to the message, address it to the survey recipients, and then send it.

To import information from a comma-delimited text file

1. On the **External Data** tab, in the **Import** group, click the **Text File** button.

2. In the **Get External Data** wizard, on the **Select the source and destination of the data** page, click the **Browse** button, navigate to the location of the text file, click the file, and then click **Open**.

3. Select the **Append a copy of the records to the table** option, and in the list, click the text file you want to use. Then click **OK**.

4. In the **Import Text** wizard, click **Next**.

5. Select or clear the check boxes you want, click **Next**, and click **Finish** to import the text file into the table. Then on the **Save Import Steps** page, click **Close**.

To import information from an XML file

1. On the **External Data** tab, in the **Import** group, click the **XML File** button.

2. On the **Select the source and destination of the data** page of the **Get External Data** wizard, click the **Browse** button, and in the **File Open** dialog box, navigate to the location of the file, click the one you want to use, and then click **Open**.

3. On the **Select the source and destination of the data** page, click **OK**.

4. In the **Import XML** dialog box, select the **Structure and Data** import option, and click **OK**. Then on the **Save Import Steps** page, click **Close**.

To import information from an HTML file into an existing table

1. On the **External Data** tab, in the **Import** group, click the **More** button, and then in the list, click **HTML Document**.

2. On the **Select the source and destination of the data** page of the **Get External Data** wizard, click the **Browse** button, navigate to the file you want to use, click the file, and then click **Open**.

3. Select the **Append a copy of the records to the table** option, click the file in the list that you want to use, and then click **OK**.

4. In the **Import HTML** wizard, select the **First Row Contains Column Headings** check box, and then click **Finish**.

5. On the **Save Import Steps** page, click **Close**.

To import information from an Outlook folder into a new table in an Access database

1. On the **External Data** tab, in the **Import** group, in the **More** list, click **Outlook Folder**.

2. In the **Get External Data** wizard, with the **Import the source data into a new table in the current database** option selected, click **OK**.

3. Expand your primary mailbox folder, click the folder you want to import, and then click **Next**.

4. On the **Field Options** page, click on fields you don't want to import, select the **Do not import field (Skip)** check box, and then click **Next**.

5. On the **Primary Key** page, decide whether you want to create your own key, let Access create the key, or have no key, and click **Next**. Then click **Finish** to import the contents of the folder. On the **Save Import Steps** page, click **Close**.

To import information from a dBASE file into an existing table in an Access database

1. On the **External Data** tab, in the **Import** group, in the **More** list, click **dBase File**.

2. On the **Select the source and destination of the data** page of the **Get External Data** wizard, navigate to the file you want to use, click the file, and then click **Open**.

3. Select the **Import the source data into a new table in the current database** option, and then click **OK**. On the **Save Import Steps** page, click **Close**.

To save an import operation for reuse

→ Select the **Save Import Steps** check box, and then click **Save Import**.

To run a saved import operation

→ Click the **Saved Imports** button in the **Import** group on the **External Data** tab, click the import you want to run, and then click **Run**.

4   Sharing and Reusing Information

To export a table from one Access database to another

1. In the **Navigation Pane**, under **Tables**, select the table you would like to export.

2. On the **External Data** tab, in the **Export** group, click the **More** button, and then in the list, click **Access Database**.

3. In the **Export – Access Database** wizard, click the **Browse** button. In the **File Save** dialog box, navigate to the folder you want to export to, click it, and then click **Save**.

4. In the **Export – Access Database** wizard, click **OK**. In the **Export** dialog box, select the options you want, and then click **OK**.

5. In the **Export** dialog box, with the name of the exported table showing in the **Export to:** box, and **Definition and Data** selected under **Export Tables**, click **OK**.

6. On the **Save Export Steps** page, click **Close**.

To export a table from a database to an Excel workbook

1. Open the table in Datasheet view. Then on the **External Data** tab, in the **Export** group, click the **Export to Excel spreadsheet** button.

2. In the **Export – Excel Spreadsheet** wizard, click the **Browse** button. Then in the **File Save** dialog box, navigate to the folder you want to save the table in, and click **Save**.

3. In the **Export – Excel Spreadsheet** wizard, select the **Export data with formatting and layout** check box. Then select the **Open the destination file after the export operation is complete** check box.

4. With **Excel Workbook** selected in the **File format** list, click **OK**. On the **Save Export Steps** page, click **Close**.

To export the contents of a table to a SharePoint site

1. In the **Navigation Pane**, select (but don't open) the object you want to export.

2. On the **External Data** tab, in the **Export** group, click the **SharePoint List** button.

3. In the **Export – SharePoint Site** wizard, specify the SharePoint site where you want to create the list, change the list name and type a description if you want, and then click **OK**. Enter your SharePoint site credentials if prompted to do so.

To export a form from a database to an RTF document in Word

1. In the **Navigation Pane**, under **Forms**, double-click the form you want to export.
2. On the **External Data** tab, in the **Export** group, click the **Word** button.
3. In the **Export – RTF File** wizard, click **Browse**. In the **File Save** dialog box, navigate to the folder you want to save the form in, and then click **Save**.
4. In the **Export – RTF File** wizard, select the **Open the destination file after the export operation is complete** check box, and then click **OK**.

To export a table to a text file with formatting

1. Open the table in Datasheet view. Then on the **External Data** tab, in the **Export** group, click the **Text File** button.
2. In the **Export – Text File** wizard, click **Browse**. In the **File Save** dialog box, navigate to the folder in which you want to save the file, and then click **Save**.
3. In the **Export – Text File** wizard, select the **Export data with formatting and layout** check box. Then select the **Open the destination file after the export operation is complete** check box, and click **OK**.
4. In the **Encode As** dialog box, select the options you want, and then click **OK**.

To export a table from a database to an XML file

1. On the **External Data** tab, in the **Export** group, click the **More** button, and then in the list, click **XML File**.
2. In the **Export – XML File** wizard, click **Browse**, and in the **File Save** dialog box, navigate to the folder you want to store the file in, and click **Save**.
3. In the **Export – XML File** wizard, click **OK**.
4. In the **Export XML** dialog box, with the **Data (XML)** and **Schema of the data (XSD)** check boxes selected, click **OK**. Then in the **Export – XML File** wizard, click **Close**.

To export a report from a database to an HTML file

1. In the **Navigation Pane**, double-click the report you want to export.
2. On the **External Data** tab, in the **Export** group, click the **More** button, and then click **HTML Document**.
3. In the **Export – HTML File** wizard, click **Browse**. Then in the **File Save** dialog box, navigate to the folder you want to save the report in, and click **Save**.
4. In the **Export – HTML File** wizard, select the **Open the destination file after the export operation is complete** check box, and then click **OK**.
5. In the **HTML Output Options** dialog box, select the encoding format options you want, and then click **OK** to export the file.

To copy and paste records between an Access database table and other Office programs

1. Select the records you want to copy by pointing to the row selector of the first record you want to select, holding down the primary mouse button, and dragging to the last record you want to select.

2. On the **Home** tab, in the **Clipboard** group, click the **Copy** button.

3. Start the Office program you want to copy to, and click where you want to paste the records. Then on the **Home** tab, in the **Clipboard** group, click the **Paste** button.

5   Simplifying Data Entry by Using Forms

To create a form based on a table by using the Form tool

1. Open the table on which you want to base the form.

2. On the **Create** tab, in the **Forms** group, click the **Form** button.

To move labels on a form

→ Select the labels to be moved by dragging through them, drag them to a blank section of the form, and then release the selection.

To change the font and font size of a label on a form

1. Open the form in Design View, and click the label (not its text box) you want to change.

2. On the **Design** contextual tab, in the **Font** group, click the **Font** arrow, and then in the list, click the font you want to use.

3. With the label still selected, click the **Font Size** arrow, and then in the list, click the size you want.

To edit form control properties by using the Property Sheet pane

1. Open the form in Design view, and if the **Property Sheet** pane is not visible, right-click the desired control, and then click **Properties**.

2. In the **Property Sheet** pane, click the property you want to change, and either type the new value, or click the down arrow and select the value you want. Repeat for all properties that you want to change.

To edit multiple form control properties at once

1. Click anywhere in the **Detail** section of the form, and then drag diagonally to draw a rectangle through some portion of all the controls to select them.

2. In the **Property Sheet** pane, click the property you want to change, click the arrow that appears, and then click the option you want. Repeat for all properties that you want to change.

To set the background properties of all controls on a form

1. Select all the controls on the form. Then on the **Format** tab of the **Property Sheet** pane, click **Back Style**, and set it to the option you want.

2. Click **Back Color**, and then click the ellipsis button.

3. In the **Color Builder**, click the square of the color you want.

4. Set the **Special Effect** property to the option you want, and the **Border Color** property to the color you want.

To edit the caption of a form control

→ Click the label whose caption you want to change. Then in the **Property Sheet** pane, click the **Caption** property, change the text to what you want, and press `Enter`.

To change the layout of controls on a form

→ Drag through all the controls on the form to select them. Then on the **Arrange** tab, in the **Control Layout** group, click the **Remove** button.

To delete a form control label

→ Click the label you want to delete, and then press the `Del` key.

To select specific control labels on a form

→ Hold down the `Shift` key as you click each control or drag through just the labels you want to select.

To align form controls

→ Select the labels (but not their corresponding text boxes), and then in the **Property Sheet** pane, set the **Text Align** property to the alignment you want.

To size form control labels to fit their contents

→ Select the labels to be sized, and then on the **Arrange** contextual tab, in the **Size** group, click the **Size To Fit** button.

To insert space between form control labels and text boxes

→ Select all the text boxes (but not their corresponding labels). Then in the **Property Sheet** pane, click the **Left** property, and then change the setting to the amount of space you want.

To bind selected controls together

→ On the **Arrange** tab, in the **Control Layout** group, click the **Group** button.

To save the design of a form

→ On the **Quick Access Toolbar**, click the **Save** button.

To expand the Detail area of a form

→ Point to the right edge of the form **Detail** grid, and when the pointer changes to a double-headed arrow, drag the edge of the background to the right.

To move a label or text box control on a form

→ Click a label or text box, move the pointer over its border, and when the pointer changes to a four-way arrow, drag it to a new location.

To create an AutoFormat form template

1. On the **Arrange** contextual tab, in the **AutoFormat** group, click the **AutoFormat** button.
2. At the bottom of the **AutoFormat** gallery, click **AutoFormat Wizard**.
3. In the **AutoFormat** dialog box, click the **Customize** button.
4. In the **Customize AutoFormat** dialog box, click **Create a new AutoFormat based on the Form** option, and then click **OK**.
5. In the **New Style Name** dialog box, type a name for the new style, and then click **OK**.
6. Click **OK** to close the **AutoFormat** wizard. Then click the **Save** button, and close the form.

To add a graphic to a form control

1. In the **Navigation Pane**, under **Forms**, right-click the form you want to use, and then click **Design View**.
2. On the **Design** contextual tab, in the **Controls** group, click the **Image** button, and then click the area where you want to place the image, drag diagonally to draw a rectangle, and release the mouse button.
3. In the **Insert Picture** dialog box, navigate to the folder where the graphic you want to use is located, and then double-click the graphic.

To add a caption below a picture

1. In the **Controls** group, click the **Label** button, and then drag diagonally to draw a rectangle where you want it to appear.
2. In the active label control, type the caption text, and then press Enter .

To size a label control to fit the text

→ Click the label control, and then on the **Arrange** tab, in the **Size** group, click the **Size to Fit** button.

To add a combo box control without using a wizard

1. On the **Design** tab, in the **Controls** group, look at the **Use Control Wizards** button. If the button is active (orange), click it to deactivate it.
2. In the **Controls** group, click the **Combo Box** button, and then drag diagonally in the form to draw a rectangle where you want the combo box to appear.

To dynamically size a selected form control to fit the window

1. On the **Arrange** tab, in the **Size** group, click the **Anchoring** tool.
2. In the **Anchoring** gallery, click **Stretch Across Top**.

To copy the formatting of one control to another

→ Click the box whose formatting you want to copy, and in the **Font** group, click the **Format Painter** button. Then click the box to which you want to apply the formatting.

To add conditional formatting to a selected control

1. On the **Design** tab, in the **Font** group, click the **Conditional** button.
2. In the **Conditional Formatting** dialog box, select the criteria and the formatting you want to apply when the associated content meets the criteria.

To remove the record selector and scroll bar controls from a form

1. In Design view, click the **Form** selector (the box at the junction of the horizontal and vertical rulers), and then press `F4` to display the **Property Sheet** pane for the entire form (if the sheet is not already displayed).
2. On the **Format** tab, change **Record Selectors** to **No**, and **Scroll Bars** to **Neither**.

To create a form based on the fields in a table by using the Form wizard

1. In the **Navigation Pane**, under **Tables**, click the table in which you want to create the AutoForm.
2. On the **Create** tab, in the **Forms** group, click the **More Forms** button, and then in the list, click **Form Wizard**.
3. With the open table selected in the **Tables/Queries** list, click the **Move All** button to move all the table fields to the **Selected Fields** list, and then click **Next**.
4. On the second page of the wizard, choose the layout of the fields in the new form. On the third page, select a style option.
5. On the fourth page, with the **Open the form to view or enter information** option selected, click **Finish**.

To create a form and subform simultaneously

1. On the **Create** tab, in the **Forms** group, click the **More Forms** button, and then click **Form Wizard**.
2. On the first page of the **Form** wizard, in the **Tables/Queries** list, click the table on which you want to base the form. Then click the **Move All** button to include all the table fields in the new form.
3. To create the subform, display the **Tables/Queries** list, and then click the table on which you want to base the subform.
4. In the **Available Fields** list, double-click the fields you want to include in the subform to move them to the **Selected fields** list, and then click **Next**.
5. With your primary table and **Form with subform(s)** selected, click **Next**.

6. With **Datasheet** selected, click **Next**.

7. On the last page of the wizard, select a style, and then click **Finish**.

To add a subform to a form

1. Open the form in Design view. Then on the **Design** tab, in the **Controls** group, make sure the **Use Control Wizards** button is active (orange).

2. In the **Controls** group, click the **Subform/Subreport** button, and then drag diagonally to draw a rectangle in a section where you want to put the subform.

3. On the **Subform** wizard's first page, with the **Use existing Tables and Queries** option selected, click **Next**.

4. In the **Tables/Queries** list, click the type of item you want to use.

5. Add fields to the **Selected Fields** list by double-clicking each field. Then click **Next**, select the options you want, and click **Finish**.

6 Locating Specific Information

To sort information in one column

- Click the arrow at the right side of the column header for the column you want to sort, and then click the direction you want to sort the information.

- Click the header of the column you want to sort, and then on the **Home** tab, in the **Sort and Filter** group, click the **Ascending** or **Descending** button.

To sort information in multiple columns

→ Select the adjacent columns you want to sort, right-click the column header area of your selection, and then click how you want to sort the columns.

To move a field

→ Click the column head you want to move, and then drag it to the position you want.

To filter records by a single criterion

1. In the field, click any instance of the record you want to filter by.

2. On the **Home** tab, in the **Sort & Filter** group, click the **Selection** button, and then in the list, click **Equals** "[the term you want to filter on]".

To remove a filter

→ In the **Sort & Filter** group, click the **Toggle Filter** button.

To filter records with a text filter

1. Click the column header arrow, point to **Text Filters**, and then click the criterion you want to filter by.

2. In the Custom Filter dialog box, in the **ItemText begins with** box, type the first few letters of the text you want to filter by. Then click **OK**.

To filter records with a "does not equal" filter

→ In the column, right-click any instance of the criterion you don't want to filter, and then click **Does Not Equal** "[the item you don't want to filter]".

To use the Filter By Form command

1. In the **Navigation Pane**, under **Forms**, double-click the form you want to search.
2. On the **Home** tab, in the **Sort & Filter** group, click the **Advanced** button, and then in the list, click **Filter By Form**.
3. Click the box you want to search in, type the search criterion, and then press `Enter`.
4. In the **Sort and Filter** group, click the **Toggle Filter** button.

To use the Advanced Filter/Sort command to sort tables

1. On the **Home** tab, in the **Sort & Filter** group, click the **Advanced Filter Options** button, and then in the list, click **Advanced Filter/Sort**.
2. In the field list, double-click a field to copy it to the first cell in the first column of the design grid.
3. In the **Criteria** cell under the field you just copied, type the search criterion, and then press `Enter`.
4. Repeat Steps 2 and 3 for any other fields you want to filter on.
5. In the **Sort & Filter** group, click the **Toggle Filter** button to view the records that match the criteria.

To create a query in Design view

1. On the **Create** tab, in the **Other** group, click the **Query Design** button.
2. In the **Show Table** dialog box, on the **Tables** tab, double-click any tables you want to add to the query window. Then close the dialog box.
3. Drag the fields to be used in the query from the field lists to consecutive columns in the design grid.
4. On the **Design** contextual tab, in the **Results** group, click the **Run** button to run the query and display the results in Datasheet view.

To save a filter as a query:

1. On the **Home** tab, in the **Sort & Filter** group, click the **Advanced** button and then click **Save As Query**.
2. In the **Save As Query** dialog box, give the query and appropriate name, and then click **OK**.

To add data to a query in Design view

● To add a field from an existing table, double-click it.
● To add a field from another table, drag the table from the Navigation Pane into the upper section of the design window, and then double-click the field you want to add.

To remove data from a query in Design view

- To delete a field from a query, select the field in the lower section of the design window, and then press the **Delete** key.
- To delete a table from a query, right-click the table in the upper section of the design window, and then click **Remove Table**.

To add a Totals row to a query in Datasheet view

→ On the **Home** tab, in the **Records** group, click the **Totals** button. Then click in each cell of the **Totals** row that appears at the end of the table, and select the summary data you want to appear in that cell.

7 Keeping Your Information Accurate

To set the data type for a field in Design view

1. Click the **Data Type** cell next to the desired field.
2. Click the **Data Type** arrow, and then in the list, click the data type you want.

To view the properties of a field

→ With the table in Design view, click the field name to display its properties in the Field Properties area.

To set the Field Size property for text, number, and autonumber fields

→ With the table in Design view, click any cell in a field, and then in the **Field Properties** area, change the **Field Size** property to what you want.

To use the Input Mask wizard in Design view

1. Select a field, and then click **Input Mask** in the **Field Properties** area.
2. Click the ellipsis button to the right of the cell to start the **Input Mask** wizard. (Click **Yes** if Access prompts you to install this feature.)
3. Select an available mask in the **Input Mask** list, and then click **Next**.
4. In the **Input Mask** and **Placeholder character** boxes, make any changes you want, and then click **Next**.
5. Choose whether to store the data with the symbols, and then click **Finish**.
6. Press [Enter] to accept the mask. Then save your changes.

To set a field validation rule in Design view

1. Select a field, and then click in the **Validation Rule** box in the Field Properties area.
2. Type an expression in the **Validation Rule** box, or click the ellipsis button to use the Expression Builder.
3. Press [Enter]. Then save the table.

To test the validation rules in a table in Design view

→ Right-click the table's title bar, and click **Test Validation Rules**.

To select an entire field

→ Move the pointer to the left end of a field, and when the pointer changes to a thick cross, click the field.

To set a table validation rule

1. Right-click in the table window, and then click **Properties**.
2. Click in the **Validation Rule** box, type the information for the rule, press ⎑Enter⎑, and then save the table.

To create a lookup list with the Lookup wizard

1. Set the data type of a field to **Lookup Wizard**.
2. Select the options you want, and then click **Next**.
3. Continue selecting the options you want, clicking **Next** when you are done with each page. When you are done filling out the wizard, click **Finish**.
4. On the **Quick Access Toolbar**, click the **Save** button.

To restrict what can be entered in a lookup list

1. In Design view, in the **Field Properties** area, click the **Lookup** tab.
2. Change **Limit To List** to **Yes**.
3. Change **Allow Value List Edits** to **No**.
4. Save the table.

To create a multi-column lookup list

1. Add a new field, name it, and then set the data type to **Lookup Wizard**.
2. Select the **values** option you want, and then click **Next**.
3. Type the number of columns you want, and then enter the data you want in each column.
4. Click **Next**, and then click **Finish**.
5. Save your changes.

To prevent a column from being displayed in a multi-column lookup list

→ In Design view, on the **Lookup** tab, in the **Column Widths** box, change the width for the column you don't want displayed to 0. Then save your changes.

To filter selections in a multi-column lookup list

1. Right-click any cell in a column you want to filter, point to **Text Filters**, and then click the filter option you want.
2. In the **Custom Filter** box, type criterion you want to filter for, and then press ⎑Enter⎑.

To create a select query

1. You must first create a select query. On the **Create** tab, in the **Other** group, click the **Query Design** button.

2. In the **New Query** dialog box, with **Simple Query Wizard** selected, click **OK**.

3. In the **Tables/Queries** list, click the option you want. Then in the **Available Fields** list, double-click the fields you want to move to the **Selected Fields** list.

4. In the **Simple Query Wizard** dialog box, click **Finish** to create the select query.

To create an update query

1. First, create a select query that selects the records you want to update.

2. Open the select query in Design view. Then on the **Design** contextual tab, in the **Query Type** group, click the **Update** button.

3. In the design grid, type the expression for your update.

To create an action query

1. First, create a select query that selects the records you want to manipulate.

2. Open the select query in Design view. Then on the **Design** contextual tab, in the **Query Type** group, click the **Make Table**, **Append**, **Update**, or **Delete** button.

3. Provide the information requested for the specified query type.

To create a delete query

1. First, create a select query that selects the records you want to delete.

2. Open the select query in Design view. Then on the Design contextual tab, in the **Query Type** group, click the **Delete** button to convert this select query to a delete query.

3. In the design grid, set the delete criteria.

To back up a database

1. Click the **Microsoft Office Button**, point to **Manage**, and then click **Back Up Database**.

2. In the **Save As** dialog box, navigate to the folder in which you want to store the backup, and then click **Save**.

To compact a database

→   Click the **Microsoft Office Button**, point to **Manage**, and then click **Compact and Repair Database**. Acknowledge the safety warning if prompted to do so.

To analyze the performance of a database

1. On the **Database Tools** tab, in the **Analyze** group, click the **Analyze Performance** button.

2. In the **Performance Analyzer** dialog box, on the **All Object Types** tab, click **Select All**, and then click **OK**.

3. Click each result in the **Analysis Results** box to display more information about that result in the **Analysis Notes** area.

To document a database

1. On the **Database Tools** tab, in the **Analyze** group, click the **Database Documenter** button.
2. In the **Documenter** dialog box, select the options you want on each tab. Then click **OK** to start the documentation process.

8   Working with Reports

To create a report by using the Report wizard

1. On the **Create** tab, in the **Reports** group, click the **Report Wizard** button.
2. On the field selection page, click the **Tables/Queries** arrow, and then in the list, click the table or query that you want to base your report on.
3. In the **Available Fields** list, double-click the fields you want to move to the **Selected Fields** list.
4. To select fields from additional tables or queries, repeat Steps 2 and 3.
5. On the field selection page, click **Next**.
6. On the grouping page, select how you want to view your data, and then click **Next**.
7. On the grouping levels page, add up to four grouping levels by double-clicking field names to move them to the top of the preview pane. Then click the **Grouping Options** button.
8. In the **Grouping Intervals** dialog box, click the **Grouping intervals** arrow next to each grouping level and select the desired interval, click **OK**, and then click **Next**.
9. On the sort order page, click the arrow to the right of the first box, and select a field to sort on; repeat for each field you want to sort on, and then click **Next**.
10. On the layout page, select the options you want, and then click **Next**.
11. On the style selection page, click the style you want, and then click **Next**.
12. In the title box, type a title for the report, and then with the **Preview the report** option selected, click **Finish**.

To preview a print version of a report

→ In the **Navigation Pane**, right-click the desired report, and then click **Print Preview**.

To adjust the height of a report section

1. In the **Navigation Pane**, right-click the desired report, and then click **Design View**.
2. Point to the top edge of a section selector.
3. When the pointer changes to a two-headed vertical arrow, drag the selector in the direction you want.

To insert the current date in a report

1. In Design view, on the **Design** contextual tab, in the **Controls** group, click the **Date & Time** button.

2. In the **Date And Time** dialog box, select a date format option, and clear the **Include Time** check box if you want to include only the date. Then click **OK**.

To reposition a text box in a report

→ In Design view, select the text box, then drag it to the desired location.

To align text in a report

→ In Design view, select the text box, and in the **Font** group, click one of the alignment buttons.

To delete a text box from a report

→ In Design view, click the text box to select it, and then press ⌨Del⌨.

To move controls as a group

1. In Design view, drag diagonally to draw a rectangle through some portion of all the labels and the text boxes you want to move.

2. Drag the selected controls to where you want them.

To change the page width of a report

1. In Design view, click the Report Selector. Then press ⌨F4⌨ to display the **Property Sheet** pane.

2. On the **Format** tab, change the **Width** setting.

To group and sort data in a report

1. Switch to Design view.

2. On the **Design** tab, in the **Grouping & Totals** group, click the **Group & Sort** button.

3. In the **Group, Sort, and Total** pane, in the **Group on** bar, click **More** to see additional options, and then choose the ones you want.

4. Click the **Group & Sort** button to close the **Group, Sort, and Total** pane.

To insert a horizontal line in a report

1. In Design view, in the **Controls** group, click the **Line** button.

2. Click the location where you want the horizontal line to appear.

3. Press ⌨F4⌨ to display the **Property Sheet** pane. Then set the **Left**, **Width**, and **Border Color** properties as desired.

To align the columns of a report

1. In Design view, select the label and text box for the column you want to align.

2. Press ⌨F4⌨ to display the **Property Sheet** pane. Then set the **Left** and **Width** properties to precisely align the column on the page.

3. Repeat Step 2 for each column you want to align.

To change the Design view grid for a report

1. In Design view, click the **Report** selector, and then press ⌨F4 to open the **Property Sheet** pane.

2. On the **Format** tab, change the **Grid X** and **Grid Y** properties to the number of dots per inch that you want to show on the grid.

To set the height of a section in a report

→ Click the section, and on the **Format** tab in the **Property Sheet** pane, set the **Height** property to the measurements you want.

To save a new report

1. On the **Quick Access Toolbar**, click the **Save** button.

2. In the **Save As** dialog box, type a name for the new report in the **Report Name** box, and then click **OK**.

To insert a title in a report

→ Open the report in Design view. Then on the **Design** contextual tab, in the **Controls** group, click the **Title** button.

To insert a page number in a report

1. Open the report in Design view. Then in the **Controls** group, click the **Insert Page Number** button.

2. In the **Page Numbers** dialog box, select the desired format, position, and alignment options. Then click **OK**.

To insert a subreport in a report

1. Open the main report in Design view. Then double-click the **Report Selector** to display the **Property Sheet** pane.

2. On the **Data** tab, click the **Record Source** arrow, and select the table or query on which the subreport will be based.

3. On the **Design** contextual tab, in the **Controls** group, click the **Subform/Subreport** button, and then click a point on the main report.

4. In the **Subreport** wizard, with the **Use existing Tables and Queries** option selected, click **Next**.

5. In the **Tables/Queries** list, click the query you want to use.

6. In the **Available Fields** list, double-click the fields you want to use to move them to the **Selected Fields** list, and then click **Next**.

7. Select the appropriate options to define the fields you want to include in the subform.

8. Click **Next**, and then click **Finish**.

To view a report in Print Preview mode

- If the report is not open, right-click it in the **Navigation Pane**, and then click **Print Preview**.

- If the report is open, on the **Home** tab, in the **Views** group, click the **View** arrow, and then click **Print Preview**, or click the **Print Preview** button on the **View** toolbar.

To view a report in Layout View mode

- If the report is not open, right-click it in the **Navigation Pane**, then click **Layout View**.

- If the report is open, on the **Home** tab, in the **Views** group, click the **View** arrow, and then click **Layout View**, or click the **Layout View** button on the **View** toolbar.

To print a report

1. Either open the report or select it in the **Navigation Pane**.

2. Click the **Microsoft Office Button**, and then click **Print**.

3. In the **Print** dialog box, set the properties you want, and then click **OK**.

9 Making Your Database Easy to Use

To create a switchboard

1. On the **Database Tools** tab, in the **Database Tools** group, click the **Switchboard Manager** button, and then click **Yes** if Access asks whether you want to create a switchboard.

2. With **Main Switchboard (Default)** selected in the **Switchboard Pages** list, click **Edit**.

3. In the **Switchboard Name** box, replace *Main Switchboard* with a name for your switchboard. Then click **Close**.

To add a new page to a switchboard

1. On the **Database Tools** tab, in the **Database Tools** group, click the **Switchboard Manager** button.

2. In the **Switchboard Manager** window, select the type of switchboard you want, and then click **New**.

3. Replace the default new switchboard page name with the name you want, and then click **OK**.

To create a button on a switchboard page

1. On the **Database Tools** tab, in the **Database Tools** group, click the **Switchboard Manager** button.

2. With the switchboard selected in the **Switchboard Pages** list, click **Edit**.

3. In the **Edit Switchboard Page** window, click **New**.

4. In the **Edit Switchboard Item** dialog box, in the **Text** box, type a name for the button label.

5. If you want to change the command assigned to the button, click the **Command** arrow, and then click your selection in the list.

6. If there is a box below the **Command** box, click the arrow next to it, and in the list, select the appropriate option. Then click **OK**.

7. In the **Edit Switchboard Item** dialog box, click **OK**.

To create a custom category

1. Right-click the category header at the top of the **Navigation Pane**, and then click **Navigation Options**.

2. In the **Grouping Options** area of the **Navigation Options** dialog box, click the **Add Item** button.

3. Replace the default name of the new category with the name you want, and then press Enter .

4. Click the **Add Group** button, and then in the **Groups** list, replace *Custom Group 1* with the new group name.

5. In the **Navigation Options** dialog box, click **OK**.

To add shortcuts to a category

1. Click the category header at the top of the **Navigation Pane**, and then click the custom category that you want to add shortcuts to.

2. In the **Unassigned Objects** group, click the object you want to add to a custom group, and drag the object on top of the desired group header to add a shortcut to the group; or right-click the desired object, point to **Add to group**, and click the group you want to add the shortcut to.

To add any command to the Quick Access Toolbar

1. At the right end of the **Quick Access Toolbar**, click the **Customize Quick Access Toolbar** button.

2. Near the bottom of the **Customize Quick Access Toolbar** menu, click **More Commands**.

3. In the **Access Options** window, click the **Choose commands from** arrow, and in the list, click the area from which you want to add a command.

4. In the available commands list, locate and click the command you want to add to the Quick Access Toolbar. Then between the two command lists, click **Add**.

5. At the bottom of the **Customize** page, click **OK**.

To reposition commands on the Quick Access Toolbar

1. On the **Customize** page of the **Access Options** window, click the command you want to move, and then click the **Move Up** or the **Move Down** button until the command is in the position you want.

2. At the bottom of the **Customize** page, click **OK**.

To add a command from the Ribbon to the Quick Access Toolbar

→ Right-click the command on the Ribbon, and then click **Add to Quick Access Toolbar**.

To remove a command from the Quick Access Toolbar

1. At the right end of the **Quick Access Toolbar**, click the **Customize Quick Access Toolbar** button.

2. Near the bottom of the **Customize Quick Access Toolbar** menu, click **More Commands**.

3. In the toolbar commands list, click the command you want to remove. Then between the two command lists, click **Remove**.

4. At the bottom of the **Customize** page, click **OK**.

10 Securing and Sharing Information

To assign a password to a database

1. Start Access 2007.

2. Click the **Microsoft Office Button**, and then on the menu, click **Open**.

3. In the **Open** dialog box, navigate to the folder where the database is located, and click the database to select it. Then click the **Open** arrow, and in the list, click **Open Exclusive**.

4. On the **Database Tools** tab, in the **Database Tools** group, click the **Encrypt with Password** button.

5. In the **Password** box of the **Set Database Password** dialog box, type a password, and then press the `Tab` key.

6. In the **Verify** box, type the same password you typed in the **Password** box. Then click **OK**.

To test a database password

1. Open the database.

2. In the **Enter database password** box of the **Password Required** dialog box, type an incorrect password, and then click **OK**.

3. In the **Microsoft Office Access** message box warning you that the password you entered is not valid, click **OK**.

4. In the **Password Required** dialog box, type the correct password, and then click **OK**.

To remove a password from a database

1. Start Access 2007.

2. Click the **Microsoft Office Button**, and then on the menu, click **Open**.

3. In the **Open** dialog box, navigate to the folder where the database is located, and click the database to select it. Then click the **Open** arrow, and in the list, click **Open Exclusive**.

4. On the **Database Tools** tab, in the **Database Tools** group, click the **Decrypt Database** button.

5. In the **Password** box of the **Unset Database Password** dialog box, type the current password, and then click **OK**.

To secure VBA code in a database by using a password

1. Open a database, and on the **Database Tools** tab, in the **Macro** group, click the **Visual Basic** button.

2. On the **Tools** menu of the Visual Basic Editor, click **Base Properties**.

3. On the **Protection** tab of the **Project Properties** dialog box, select the **Lock project for viewing** check box.

4. In the **Password** box, type a password, and then press the ⌞Tab⌟ key.

5. In the **Confirm Password** box, type the same password you entered in the **Password** box, and then click **OK**.

6. Close the Visual Basic Editor, and then close the database.

To test a VBA-securing password

1. Open the database.

2. On the **Database Tools** tab, in the **Macro** group, click the **Visual Basic** button (or press ⌞Alt⌟+⌞F11⌟).

3. Click the **Expand** button to the left of the database project.

4. In the **Password** dialog box, type the password for the database, and then click **OK**.

To remove the security from the VBA code in a database

1. On the Visual Basic Editor **Tools** menu, click **Base Properties**.

2. On the **Protection** tab, clear the **Lock project for viewing** check box, and delete the asterisks from the two password boxes. Then click **OK**.

To secure a database by saving it as a distributable ACCDE file

1. Open a database, and on the **Database Tools** tab, in the **Database Tools** group, click the **Make ACCDE** button.

2. In the **Save As** dialog box, navigate to the folder you want to save the file in, and then click **Save**.

To split a database:

1. Make a copy of the database on your computer, and then open it.

2. On the **Database Tools** tab, in the **Move Data** group, click the **Access Database** button.

3. In the Database Splitter wizard, click **Split Database**.

4. In the **Create Back-end Database** dialog box, specify a name and storage location for the back-end database, click **Split**, and then click **OK** in the message box telling you that the split was successful.

Chapter at a Glance

Work in Access 2007, **page 2**

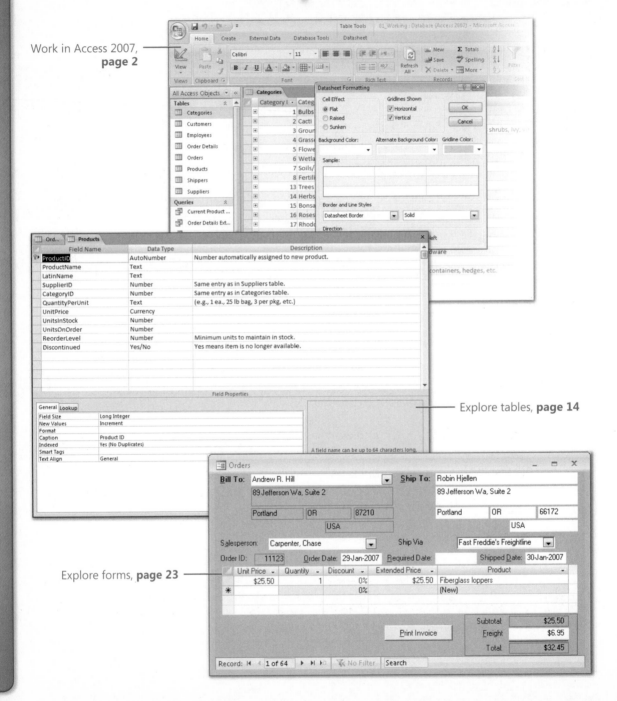

Explore tables, **page 14**

Explore forms, **page 23**

1 Exploring Access 2007

In this chapter, you will learn to:

✔ Work in Access 2007.

✔ Understand database concepts.

✔ Open an existing database.

✔ Explore tables, queries, forms, reports, and other Access objects.

✔ Preview and print Access objects.

Microsoft Office Access 2007 is part of the 2007 Microsoft Office system, so the basic interface objects—such as the Office menu, the Quick Access Toolbar, the Ribbon, and dialog boxes—will be familiar if you have used other Office 2007 products. However, Access has more dimensions than most of those other products or programs, so it might seem more complex until you become familiar with it.

If you are upgrading from an earlier version of Access, then you should review "Introducing Access 2007" in the front of this book to learn about differences between earlier versions and Access 2007.

In this chapter, you will learn to work in the Access program window and learn about the concepts and structure of data storage in Access, including types of databases, types of Access objects, and relationships between objects. You will experiment with a complete working database, learning about interesting features of Access as well as functionality that you will explore in more depth in later chapters.

See Also Do you need only a quick refresher on the topics in this chapter? See the Quick Reference section at the beginning of this book.

Important Before you can use the practice files in this chapter, you need to install them from the book's companion CD to their default location. See "Using the Companion CD" at the beginning of this book for more information.

> **Troubleshooting** Graphics and operating system–related instructions in this book reflect the Windows Vista user interface. If your computer is running Windows XP and you experience trouble following the instructions as written, please refer to the "Information for Readers Running Windows XP" section at the beginning of this book.

Working in Access 2007

When you create or open a database, it opens in a *database window*. The new Access database window interface is designed to more closely reflect the way people generally work with a database or database object.

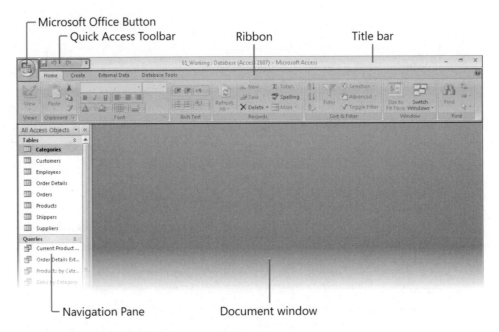

The interface includes the following elements:

- Commands related to managing databases (such as creating, saving, printing, backing up, and publishing) are available from the menu that appears when you click the *Microsoft Office Button* in the upper-left corner of the program window. This menu, which we refer to throughout this book as the *Office menu*, takes the place of the File menu that appeared in pre-vious versions of Access.

- Some commands are represented by buttons on the *Quick Access Toolbar* to the right of the Microsoft Office Button. By default, the database window Quick Access Toolbar displays the Save, Undo, and Redo buttons. You can add commands to the

Quick Access Toolbar so that they are available regardless of which tab or object is currently active in the database window.

See Also For information about customizing the Quick Access Toolbar commands and location, see "Making Favorite Access Commands Quickly Available" in Chapter 9, "Making Your Database Easy to Use."

- The *title bar* displays the name of the active database object (if it is maximized). At the right end of the title bar are the three familiar buttons that have the same function in all Windows programs. You can temporarily hide the Access window by clicking the Minimize button, adjust the size of the window by clicking the Restore Down/Maximize button, and close the active window or exit Access by clicking the Close button.

- Below the title bar is the *Ribbon*, a new feature in many of the programs in the Office system. Commands are presented on the Ribbon rather than on the more-traditional menus or toolbars so that you can work most efficiently within the window. The Ribbon is organized into task-specific *tabs*, which are further divided into feature-specific or task-specific *groups* of commands.

- The buttons in each group change size depending on the width of the program window. They might be large, small, or wide, and might be labeled with the button name, icon, or both. Pointing to any button displays the button name in a *ScreenTip* that sometimes also describes the button's function.

  Some buttons have arrows, but not all arrows function the same way. If you point to a button that has an arrow is incorporated into the button body, clicking the button will display a list of options for you to choose from. If the arrow is separate from the button body, clicking the arrow will display a list of options and clicking the button will perform the currently selected action.

Dialog Box
Launcher

- Related but less common commands are not represented in a group as buttons. Instead they are available from a dialog box, which you can display by clicking the *Dialog Box Launcher* at the right end of the group title bar.

- The **Microsoft Office Access Help** button appears at the right end of the Ribbon.

- The *Navigation Pane* displays filtered lists of database objects. You can change the objects included in the list by clicking the list header and then clicking the category or group of objects you want to display.

The goal of the redesigned environment is to make working within an item window more intuitive. Commands for tasks you perform often are no longer hidden on menus and in dialog boxes, and features that you might not have discovered before are now plainly visible.

By default, Access 2007 displays database objects as *tabbed documents* in the document window. If you prefer to display each object in a separate window rather than on a separate tab, you can do so by clicking Access Options on the Office menu, and then on the Current Database page, selecting the Overlapping Windows option.

When displaying Tabbed Documents, a Close button for the active database object appears to the right of the document tabs. When displaying Overlapping Windows, in a maximized database object window, the Minimize, Maximize/Restore Down, and Close buttons for the object window appear on the right end of the Ribbon, and the Access icon appears to the left of the Home tab. Clicking the Access icon opens the control menu, displaying a list of commands related to managing the active object window: Restore, Move, Size, Minimize, Maximize, and Close. When not maximized, clicking the object icon at the left end of the object window title bar displays the control menu.

In this exercise, you will take a tour of the command structure in an Access 2007 database window.

> **USE** the *Working* database. This practice file is located in the *Documents\Microsoft Press\Access2007SBS\Exploring* folder.

1. On the **Start** menu, click **Documents**. Then in your *Documents* folder, browse to the *Microsoft Press\Access2007SBS\Exploring* subfolder, and double-click the *Working* database.

   The database opens, with the Navigation Pane displaying the All Access Objects list. In the database window, the Ribbon includes four tabs:

   - Home
   - Create
   - External Data
   - Database Tools

   > **Tip** Depending on what programs are installed on your computer, tabs and groups other than those described here might also appear on the Ribbon.

The Home tab is active by default. Because no database object is currently open, only a few buttons on the Home tab are available.

Microsoft Office
Button

2. In the upper-left corner of the database window, click the **Microsoft Office Button.**

The Office menu opens.

You can create a database, but not a database object, from this menu. We'll talk about the commands available from the Office menu in other chapters of this book.

3. Click away from the Office menu to close it.

4. In the **Navigation Pane**, under **Tables**, double-click **Categories**.

The Categories table opens, an associated Table Tools contextual tab (Datasheet) appears, and more of the Home tab becomes active.

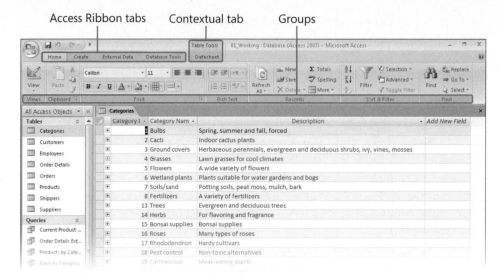

Buttons representing commands related to working with database content are organized on this tab in seven groups:

- Views
- Clipboard
- Font
- Rich Text
- Records
- Sort & Filter
- Find

Only the buttons for the commands that can be performed on the currently selected database object are active.

> **Important** Depending on your screen resolution and the size of the database window, you might see more or fewer buttons in each of the groups, the buttons you see might be represented by larger or smaller icons than those shown, or the group might be represented by a button that you click to display the group's commands. Experiment with the size of the database window to understand the effect on the appearance of the tabs.

Dialog Box
Launcher

5. On the **Home** tab, click the **Font** Dialog Box Launcher.

The Datasheet Formatting dialog box opens.

You can access certain settings not available from the Font group, such as Cell Effect and Border Styles, from this dialog box.

6. In the **Datasheet Formatting** dialog box, click **Cancel**.

7. Click the **Create** tab.

Buttons representing commands related to creating database objects are organized on this tab in four groups:

- Tables
- Forms
- Reports
- Other

8. Double-click the **Create** tab.

Double-clicking the active tab hides the Ribbon and provides more space for the active database object.

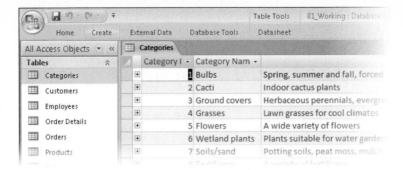

9. Click the **External Data** tab.

The Ribbon reappears, with the External Data tab active.

Buttons representing commands related to moving information between a database and other sources are organized on this tab in four groups:

- Import
- Export
- Collect Data
- SharePoint Lists

10. Click anywhere in the open table.

The Ribbon hides again. When you hide the Ribbon, it remains hidden except when active, until you again double-click a tab.

11. Double-click the **Database Tools** tab to display the tab and redisplay the Ribbon.

Buttons representing commands related to managing, analyzing, and protecting information are organized on this tab in five groups:

- Macro
- Show/Hide
- Analyze
- Move Data
- Database Tools

 CLOSE the *Working* database.

Understanding Database Concepts

Simple *database programs*, such as the Database component of Microsoft Works, can store information in only one table. These simple databases are often called flat file databases, or just *flat databases*. More complex database programs, such as Access, can store information in multiple related tables, thereby creating what are referred to as *relational databases*. If the information in a relational database is organized correctly, you can treat these multiple tables as a single storage area and pull information electronically from different tables in whatever order meets your needs.

A table is just one of the types of *objects* that you can work with in Access. Other object types include queries, forms, reports, pages, macros, and modules.

Of all these object types, only one—the table—is used to store information. The rest are used to manage, manipulate, analyze, retrieve, display, or publish information stored in a table—in other words, to make the information as accessible and therefore as useful as possible.

> **Tip** Access 2007 introduces a new file storage format that uses the *.accdb* extension. You can open old Access databases (with an *.mdb* extension) in Access 2007 and save them in the new format, but after they're converted, you will not be able to open them with a previous version of Access.
>
> The new format supports many new features. For more information about this format, search Access Help for *accdb*.

Over the years, Microsoft has put a lot of effort into making Access not only one of the most powerful consumer database programs available, but also one of the easiest to learn and use. Because Access is part of the Microsoft Office system, you can use many of the techniques you know from using other Office programs, such as Microsoft Office Word and Microsoft Office Excel, when using Access. For example, you can use familiar commands, buttons, and keyboard shortcuts to open and edit the information in Access tables. And because Access is integrated with other members of the suite, you can easily share information between Access and Word, Excel, or other programs.

In its most basic form, a database is the electronic equivalent of an organized list of information. Typically, this information has a common subject or purpose, such as the list of employees shown here:

ID	Last name	First name	Title	Hire date
1	Anderson	Nancy	Sales Rep	May 1, 2003
2	Carpenter	Chase	Sales Manager	Aug 14, 2001
3	Emanuel	Michael	Sales Rep	Apr 1, 1999
4	Furse	Karen	Buyer	May 3, 2004

This list is arranged in a *table* of columns and rows. Each column represents a *field*—a specific type of information about an employee: last name, first name, hire date, and so on. Each row represents a *record*—all the information about a specific employee.

If a database did nothing more than store information in a table, it would be no more useful than a paper list. But because the database stores information in an electronic format, you can manipulate the information in powerful ways to extend its utility.

For example, if you want to locate a person or a business in your city, you can do so because the information in the telephone book is organized in an understandable manner. If you want to get in touch with someone a little further away, you can go to the public library and use its collection of phone books, which probably includes one for each major city in the country. However, if you want to find the phone numbers of all the people in the country with your last name, or if you want to find the phone number of your grandmother's neighbor, these phone books won't do you much good because they aren't organized in a way that makes that information easy to find.

When the information published in a phone book is stored in a database, it takes up far less space, it costs less to reproduce and distribute, and, if the database is designed correctly, the information can be retrieved in many ways. The real power of a database isn't in its ability to store information; it is in your ability to quickly retrieve exactly the information you want from the database.

Because you can use standard Web programming code to easily manipulate the information in an Access 2007 database, you can create Web sites based on the information in your database or share that information with visitors to your site.

Opening an Existing Database

Throughout this book, you will be working with databases that contain information about the employees, products, suppliers, and customers of a fictional company. As you complete the exercises in this book, you will develop an assortment of queries, forms, reports, data access pages, macros, and modules that can be used to enter, edit, and manipulate the information in many ways.

When you start Access without opening a database, you see the Getting Started With Microsoft Office Access window. You can return to this window at any time by clicking the Microsoft Office Button and then clicking New.

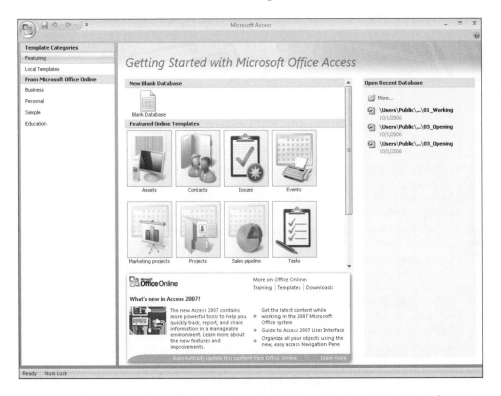

From this window you can open a blank database, create a new database from one of the many templates supplied with Access, from a template you download from the Microsoft Office Online Web site, or from a custom template saved on your computer or on a network share. You can also open a database you worked in recently, or navigate to any database on your computer and open it.

From the section at the bottom of the Getting Started window, you can link to the Microsoft Office Online Web site, where you can find information about all aspects of Office and download useful tools.

Enabling Macros and Other Database Content

Some databases, such as those provided for your use in this book, contain Microsoft Visual Basic for Applications (VBA) macros that can run code on your computer. In most cases, the code is there to perform a database-related task, but hackers can also use macros to spread a virus to your computer.

When you open a database containing one or more macros, if the database is not stored in a Trusted Location or signed by a Trusted Publisher, Access displays a *security warning* just below the Ribbon.

 Security Warning   Certain content in the database has been di... | Options... |

While the security warning is displayed, the macros in the database are disabled. You can enable macros in three ways:

- By enabling the macros in the database for use in the current database session.
- By adding the database *publisher* to a list of Trusted Publishers. Access will automatically enable macro content in any database *signed* by that publisher.
- By placing the database in a Trusted Location. Access will automatically enable macro content in any database saved in that location. The Trusted Locations you specify within Access are not also trusted by other Office programs.

To enable macros for the current database session only:

1. In the **Security Warning** area, click **Options**.
2. In the **Microsoft Office Security Options** dialog box, click **Enable this content**, and then click **OK**.

To add the publisher of a digitally signed database to the Trusted Publishers list:

1. In the **Security Warning** area, click **Options**.
2. In the **Microsoft Office Security Options** dialog box, click **Trust all documents from this publisher**, and then click **OK**.

To add the location of this database to the Trusted Locations list:

1. In the **Microsoft Office Security Options** dialog box, click **Open the Trust Center**.
2. In the page list in the left pane of the **Trust Center**, click **Trusted Locations**.
3. On the **Trusted Locations** page, click **Add new location**.

4. In the **Microsoft Office Trusted Location** dialog box, click **Browse**.

5. In the **Browse** dialog box, browse to the folder containing the current database, and then click **OK**.

6. In the **Microsoft Office Trusted Location** dialog box, select the **Subfolders of this location are also trusted** check box if you want to do so, and then click **OK** in each of the open dialog boxes.

If you prefer, you can change the way Access handles macros in all databases:

1. Click the **Microsoft Office Button**, and then click **Access Options**.

2. On the **Trust Center** page of the **Access Options** dialog box, click **Trust Center Settings**.

3. On the **Macro Settings** page of the **Trust Center**, select the option for the way you want Access to handle macros:

   ● **Disable all macros without notification**. If a database contains macros, Access disables them and doesn't display the security warning to give you the option of enabling them.

   ● **Disable all macros with notification**. Access disables all macros and displays the security warning.

   ● **Disable all macros except digitally signed macros**. Access automatically enables digitally signed macros.

   ● **Enable all macros**. Access enables all macros.

4. Click **OK** in the **Trust Center** and in the **Access Options** dialog box.

In this exercise, you will open a database, explore some of the objects it contains, and then close the database.

USE the *Opening* database. This practice file is located in the *Documents\Microsoft Press\Access2007SBS\Exploring* folder.

BE SURE TO start your computer, but don't start Access before starting this exercise.

1. On the **Start** menu, point to **All Programs**, click **Microsoft Office**, and then click **Microsoft Office Access 2007**.

   The Getting Started With Microsoft Office Access window opens.

2. In the **Open Recent Database** list, click **More**.

3. In the **Open** dialog box, navigate to your *Documents\Microsoft Press\ Access2007SBS\Exploring* folder, and then double-click the *Opening* database.

The database window opens.

> **Troubleshooting** If this is the first time you've run Access, you might see a security warning below the Ribbon. Just ignore this warning for the moment, but be sure to read the sidebar "Enabling Macros and Other Database Content" to learn about Access security options.

The Navigation Pane on the left side of the program window lists the Access database objects. You can use the Navigation Pane to group and filter these objects in various ways. You can display only one type of object (for example, all tables) by clicking the list title bar and then the category or group of objects you want to display.

Shutter Bar Open/Close

If the Navigation Pane is in your way, you can click the Shutter Bar Open/Close button in its upper-right corner, or press F11, to minimize it. To redisplay the Navigation Pane, click the Shutter Bar Open/Close button or press F11.

> **Tip** For more information about the Navigation Pane, search Access Help for *navigation pane* and read the topic *Guide to the Navigation Pane*.

4. Click the **Microsoft Office Button**, and then click **Close Database**.

When you close a database in this way, you return to the Getting Started window.

> **Tip** You can close Access entirely by clicking the Close button in the upper-right corner of the window, or by clicking the Microsoft Office Button and then clicking Exit Access.

Exploring Tables

Tables are the core database objects. Their purpose is to store information. The purpose of every other database object is to interact in some manner with one or more tables. An Access database can contain thousands of tables, and the number of records each table can contain is limited more by the space available on your hard disk than by anything else.

> **Tip** For detailed information about Access specifications, such as the maximum size of a database or the maximum number of records in a table, search Access Help for *"Access 2007 specifications"* (including the quotes).

Every Access object has two or more *views*. For tables, the two most common views are *Datasheet view*, in which you can see and modify the table's data, and *Design view*, in which you can see and modify the table's structure. To open a table in Datasheet view, either double-click its name in the Navigation Pane, or right-click its name and then click Open. To open a table in Design view, right-click its name and then click Design View. After an object is open, you can switch between views by clicking one of the View icons in the lower-right corner of the program window, or by clicking the View arrow in the Views group on the Home tab, and then selecting a view from the list. If you simply click the View button Access switches between views in a manner that at times seems logical. If the current view is not Design view, it switches to Design view. If you click it again, the table switches to Datasheet view. When other database objects are active, clicking the View switches between views in a similar manner.

When you view a table in Datasheet view, you see the table's data in columns (fields) and rows (records).

Column

CustomerID	FirstName	LastName	Address	City	Region	PostalCode	Country	Ph
ACKPI	Pilar	Ackerman	8808 Backbay S	Bellevue	WA	88004	USA	(42
ADATE	Terry	Adams	1932 52nd Ave.	Vancouver	BC	V4T 1Y9	Canada	(60
ALLMI	Michael	Allen	130 17th St.	Vancouver	BC	V4T 1Y9	Canada	(60
ASHCH	Chris	Ashton	89 Cedar Way	Redmond	WA	88052	USA	(42
BANMA	Martin	Bankov	78 Riverside Dr	Woodinville	WA	88072	USA	(42
BENPA	Paula	Bento	6778 Cypress P	Oak Harbor	WA	88277	USA	(2!
BERJO	Jo	Berry	407 Sunny Way	Kirkland	WA	88033	USA	(4!
BERKA	Karen	Berg	PO Box 69	Yakima	WA	88902	USA	(5!
BOSRA	Randall	Boseman	55 Grizzly Peak	Butte	MT	49707	USA	(5!
BRETE	Ted	Bremer	311 87th Pl.	Beaverton	OR	87008	USA	(5!
BROKE	Kevin F.	Browne	666 Fords Land	Seattle	WA	88121	USA	(2!
CAMDA	David	Campbell	22 Market St.	San Francisco	CA	84112	USA	(4!
CANCH	Chris	Cannon	89 W. Hilltop D	Palo Alto	CA	84306	USA	(4!
CHANE	Neil	Charney	1842 10th Aven	Sidney	BC	V7L 1L3	Canada	(60
CLAMO	Molly	Clark	785 Beale St.	Sidney	BC	V7L 5A6	Canada	(60
COLPA	Pat	Coleman	876 Western A	Seattle	WA	88119	USA	(20
CORCE	Cecilia	Cornejo	778 Ancient Rd	Bellevue	WA	88007	USA	(4!
COXBR	Brian	Cox	14 S. Elm Dr.	Moscow	ID	73844	USA	(2!
CULSC	Scott	Culp	14 E. University	Seattle	WA	88115	USA	(20
DANMI	Mike	Danseglio	55 Newton	Seattle	WA	88102	USA	(20
DANRY	Ryan	Danner	33 Neptune Cir	Langley	WA	88260	USA	(2!
DOYPA	Patricia	Doyle	1630 Hillcrest V	Carmel Valley	CA	83924	USA	(4!
ERIGA	Gail A.	Erickson	908 W. Capital	Tacoma	WA	88405	USA	(2!
ESTMO	Modesto	Estrada	511 Lincoln Ave	Burns	OR	87710	USA	(5
FENHA	Hanying	Feng	587 Orchard H	Victoria	BC	V8C 3Z1	Canada	(60

Row

If two tables have one or more fields in common, you can embed the datasheet from one table in another. By using an embedded datasheet, called a *subdatasheet*, you can see the information in more than one table at the same time. For example, you might want to embed an Orders datasheet in a Customers table so that you can see the orders each customer has placed.

In this exercise, you will open existing database tables and explore the table structures in different views.

> **USE** the *Tables* database. This practice file is located in the *Documents\Microsoft Press\Access2007SBS\Exploring* folder.
>
> **BE SURE TO** start Access and display the Getting Started window before beginning this exercise.

> **Tip** In this database, the Navigation Pane filter has been set to display all Access objects, but the Queries, Forms, and Reports object groups are collapsed. You can collapse and expand groups to display only the ones you want, or you can filter the database objects by clicking the list header, and then clicking the option you want under Filter By Group.

1. Click the **Microsoft Office Button**, and then click **Open**.

2. In the **Open** dialog box, browse to the *Documents\Microsoft Press\Access2007SBS\Exploring* folder, and double-click the *Tables* database.

    The database opens.

3. In the **Navigation Pane**, double-click **Categories**.

    The Categories table opens in Datasheet view.

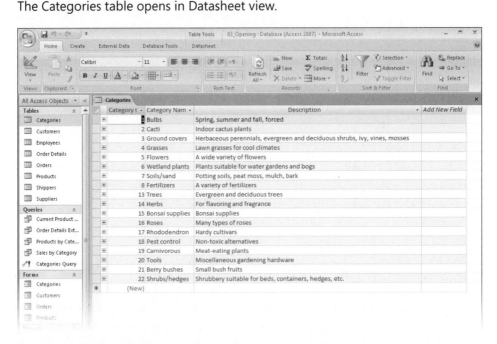

This table contains a list of product categories and fields such as Category ID, Category Name, and Description.

> **Tip** You can open any database object by right-clicking it in the Navigation Pane and then clicking the view you want to open it in. Clicking Open opens the object in its default Datasheet.

> **Tip** You can resize a table column by dragging the vertical bar in the header that separates it from the column to its right. You can set the width of a column to the width of its widest entry by double-clicking the vertical bar.

⊞
Expand

4. Maximize the table window if it isn't already maximized. Then in the datasheet, click the **Expand** button at the left end of the record for the Bulbs category.

   The Bulbs category expands to reveal an embedded subdatasheet. Access displays the category records from the Categories table and product records from the Products table simultaneously.

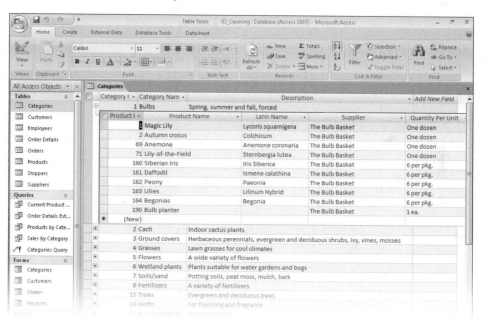

⊟
Collapse

5. Click the **Collapse** button to the left of the Bulbs category to hide the subdatasheet.

6. Click the **Close Window** button in the upper-right corner of the table, to the right of its tab (not the Close button in the upper-right corner of the program window) to close the Categories table. If Access prompts you to save changes to the table layout, click **Yes**.

7. In the **Navigation Pane**, double-click the **Orders** table to open it in Datasheet view.

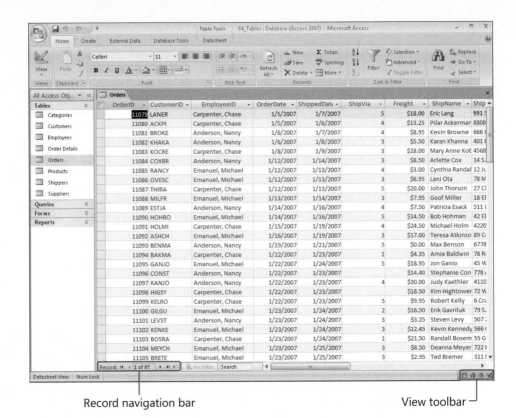

Record navigation bar   View toolbar

The record navigation bar at the bottom of the window indicates that this table contains 87 records, and that the active record is number 1 of 87.

Next Record

8. Move through the table one record at a time by clicking the **Next Record** button several times.

The selection moves down the OrderID field, because that field contains the insertion point.

> **Tip** You can move the selection one record at a time by pressing the Up Arrow or Down Arrow key, one screen at a time by pressing the Page Up or Page Down key, or to the first or last field in the table by pressing Ctrl+Home or Ctrl+End.

9. Move directly to record 40 by selecting the current record number in the record navigation bar, typing 40, and then pressing Enter.

10. In the **Navigation Pane**, double-click the **Products** table to open it in Datasheet view.

Notice that the table contains 189 records.

11. On the **View** toolbar, click the **Design View** button.

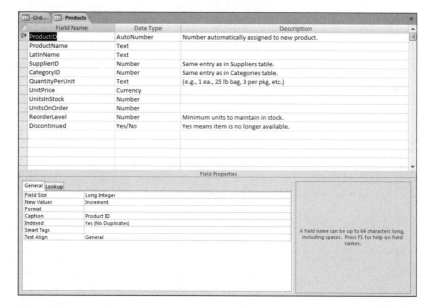

Datasheet view displayed the data stored in the table, whereas Design view displays the underlying table structure.

CLOSE the Products and Orders tables without saving your changes, and then close the *Tables* database to return to the Getting Started window.

Exploring Queries

You can locate specific information stored in a table, or in multiple tables, by creating a *query* specifying the parameters of the information you want to find. For example, you might want to locate all your out-of-state customers who have purchased gloves within the last three months. You could find this information by sorting, filtering, and cross-referencing table data, but that would be a difficult and time-consuming task. It is far simpler to create a query that returns all records in the Customers table with billing addresses not in your state, whose customer IDs map to records that appear in the Transactions table within the past quarter and include item IDs that map to records in the Inventory table that are classified as gloves. That might sound complicated, but the process of creating a query to return the results described in this example is quite simple.

Running a query (also called *querying the database*) displays a datasheet containing the records that fit your search criteria. You can use the query results as the basis for further analysis, create other Access objects (such as reports) from the results, or export the results to another format, such as an Excel spreadsheet or a Microsoft SharePoint list.

If you will want to locate records matching the search criteria at any time in the future, you can save the query, and run it again from the Queries section of the Navigation Pane. Each time you run a query, Access evaluates the records in the specified table (or tables) and displays the current subset of records that match the criteria you have defined.

Don't worry if this all sounds a bit complicated at the moment. When you approach queries logically, they soon begin to make perfect sense. You can easily create queries by using the Query wizard that is available to help you structure the query, and if you create a query that you are likely to run more than once, you can save it. It then becomes part of the database and is displayed when you click Queries in the Navigation Pane.

See Also For more information about queries, see Chapter 6, "Locating Specific Information."

In this exercise, you will explore two existing queries.

USE the *Queries* database. This practice file is located in the *Documents\Microsoft Press\ Access2007SBS\Exploring* folder.
OPEN the *Queries* database.

1. In the **Navigation Pane**, click **Queries**.

    The database window displays all the queries that have been saved as part of this database.

2. Right-click the **Current Product List** query, and then click **Object Properties**.

Access displays the properties of the Current Product List query, including a description of its purpose. The icon shown on the General tab matches the icon shown for this query in the Navigation Pane, and is an indication of the query's type. The query type is also specified in the Properties dialog box: this is a Select Query.

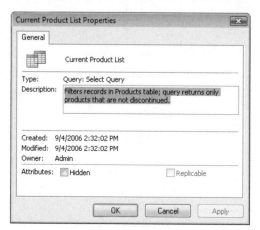

3. In the **Properties** dialog box, click **Cancel**.

4. Right-click the **Products by Category** query, and then click **Open**.

Access processes the query (commonly referred to as *running the query*) and produces a datasheet displaying the results.

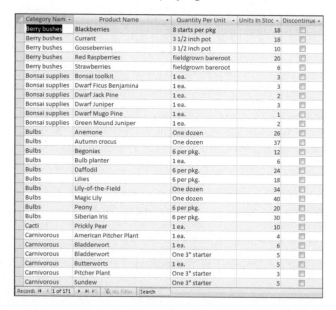

The record navigation bar indicates that 171 records are displayed; the database actually contains 189 records. To find out why 18 of the records are missing, you need to look at this query in Design view.

Design View

5. On the **View** toolbar, click the **Design View** button.

Access displays the query in Design view.

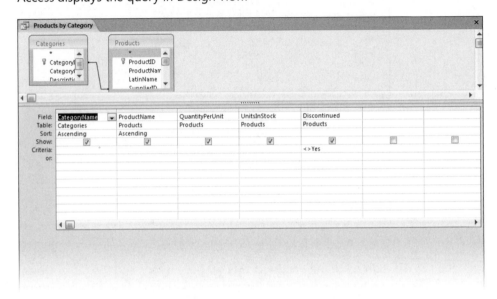

Two boxes in the top part of the query window list the fields in the tables this query is designed to work with. The query is formed in the design grid at the bottom of the query window. Each column of the grid can refer to one field from one of the tables above. Notice that <> *Yes* (not equal to Yes) has been entered in the Criteria row for the Discontinued field. This query finds all the records that don't have a value of *Yes* in that field (in other words, all the records that have not been discontinued).

Run

6. As an experiment, in the **Criteria** row of the **Discontinued** field, replace <> with =, and then on the **Design** contextual tab, in the **Results** group, click the **Run** button.

> **Tip** You can also run a query by switching to Datasheet view.

This time, the query finds all the records that have been discontinued.

The 18 discontinued products account for the difference between the number of records in the Products table and the number of records displayed by the original query.

Category Nam ▾	Product Name	Quantity Per Unit ▾	Units In Stoc ▾	Discontinue ▾
Bonsai supplies	Bonsai mixed garden	1 ea.	0	☑
Bonsai supplies	Bonsai scissors	1 ea.	0	☑
Fertilizers	Guano	5 lb. bag	0	☑
Fertilizers	Muriate of potash	10 lb. bag	0	☑
Grasses	Decorator moss	1 tray	0	☑
Shrubs/hedges	Hedge shears 10"	1 ea.	0	☑
Soils/sand	Buckwheat hulls	5 lb bag	0	☑
Soils/sand	Oyster shells	5 lb bag	0	☑
Soils/sand	Peanut hull meal	5 lb bag	0	☑
Soils/sand	Terrarium soil	5 lb bag	0	☑
Tools	Manure fork	1 ea.	0	☑
Tools	Optional grass catcher	1 ea.	0	☑
Tools	Posthole digger	1 ea.	0	☑
Tools	Push reel lawn mower	1 ea.	0	☑
Tools	Revolving sprinkler	1 ea.	0	☑
Tools	Root waterer	1 ea.	0	☑
Tools	Shade fencing 6'	50' roll	0	☑
Tools	Sharpening kit	1 ea.	0	☑
✱				☐

CLOSE the Products By Category query without saving your changes, and then close the *Queries* database.

Exploring Forms

Access tables are dense lists of raw information. It will probably be quite simple for you to work directly with tables in a database you create for your own use, but might be overwhelming for people who don't know much about databases. To make it easier to enter, retrieve, display, and print information, you can design *forms* through which people can interact with your database.

A form is essentially a window containing *controls* that either display information to people or accept information that people enter. Access provides a collection of standard Windows controls, such as labels, text boxes, option buttons, and check boxes. With a little ingenuity, you can create forms that look and work much like the dialog boxes in all Windows applications.

A form acts as a friendly interface for a table. Through a form, you can display and edit the records of the underlying table, or create new records. As with tables and queries, you can display forms in several views. The three most common views are:

- **Form view**, in which you enter data
- **Datasheet view**, which looks essentially like a table
- **Design view**, in which you work with the elements of the form to refine the way it looks and works

Most forms link to only one table, but if you want to link to multiple tables from one form, you can embed other forms (*subforms*) within a form (then referred to as the *main form*). The form shown above in Design view includes *label controls* containing text that appears in the form in Form view, and *text box controls* that will contain data from the underlying table. Although you can create a form from scratch in Design view, you will probably use this view most often to refine forms you create by using a wizard.

In this exercise, you will explore forms, subforms, and the available form controls.

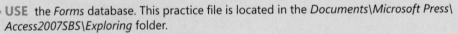

USE the *Forms* database. This practice file is located in the *Documents\Microsoft Press\Access2007SBS\Exploring* folder.

OPEN the *Forms* database.

1. In the **Navigation Pane**, under **Forms**, double-click **Orders**.

   The **Orders** form opens. This form consists of a main form and a subform. The main form displays information from the Orders table. The subform, which looks like a datasheet in the middle of the main form, displays the information from the Order Details table for the current record.

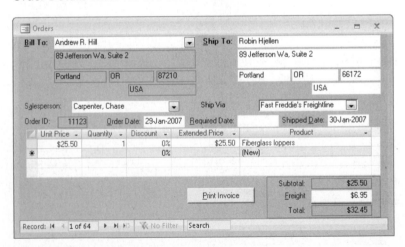

Next Record

2. In the form window, on the record navigation bar, click the **Next Record** button a few times to display the next few records.

   Notice that the subform changes with each click to display the items purchased on that order.

3. Click the **Bill To** arrow to display a list of all customers who have placed orders.

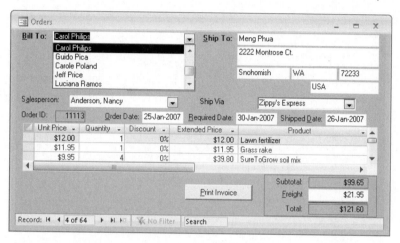

This is an example of a list box control.

4. In the **Navigation Pane**, under **Forms**, double-click **Products**.

   The Products form opens in Form view.

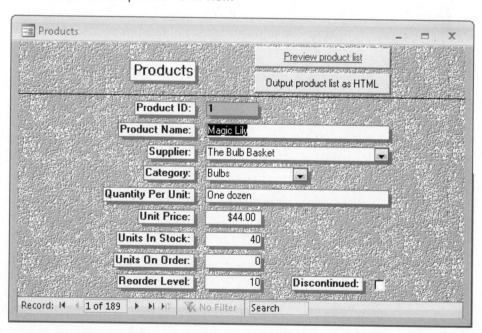

The purpose of this form is to edit or create product records.

5. On the **Home** tab, in the **Views** group, click the **View** arrow, and then in the list, click **Design View**.

This is the view in which you can add controls to a form.

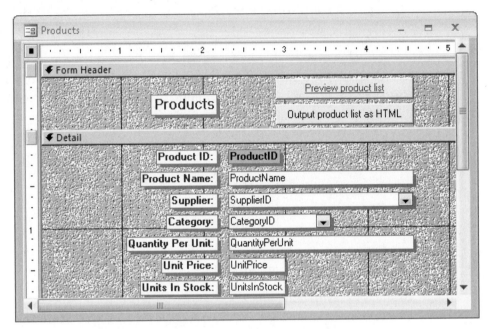

6. Note that two Form Design Tools contextual tabs, Design and Arrange, were added to the Ribbon when you switched to Design view. Switch to Form view and then back to Design view to see this happen.

Contextual tabs are available only when you are working on an object that needs the tools on it.

7. On the **Design** contextual tab, point to each of the buttons in the center section of the **Controls** group to display the name of the control in a ScreenTip. You can use these controls to assemble custom forms for your database.

CLOSE the Orders and Products forms without saving your changes, and then close the *Forms* database.

> **Tip** To change the level of detail displayed in ScreenTips, click Access Options on the Office menu. The ScreenTip Style list at the top of the Popular page displays the detail options: *Show feature descriptions in ScreenTips, Don't show feature descriptions in ScreenTips,* and *Don't show ScreenTips.*

Exploring Reports

You can display the information recorded in your tables in nicely formatted, easily accessible *reports*, either on your computer screen or on paper. A report can include items of information selected from multiple tables and queries, values calculated from information in the database, and formatting elements such as headers, footers, titles, and headings.

You can look at reports in four views:

● **Design View,** in which you can manipulate the design of a report in the same way that you manipulate a form.

● **Report View,** where you can scroll through the information in the report without the page breaks inserted when it is printed.

● **Print Preview,** in which you see your report exactly as it will look when printed.

● **Layout View,** which displays the data in the report (similar to Print Preview) but enables you to edit the layout.

In this exercise, you will preview a report as it will appear when printed.

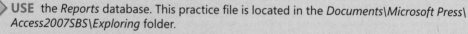

USE the *Reports* database. This practice file is located in the *Documents\Microsoft Press\ Access2007SBS\Exploring* folder.
OPEN the *Reports* database.

1. In the **Navigation Pane**, under **Reports**, right-click **Customer Labels**, and then click **Print Preview**.

   The Customer Labels report opens.

2. Click the preview document to display a larger view of it.

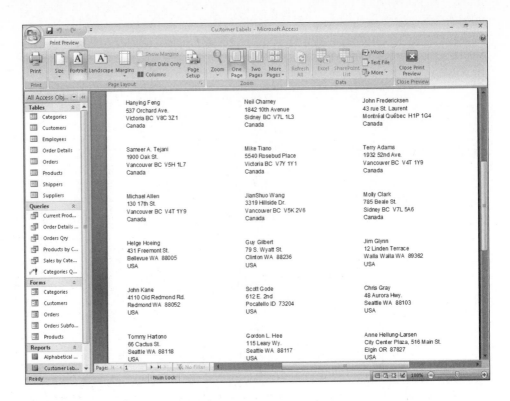

> **Tip** If the report is too small to read in Print Preview, you can adjust the zoom level by clicking the Zoom In button or dragging the Zoom slider that appears in the lower-right corner of the Print Preview window.

This report prints customer names and addresses in a mailing label format. You are looking at it in a view that is much like Print Preview in other Office programs.

> **Tip** Access provides a wizard that can help you create a mailing label report. You can also use the Customers table as a source document for the Word 2007 mail merge tool to create labels like these.

3. In the **Navigation Pane**, right-click the **Sales by Category** report, and then click **Print Preview**.

4. Scroll through a few pages of the multi-page report by clicking the navigation buttons at the bottom of the window.

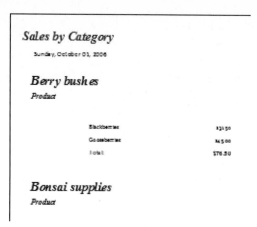

Design View

5. On the **View** toolbar, click the **Design View** button.

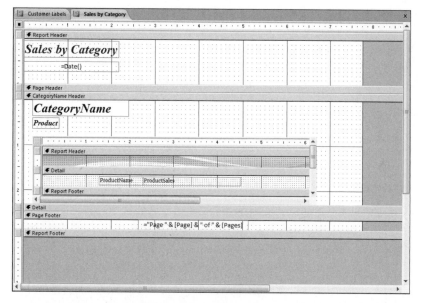

Access displays the report in Design view. In this view, the report looks similar to a form. The techniques you use to create forms can also be used to create reports.

 CLOSE the Customer Labels report and the Sales By Category report without saving your changes, and then close the *Reports* database.

Exploring Other Access Objects

Tables, queries, forms, and reports are the objects you will use most frequently in Access. You can use them to create powerful and useful databases. However, you can also use macros and modules to substantially extend the capabilities of Access.

> **Tip** Previous versions of Access included Data Access Pages. Access 2007 doesn't include these objects. If you are familiar with Data Access Pages and need something like this, you can deploy your database to a collaboration site built with Microsoft SharePoint products and technologies, and use the tools provided there.

Macros

A *macro* is a simple program that performs multiple actions. You can use a macro to have Access respond to an event such as the click of a button, the opening of a form, or the updating of a record. Macros can be particularly useful when you expect that other people who are less experienced with Access than you will work in your database. For example, you can make routine database actions, such as opening and closing forms or printing reports, available as command buttons on switchboards. And by grouping together an assortment of menu commands and having users carry them out with the click of a button, you can ensure that everyone does things the same way.

Modules

More powerful than macros, *modules* are Microsoft Visual Basic for Applications (VBA) programs. VBA is a high-level programming language developed by Microsoft for the purpose of creating Windows programs. A common set of VBA instructions can be used with all programs in the Microsoft Office system, and each program has its own set as well. Whereas macros can automate four to five dozen actions, VBA includes hundreds of commands and can be extended indefinitely with third-party add-ins. You could use VBA to carry out tasks that are too complex to be handled with macros, such as opening an Excel spreadsheet and retrieving specific information.

> **Tip** The Microsoft 2007 Office system installation CD and the online resources include a variety of sample databases that illustrate many of the principles of creating and using a database. You can use these to learn more about Access features, or as templates for your own databases.
>
> One of these, the *Northwind 2007* database, is used as an example in many topics in the Access Help system, so it is a particularly good database for you to explore. You'll find a link to this database in the Sample category in the Getting Started window.

Previewing and Printing Access Objects

Because Access is a Windows application, it interacts with your printer through standard Windows dialog boxes and drivers. This means that any printer that you can use from other programs can be used from Access, and any special features of that printer, such as color printing or duplex printing, are available in Access.

As you have seen in this chapter, you can use different Access objects—tables, forms, reports, and so on—to display the information stored in your database. Within each object there are several views available: Design view, Datasheet view, and so on. You can choose the view you want by selecting it from the View group on the Home tab (the views available will depend on the object that is active) or by clicking the buttons on the View toolbar at the right end of the status bar at the bottom of the window.

The print-related commands are available from the Microsoft Office Button or on the Ribbon when their use would be appropriate, which is determined by the object displayed and the current view of that object.

In this exercise, you will preview and print a table and a form.

USE the *Print* database. This practice file is located in the *Documents\Microsoft Press\Access2007SBS\Exploring* folder.

OPEN the *Print* database.

1. In the **Navigation Pane**, expand the **Tables** list, and then double-click the **Employees** table to open it in Datasheet view.

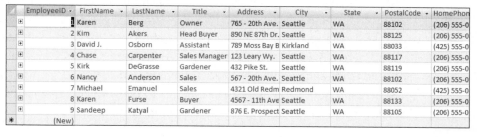

EmployeeID	FirstName	LastName	Title	Address	City	State	PostalCode	HomePhon
1	Karen	Berg	Owner	765 - 20th Ave.	Seattle	WA	88102	(206) 555-0
2	Kim	Akers	Head Buyer	890 NE 87th Dr.	Seattle	WA	88125	(206) 555-0
3	David J.	Osborn	Assistant	789 Moss Bay B	Kirkland	WA	88033	(425) 555-0
4	Chase	Carpenter	Sales Manager	123 Leary Wy.	Seattle	WA	88117	(206) 555-0
5	Kirk	DeGrasse	Gardener	432 Pike St.	Seattle	WA	88119	(206) 555-0
6	Nancy	Anderson	Sales	567 - 20th Ave.	Seattle	WA	88102	(206) 555-0
7	Michael	Emanuel	Sales	4321 Old Redm	Redmond	WA	88052	(425) 555-0
8	Karen	Furse	Buyer	4567 - 11th Ave	Seattle	WA	88133	(206) 555-0
9	Sandeep	Katyal	Gardener	876 E. Prospect	Seattle	WA	88105	(206) 555-0
(New)								

This table contains information about nine employees. You can see that there are more fields than will fit on the screen.

Microsoft Office
Button

2. To display the first page of the datasheet printout, click the **Microsoft Office Button**, point to **Print**, and then click **Print Preview**.

3. Click the preview document once to zoom in, so the table content is legible.

Next Page

4. At the bottom of the **Print Preview** window, click the **Next Page** button.

This datasheet will print as three short pages if you print it with the current settings. Notice that the information on the second and third pages is a continuation of the table started on the first page.

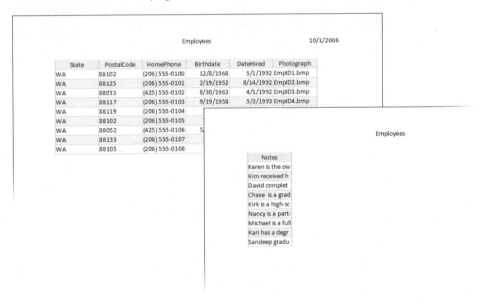

5. On the **Print Preview** tab, in the **Page Layout** group, click the **Landscape** button.

In Landscape orientation, the datasheet fits onto two pages.

> **Tip** In this book, when we give instructions to implement a command we tell you on what tab and in which group the command button appears. When directing you to use multiple command buttons on the same tab, we might omit the tab name to avoid needless repetition.

Print

6. In the **Print** group, click the **Print** button.

The Print dialog box opens. You can select the printer and set print options (such as the range of pages, specific records, or number of copies to be printed) from this dialog box.

> **Tip** If you just want to send this datasheet to your default printer, click the Microsoft Office Button, point to Print, and then click Quick Print.

Close Print
Preview

7. Close the **Print** dialog box and then in the **Close Preview** group, click the **Close Print Preview** button.

8. In the **Navigation Pane**, under **Forms**, double-click **Employees**.

The Employees form opens in Form view.

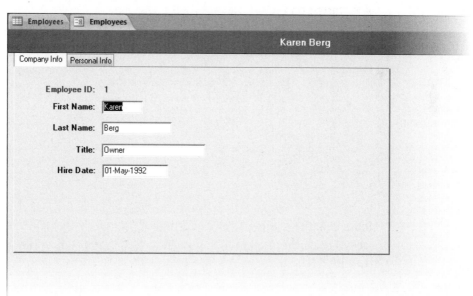

The information for each employee appears on its own page. Notice that there are two tabs at the top of the page, one for company information and one for personal information.

9. Click the **Personal Info** tab to see the information that is listed there, and then return to the **Company Info** tab.

10. Click the **Microsoft Office Button**, point to **Print**, and then click **Print Preview** to preview the printout.

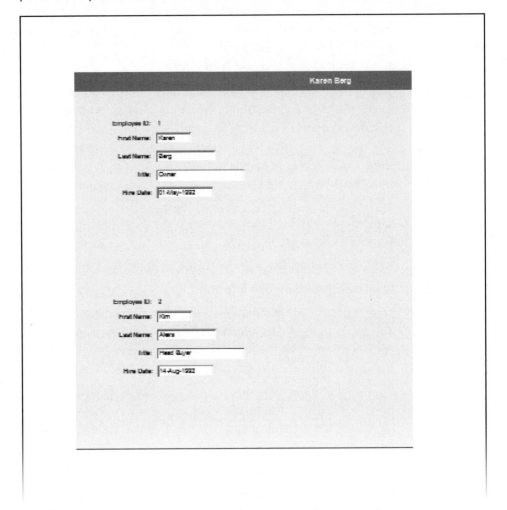

Notice that the preview shows information from only the active form tab. If you want to print information that appears on a different tab, you first need to select that tab.

11. On the **View** toolbar, click the **Form View** button to return to that view.

Form View

See Also You use essentially the same methods to print information displayed in different Access objects. For more information, see "Previewing and Printing a Report" in Chapter 8, "Working with Reports."

CLOSE the Employees table and the Employees form without saving your changes, and then close the *Print* database.

Key Points

- Access is part of the Microsoft Office system, so the basic interface objects—menus, toolbars, dialog boxes—work much the same as other Office products or other Windows applications.

- A database is the computer equivalent of an organized list of information. The power of a database is in your ability to organize and quickly retrieve precise information from it, and then to manipulate, share, and distribute or use this information in various ways. In Access, data is organized in tables comprised of columns and rows, called fields and records. Access is a relational database, so you can treat the multiple tables in one database as a single storage area and easily pull information from different tables in whatever order and format that suits you.

- The types of objects you can work with in Access include tables, queries, forms, reports, macros, and modules. Tables are the core database objects and the purpose of every other database object is to interact with one or more tables.

- Every Access object has two or more views. For example, you view data in a table in Datasheet view and define how the data is displayed in Design view.

- One way to locate information in an Access database is to create and run a query. You use queries to find information so that you can view, change, or analyze it in various ways. You can view queries in Datasheet view or Design view. You can use the results of a query as the basis for other Access objects, such as a form or report.

- Forms make it easy for users to enter, retrieve, display and print information stored in tables. A form is essentially a window in which you can place controls that either give users information or accept information they enter. Forms can be viewed in Form view, Datasheet view, or Design view.

- Reports display information from your tables in a nicely formatted, easily accessible way, either on your computer screen or on paper. A report can include items of information from multiple tables and queries, values calculated from information in the database, and formatting elements such as headers, footers, titles, and headings. Reports can be viewed in Design view, Print Preview, and Layout Preview.

- Macros and modules substantially extend the capabilities of Access. Macros can be used to make routine database actions available as command buttons in forms, which help less experienced users work in your database. Modules are VBA programs. Whereas macros can automate many actions, VBA can be used to carry out tasks that are too complex to be handled with macros.

Chapter at a Glance

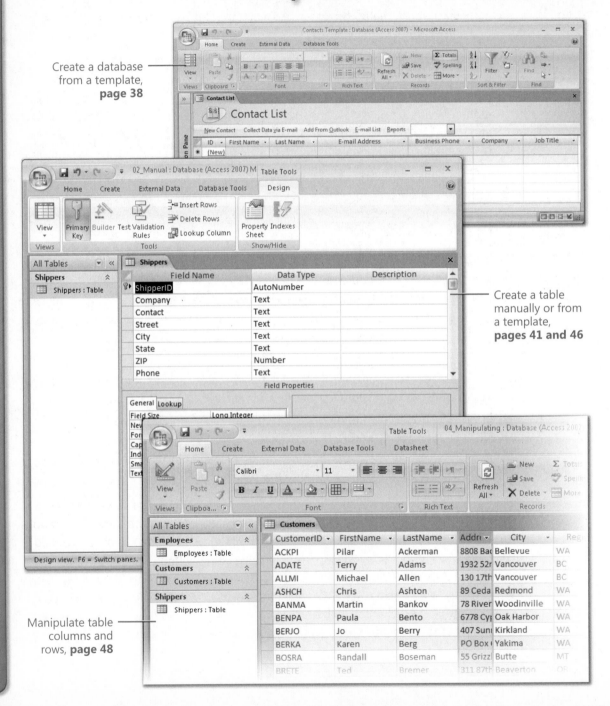

Create a database from a template, **page 38**

Create a table manually or from a template, **pages 41 and 46**

Manipulate table columns and rows, **page 48**

2 Creating a Database

In this chapter, you will learn to:

✔ Create a database from a template.

✔ Create a table manually or from a template.

✔ Manipulate table columns and rows.

Creating the structure for a database is easy. But an empty database is no more useful than an empty document or worksheet. It is only when you fill, or *populate*, a database with data in tables that it starts to serve a purpose. As you add queries, forms, and reports, it becomes easier to use. If you customize it with a switchboard or custom categories and groups, it moves into the realm of being a *database application*.

Not every database has to be refined to the point that it can be classified as an application. Databases that only you or a few experienced database users will work with can remain fairly rough-hewn. But if you expect an administrative assistant to enter data or your company's executives to generate their own reports, spending a little extra time in the beginning to create a solid database application will save a lot of work later. Otherwise, you'll find yourself continually repairing damaged files or walking people through seemingly easy tasks.

Microsoft Office Access 2007 takes a lot of the difficult and mundane work out of creating and customizing a database by providing database applications in the form of *templates* that you modify and fill with your own information. Access 2007 also provides templates for common types of tables, and improved ways to import content from other applications to instantly create and populate tables. Using one of these methods to create something that is similar to what you need and then modifying your creation is generally easier than creating the same thing manually. If none of the templates or import methods match your needs, you can create tables manually—another process that has been improved in this version of Access.

In this chapter, you will create a database from a template, create a table manually, and create a single table from a template. Then, you'll adjust the display of a data table to fit your needs. By the end of this chapter, you will have a database containing three tables that will serve as the foundation for many of the exercises in this book.

See Also Do you need only a quick refresher on the topics in this chapter? See the Quick Reference section at the beginning of this book.

Important Before you can use the practice files in this chapter, you need to install them from the book's companion CD to their default location. See "Using the Companion CD" at the beginning of this book for more information.

Troubleshooting Graphics and operating system–related instructions in this book reflect the Windows Vista user interface. If your computer is running Windows XP and you experience trouble following the instructions as written, please refer to the "Information for Readers Running Windows XP" section at the beginning of this book.

Creating a Database from a Template

A few years ago (the distant past in computer time), creating a database structure in-volved first analyzing your needs and then laying out the database design on paper. You would decide what information you needed to track and how to store it in the data-base. Creating the database structure could be a lot of work, and after you created it and entered data, making changes could be difficult. Templates have changed this process. Committing yourself to a particular database structure is no longer the big decision it once was. By using pre-packaged templates, you can create a dozen database applications in less time than it used to take to sketch the design of one on paper. Access templates might not create exactly the database application you want, but they can quickly create some-thing very close that you can tweak to fit your needs.

Tip Access creates new databases in your *Documents* folder. You can change the location as you create each database, or change the default save location. To do so, click the Microsoft Office Button, click Access Options, and then on the Personalize page, under Creating Databases, click the Browse button. In the Default Database Path dialog box, browse to the new default database storage folder. Then click OK in each of the open dialog boxes.

In this exercise, you will open and explore a database application based on the Contacts template. This template is typical of those provided with Microsoft Office Access 2007, in that it looks nice and demonstrates a lot of the neat things you can do in a database, such as adding command buttons and embedded macros to link to other Office applications or Windows commands. Due to the complexity of these templates, you probably shouldn't try to modify them until you are comfortable working with simpler tables and forms in Design view. There are no practice files for this exercise.

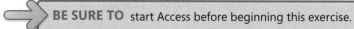

BE SURE TO start Access before beginning this exercise.

1. In the **Template Categories** list, click **Local Templates**.

> **Tip** When you are connected to the Internet, you can find additional templates and other resources in the From Office Online area of the Getting Started screen.

Access displays a list of the templates that are available from the default template location (*C:\Program Files\Microsoft Office\Templates\1033\Access*).

> **Tip** When you point to a template icon, Access displays a description of the database in a pop-up window, called a ScreenTip. For more information about these templates, search Access Help for *Guide to the Access 2007 templates*.

2. Click the **Contacts** template icon.

A description of the template appears on the right side of the program window, along with a box in which you can assign a name to the database and a folder button to browse to the place you want to store the database.

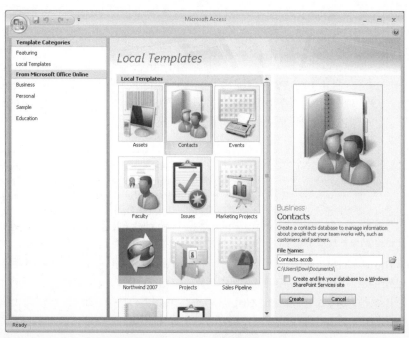

3. In the **File Name** box, type Contacts Template, and note the default path.

> **Tip** Naming conventions for Access database files follow those for Windows files. A file name, including its path, can contain up to 260 characters, including spaces, but creating a file name that long is not recommended. File names cannot contain the following characters: \ / : * ? " < > |.
>
> The extension for an Access 2007 database file is .*accdb*, instead of the .*mdb* extension used for previous versions. For information about the differences between the two formats, search Access Help for *accdb*.

4. Click the **Create** button.

Access briefly displays a progress bar, and then your new database opens.

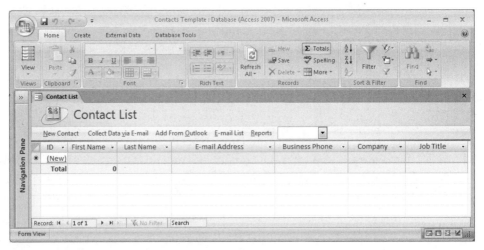

5. If the **Navigation Pane** is closed, press F11 to open it.

The Navigation Pane displays a custom category named Contacts, and a custom group named Supporting Objects. The commands above the column headers are examples of the embedded macros that make this an application rather than a database.

> **Tip** Access stores embedded macros as properties of the object to which they are attached, rather than as a macro common to all database objects. Any modifications you make to an embedded macro are specific to the active object.
>
> Restricting the scope of a macro by embedding it ensures that Access will not consider its actions "unsafe" and therefore will not block it.

6. Enter your own contact information into the first record.

7. Explore the *Contacts Template* database on your own.

CLOSE the Contacts Template database.

BE SURE TO delete the Contacts Template database from the default storage location if you don't want to use it again.

Creating a Table Manually

In the previous exercise, you created a contact management database application based on an Access 2007 template. The database had all the tables, forms, reports, and code needed to import, store, and use basic information about people. But suppose you need to store different types of information for different types of contacts. For example, you might want to maintain different types of information about employees, customers, and suppliers. In addition to the standard information—such as names, addresses, and phone numbers—you might want to track these other kinds of information:

- Employee identification numbers, hire dates, marital status, deductions, and pay rates
- Customer orders and account status
- Supplier contacts, current order status, and discounts

You could start with the template, add fields to the Contacts table, and then fill in only the ones you want for each contact type; but cramming all this information into one table would soon get pretty messy. In this instance, it's better to manually create a database that includes one table for each contact type: employee, customer, and supplier.

> **Tip** In a well-designed database, unique data is recorded only once. If you're capturing the same information in multiple places, it should probably go in a separate table.

See Also For information about ways of controlling table content, see Chapter 7, "Keeping Your Information Accurate."

Design your database content to comply with accepted *normalization rules*. Tables should adhere to the third normalization form rule, which requires that all non-key fields in a record be dependent on one (and only one) other field--the primary key. Data that is not dependent on the *primary key* should be stored in another table, or calculated. (Calculate values that are likely to change.)

See Also For information about normalization rules, see the Access Help system topic "Database design basics." For information about standard, composite, and multi-field primary keys, see the Access Help system topic "Add, set, change, or remove the primary key."

> **Important** With most computer programs, it's important to save your work frequently. With Access, it is not only *not* important to save your data, it is *not possible* to manually save it. When you move out of a record after entering or editing information, Access saves that record. You don't have to worry about losing your changes, but you do have to remember that most data entry changes you make are permanent and can be undone only by editing the record again.
>
> Note, however, that changes to properties and layout are not saved automatically. If you create a new table, form, or report, or modify the properties or layout of an existing one, you will be prompted to save the changes before closing the object or the database.

You can store more than one value in a field (for example, to assign more than one representative to an account) by creating a multivalued field. (Multivalued fields are not natively supported by Microsoft SQL Server, so don't use them if you anticipate exporting the database to SQL Server.)

See Also For more information, see the Access Help system topic "Guide to multivalued fields."

In this exercise, you will open a blank database, create a table, manually add a record, and import some records. There are no practice files for this exercise.

BE SURE TO start Access before beginning this exercise.

1. On the **Getting Started with Microsoft Access** page, under **New Blank Database**, click **Blank Database**.

   Access displays information about the selected template on the right side of the program window.

Browse for a location

2. In the **File Name** box, type Manual, click the **Browse for a location** button, browse to the *Documents\Microsoft Press\Access2007SBS\Creating* folder, and click **OK**.

   > **Important** You can't create a blank database without saving it. If you don't provide a path and file name in the File Name box, Access saves the file in a default location and with a sequentially-numbered default name. The usual location is in the *Documents* folder, and the name is in the format *Database1.accdb*.

3. Click **Create** to create the blank database in the specified location.

   The database opens, displaying a new blank table named Table1, in a group named Table1.

   > **Tip** If you already have a table set up the way you want, you can copy its structure into a new table. To do so, right-click the existing table in the Navigation Pane, and then click Copy. On the Home tab, in the Clipboard group, click the Paste button. In the Paste Table As dialog box, supply a unique name for the table, click Structure Only, and then click OK.

Tip Notice that the first column is titled ID and the second is titled Add New Field. Access automatically creates the ID field—you can delete it if you don't need it. The ability to add fields to a table by simply typing data in the first row is new with Access 2007. As you enter information in the cells, Access adds fields to the table and guesses at the data type and other properties.

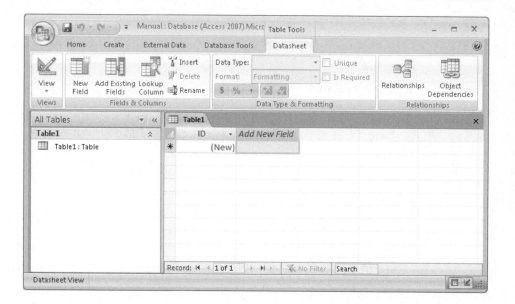

Troubleshooting At press time, there was an unresolved bug in the process for adding the first record to a table. The result of the bug is that if you don't save the first record after adding the first field, and before adding the second field, then Access increments the record ID value for each field you add to the first record. If you add seven fields, Access assigns the value "7" to the ID field of the first record. To avoid this bug, simply click the record selector after adding a value to the first field of the first record in the table. This will save the record and Access will assign a value of "1" to the ID field. Then continue adding the rest of your fields.

4. Click in the empty cell below **Add New Field**, type Big Things Freight, and then press Tab to move to the next cell.

   Access automatically assigns the value "1" to the ID field, assigns the name "Field1" to the first column, and moves the Add New Field heading to the third column. The Unsaved Record icon (two dots followed by a pencil) in the Record Selector box at the left of the record indicates that this record has not yet been saved.

   Tip You can rename or delete a table by right-clicking the table in the Navigation Pane and then clicking the relevant command.

5. Type the following information into the next six cells, pressing ⎯Tab⎯ after each entry:

   John Woods
   345 S. 34th St.
   Ventura
   CA
   83003
   805 555-0154

   As the insertion point moves out of each cell, its name changes to *Field* followed by a number.

6. Double-click the **ID** column name, and then type ShipperID to rename it.

7. Repeat step 6 for the other columns, changing the column names to the following:

Field1	Company	Field4	City	Field6	ZIP
Field2	Contact	Field5	State	Field7	Phone
Field3	Street				

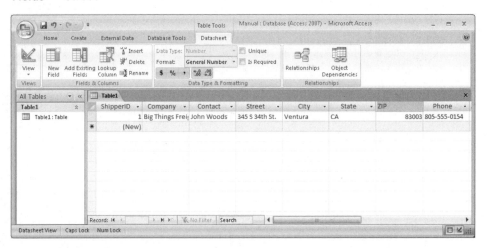

Design View

8. On the **View** toolbar in the lower-right corner of the program window, click the **Design View** button to switch to Design view.

   > **Tip** The buttons displayed on the View toolbar change depending on the type of object that is active. They are a handy way to switch views if the pointer is near the bottom of the window. Most instructions to switch views in this book refer to the View button in the Views group on the Home tab.

   Access prompts you to provide a name, because you need to save the table before changing to Design view.

9. In the **Save As** dialog box, type Shippers, and then click **OK**.

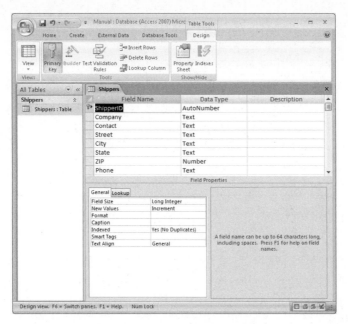

In Design view, the top portion of the window contains a list of the table's fields. The Field Name column contains the names you specified when you created the table. The Data Type column specifies the type of data that the field can contain. The Description column can contain a description of the field.

> **Tip** You can use field names that include spaces, but this can affect how queries and modules have to be written, so it is best not to do so.

Notice the Primary Key icon (a key and right-pointing arrow) to the left of the ShipperID field. The value in the primary key field is used to uniquely identify each record; that is, no two records can have the same value in this field. You can enter this value yourself, or you can let Access help you with this chore. When the data type of a field is set to AutoNumber, as it is here, Access fills this field in every new record with the next available number.

> **Tip** If you don't want a table to have a primary key, select the field designated as the primary key, and on the Design tab, click Primary Key. If you want to change the primary key field, select the new field, and click Primary Key on the Design tab.

10. Click the **Data Type** for the *ZIP* field, click the arrow that appears, and then in the list, click **Text**.

> **See Also** For information about table field types, see the Access Help system topic "Modify or change the data type setting for a field."

> **Tip** If you use only five-digit ZIP codes, the numeric data type would be fine. But setting it to Text is a good idea so users can enter ZIP codes in the ZIP + 4 format.

11. Click each field name in turn, and then in the **Field Properties** area, change the **Field Size** to the following:

Company	40	**City**	50	**Phone**	24
Contact	50	**State**	2		
Street	50	**ZIP**	10		

> **Troubleshooting** If you change any field properties that might cause data to be lost (for example, making the size of the field smaller), Access will warn you of this when you attempt to save the table.

 CLOSE the table, saving your changes, and then close the database.

Attaching Files to Database Records

New in Access 2007 is the ability to attach actual files to database records. (Prior versions of Access used OLE to store bitmap representations of files.) To attach a file to a record you must create a field and set it to the Attachment data type. This can be done only when the field is first created; you can't change an existing field to an Attachment field (nor can you change an Attachment field to another data type).

See Also For more information about the Attachment data type, see the Access Help system topic "Attach files and graphics to the records in your database."

Creating a Table from a Template

Although manually creating a table is relatively easy, if one of the available table templates is close to what you want, using it might save you a little time and effort.

In this exercise, you will use a template to add a table to an existing database.

 USE the *TableTemplate* database. This practice file is located in the *Documents\Microsoft Press\Access2007SBS\Creating* folder.

OPEN the *TableTemplate* database.

Table
Templates ▾

View
▾

1. On the **Create** tab, in the **Tables** group, click the **Table Templates** button to display the list of available templates, and then click **Contacts**.

   A new table opens. This table contains fields appropriate for many common kinds of contact information, but some aren't needed and you will need a few more.

2. On the **Datasheet** contextual tab, in the **Views** group, click the upper half of the **View** button. In the **Save As** dialog box that appears, type Employees, and then click **OK**.

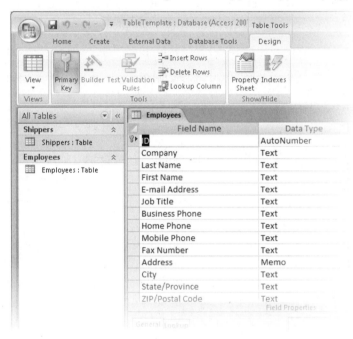

3. Right-click anywhere in the **Company** row, and then click **Delete Rows**.

4. Repeat the previous step to delete the E-Mail Address, Business Phone, Mobile Phone, Fax Number, Country, and Web Page rows.

   > **Tip** You can select and delete adjacent records by clicking one and then shift-clicking another. You can't select multiple non-adjacent records.

5. In the **Job Title** field name, select *Job* and then press the ⌈Del⌋ key, so the field name is just *Title*.

6. Change the **ID** field name to EmployeeID.

   Changing the name of the ID field makes it easier to differentiate the ID field of this table from the ID field of other tables.

7. Change the **Attachments** field name to Photograph.

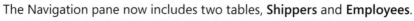

> **Tip** The ability to store and display attachments in a database is new in Access 2007.

8. Click in the first blank **Field Name** cell and type BirthDate. Then press [Enter], type d to scroll the list to **Date/Time,** and press [Tab] twice.

The selection moves to the first column in the next row.

9. Repeat the previous step to add a field named DateHired.

Save

10. On the **Quick Access Toolbar**, click the **Save** button.

The Navigation pane now includes two tables, **Shippers** and **Employees**.

> **CLOSE** the *TableTemplate* database.

Manipulating Table Columns and Rows

When you refine a table's structure by adding fields and changing field properties, you affect the data that is stored in the table. But sometimes you will want to reorganize the table itself to get a better view of the data. If you want to look up a phone number, for example, but the names and phone numbers are several columns apart, you will have to scroll the table window to get the information you need. You might want to rearrange or hide a few columns to be able to see the fields you are interested in at the same time.

You can manipulate the columns and rows of an Access table without affecting the under-lying data in any way. You can size rows and size, hide, move, and freeze columns. You can save your table formatting so that the table will look the same the next time you open it, or you can discard your changes without saving them.

In this exercise, you will open a table and manipulate its columns and rows.

>
> **USE** the *Manipulating* database. This practice file is located in the *Documents\Microsoft Press\Access2007SBS\Creating* folder.
> **OPEN** the *Manipulating* database.

1. In the **Navigation Pane**, double-click the **Customers** table to open it in Datasheet view.

2. Drag the vertical bar at the right edge of the **Address** column header to the left until the column is about a half inch wide.

The column is too narrow to display the entire address.

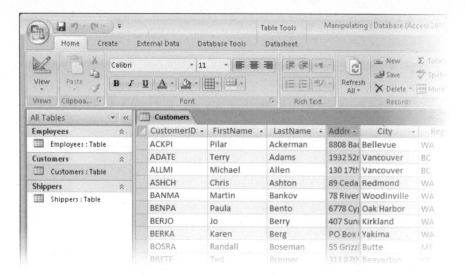

3. Point to the vertical bar between the **Address** and **City** column headers, and when the pointer changes to a double-headed arrow, double-click the vertical bar.

   Access resizes the column to the left of the vertical bar to the minimum width that will display all the text in that field in all records. This technique is particularly useful in a large table where you can't easily determine the length of a field's longest entry.

4. On the left side of the datasheet, drag the horizontal bar between any two record selectors downward to increase the height of all rows in the table.

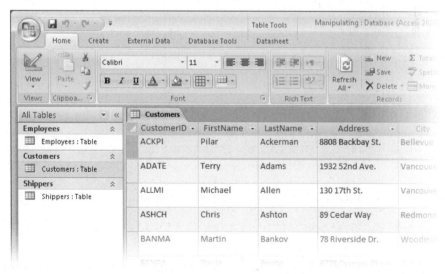

5. On the **Home** tab, in the **Records** group, click the **More** button, and then click **Row Height**.

6. In the **Row Height** dialog box, select the **Standard Height** check box, and then click **OK**.

   Access resets the height of all rows to the default setting. (You can also set the rows to any other height in this dialog box.)

7. Click anywhere in the **First Name** column. In the **Records** group, click the **More** button, and then click **Hide Columns**.

   The First Name column disappears, and the columns to its right shift to the left.

   > **Tip** If you select several columns before clicking Hide Columns, they all disappear. You can select adjacent columns by clicking in the header of one, holding down the Shift key, and then clicking in the header of another. The two columns and any columns in between are selected.

8. To restore the hidden field, in the Records group, click the **More** button, and then click **Unhide Columns**.

   The Unhide Columns dialog box opens.

9. In the **Unhide Columns** dialog box, select the **First Name** check box, and then click **Close**.

   Access redisplays the First Name column.

10. Drag the right side of the database window to the left to reduce its size so that you cannot see all fields in the table.

11. Point to the **Customer ID** column header, hold down the mouse button, and drag through the **First Name** and **Last Name** column headers. With the three columns selected, click the **More** button in the **Records** group, and then click **Freeze**.

12. Scroll the window to the right.

   The first three columns remain in view.

13. In the **Records** group, click **More,** and then click **Unfreeze** to restore the columns to their normal condition.

> **Tip** The commands to hide, unhide, freeze, or unfreeze columns are available from the shortcut menu that appears when you right-click a column header.

 CLOSE the table without saving your changes, and then close the *Manipulating* database. If you are not continuing directly on to the next chapter, quit Access.

Key Points

- Access 2007 includes templates to help you quickly and easily create databases and tables.

- In Design view, you can modify any object you created manually or from a template.

- Rather than storing all information in one table, you can create different tables for each type of information, such as employee, customer, and supplier contact information, or book, video, and CD catalog information.

- Properties determine what data can be entered in a field, and how the data will look on the screen. In Design view, you can change some properties without affecting the data stored in the table; but changing some might affect the data, so you must exercise caution when modifying properties.

- You can adjust the structure of a table—by manipulating or hiding columns and rows—without affecting the data stored in the table.

Chapter at a Glance

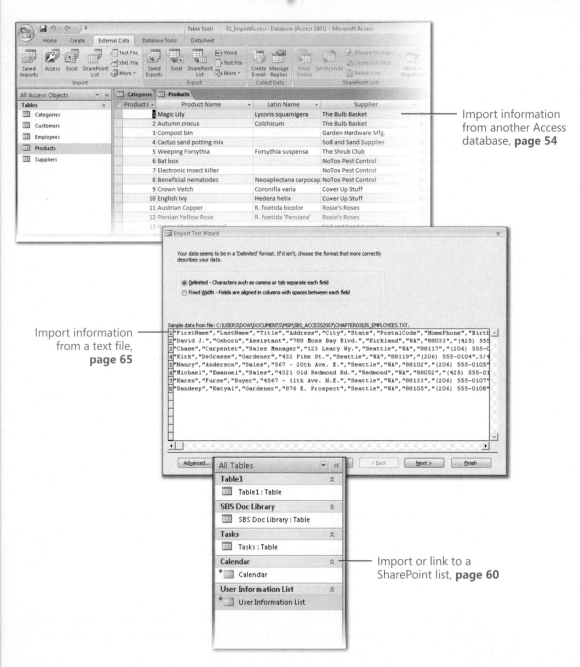

Import information from another Access database, **page 54**

Import information from a text file, **page 65**

Import or link to a SharePoint list, **page 60**

3 Populating a Database

Not many people enjoy typing information into a database table, so an important goal when designing a relational database is to structure the tables in such a way that the database user never has to enter the same information more than once. If, for example, you are designing a database to track customer orders, you don't want sales clerks to have to type the name of the customer in each order. You need a customer table to hold all the pertinent information about each customer, and you can then simply reference the customer ID in the order form. If information about a customer changes, it is updated in only one place in the database: the customer table. In this way, the only item of customer information in the order records (the ID) remains accurate. An added benefit of this system is that you reduce the confusion that can result from typographical errors and from having the same information appear in different formats throughout the database.

Good database design saves keystrokes when you're entering new information and maintaining the database, but you can save even more time and effort in another way. Microsoft Office Access 2007 can easily share information with the other programs in the Microsoft Office system. This makes it easy to populate a database by *importing* information from existing files in other formats.

If the information that you intend to store in an Access database already exists in almost any other electronic document, it is quite likely that you can move it into Access without retyping it.

If your information is still being actively maintained in another program and you want to bring it into Access to analyze it, create reports, or export it to another format, you should consider *linking* your Access database to the existing information in its original program rather than importing the information. When you link to data in another program, you can view and edit it in both programs, and what you see in Access is always up to date.

In this chapter, you will experiment with different ways of getting information into an Access database, including importing information from another database, from a Microsoft SharePoint site, from Microsoft Office Outlook, and from a text, XML, or HTML file. You will learn how to collect data through e-mail and link to data. You will also learn how to migrate an existing database created in an earlier version of Access to Access 2007.

See Also Do you need only a quick refresher on the topics in this chapter? See the Quick Reference section at the beginning of this book.

> **Important** Before you can use the practice files in this chapter, you need to install them from the book's companion CD to their default location. See "Using the Companion CD" at the beginning of this book for more information.

Importing Information from Another Access Database

Suppose you already have an Access database that includes tables of information about products and orders, and another that includes contact information, but you want to have just one database containing all the information you use on a regular basis. You can save time by importing the product and order information into the contacts database (or vice versa), rather than re-creating it all.

You can easily import any of the standard Access objects: tables, queries, forms, reports, pages, macros, and modules. When importing a table, you have the option of importing only the table definition (the structure that you see in Design view), or both the definition and the data. When importing a query, you can import it as a query or you can import the results of the query as a table.

When you import an Access object, the entire object is imported as an object of the same name in the active database. You don't have the option of importing selected fields or records. If the active database already has an object of the same name, Access imports the new object with a number appended to the end of its name.

> **Tip** If you need only some of the fields or records from a table in another database, you can create a query in the other database to select only the information you need and then import the results of the query as a table. Alternatively, you can import the table and either edit it in Design view or clean it up by using queries.

In this exercise, you will import tables from one Access database into another.

USE the *ImportAccess* and *Products* databases. These practice files are located in the *Documents\Microsoft Press\Access2007SBS\Populating* folder.

OPEN the *ImportAccess* database.

Access

1. On the **External Data** tab, in the **Import** group, click the **Access** button.

   The Get External Data wizard starts. The pages of the wizard are specific to the import operation you selected—in this case, Access Database appears in the title bar.

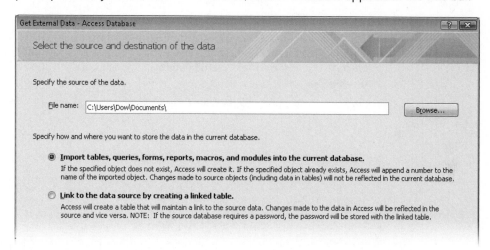

2. On the **Select the source and destination of the data** page, click **Browse**.

3. In the **File Open** dialog box, navigate to the *Documents\Microsoft Press\ Access2007SBS\Populating* folder, click the *Products* database, and then click **Open**.

4. On the **Select the source and destination of the data** page, with the **Import tables, queries, forms, reports, macros, and modules into the current database** option selected, click **OK**.

   The Import Objects dialog box opens.

5. Click **Select All** to select both tables in the list (*Categories* and *Products*). Then click **OK** to import the tables.

    Access offers you the option of saving the import steps. There is no need for this exercise, but if you repeat this process often, you will save some time by doing so.

    > **Tip** To save an import operation for reuse, select the Save Import Steps check box, and then click Save Import. To run a saved import operation, click the Saved Imports button in the Import group on the External Data tab, click the import you want to run, and then click Run.
    >
    > **See Also** For more information, see the Access Help system topic "Run a saved import or export operation."

6. On the **Save Import Steps** page, click **Close**.

7. From the **All Tables** list, open the **Categories** and **Products** tables to confirm that records were imported into the database.

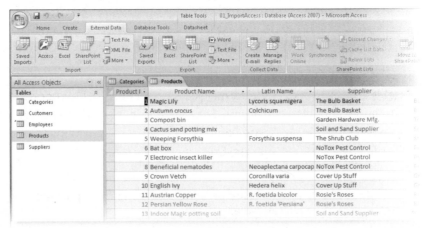

CLOSE the *ImportAccess* database.

Migrating a Database from a Previous Version of Access

Access 2007 stores data in a format that is different from earlier versions. Access 2007 can open databases created in earlier versions and save information to the earlier versions, but earlier versions of Access cannot open a database saved in the 2007 format.

If there is a chance that you or someone else will need to work on a database using a previous version of Access, then you might want to leave it in that format—Access 2007 will open it and automatically save it in the same format. However, some of the features that are new in Access 2007 won't be available unless you update the database to the new format.

Follow these steps to migrate a database from an earlier version of Access:

Microsoft Office
Button

1. Open the database.

2. Click the **Microsoft Office Button**, point to the **Save As** arrow, and then click **Access 2007 File Format**.

3. In the **Convert Database Into** dialog box, specify a name and location for the database, and then click **Save**.

    A message box appears, informing you that the database has been saved in the Access 2007 format and cannot be opened by previous versions of Access.

Importing Information from an Excel Worksheet

Access works well with Microsoft Office Excel. You can import entire *worksheets* or a *named range* from a worksheet into either a new table (one that is created during the import) or an existing table. You can also import specific fields from a worksheet or range.

Excel is a good intermediate format to use when importing information that isn't set up to import directly into Access. For example, if you want to add or remove fields, combine or split fields, or use complex mathematical functions to manipulate data before importing it into Access, Excel is a great place to do it.

> **Tip** The Table Analyzer Wizard provides an easy way to import data from a worksheet into one or more related tables.
>
> **See Also** For more information, see the Access Help system topic "Getting started with Access 2007."

In this exercise, you will import customer information from an Excel worksheet into an existing table in an Access database.

USE the *ImportExcel* database and the *Customers* workbook. These practice files are located in the *Documents\Microsoft Press\Access2007SBS\Populating* folder.

OPEN the *ImportExcel* database.

1. On the **External Data** tab, in the **Import** group, click the **Excel** button.

   The Get External Data wizard starts.

2. On the **Select the source and destination of the data** page, click **Browse**.

3. In the **File Open** dialog box, navigate to the *Documents\Microsoft Press\ Access2007SBS\Populating* folder, click the *Customers* workbook, and then click **Open**.

4. On the **Select the source and destination of the data** page, select the **Append a copy of the records to the table** option, click **Customers** in the list, and then click **OK**.

   The Import Spreadsheet wizard starts.

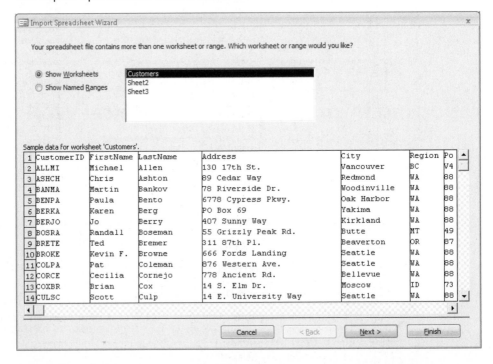

> **Important** When importing information into an existing table, all the field names and data types must match exactly; otherwise, Access can't import the file and displays an error. If the structure matches but data in a field is too large or has some other minor problem, Access might import the record containing the field into an ImportError table, rather than into the intended table. You can fix the problem in the ImportError table, and then copy and paste the record into the correct table.

On the first page of the wizard, you can browse the contents of any worksheets or named ranges in the selected worksheet. Sample data from the selected worksheet or named range appears at the bottom of the page.

5. With **Customers** selected in the **Show Worksheets** list, click **Next**.

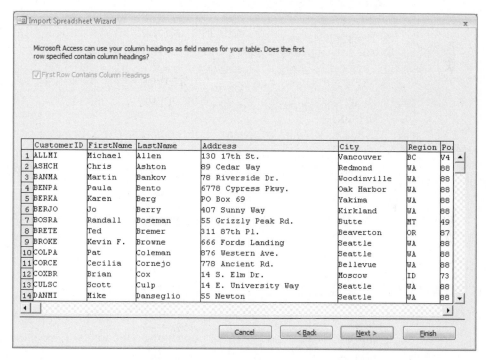

6. Select the **First Row Contains Column Headings** check box if it is not already selected.

7. Click **Next**, and then click **Finish**.

Access imports the worksheet into the Customers table.

8. On the **Save Import Steps** page, click **Close**.

9. Open the **Customers** table to confirm that Access imported the customer list.

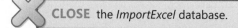

CLOSE the *ImportExcel* database.

Linking to Information

Instead of importing data into an Access database from another program, you can leave the data in the other program and link to it. Although working with data that is stored in your own database is faster, safer, and more flexible, sometimes linking is preferable.

The most common reason for linking to data in another Access database or a different program is because you don't own the data. Perhaps another department in your organization maintains the data in a *SQL database*, and they are willing to give you permission to read the tables and queries but not to change them. Other reasons are security and ease of data distribution.

You can usually link to information in any application from which you can import information. The only difference in the process is the option you select on the Select The Source And Destination Of The Data page of the Get External Data wizard. Rather than the Import or Append option, select the Link To The Data Source By Creating A Linked Table option.

If you link to a file on a *local area network (LAN)*, be sure to use a *universal naming convention (UNC) path*, rather than a *mapped network drive*. A UNC path includes the computer name as well as the drive letter and folder names, so it is less likely to change.

Access indicates a linked table by an arrow to the left of the table icon.

Importing or Linking to a SharePoint List

If your organization utilizes a collaboration site built with Microsoft SharePoint products and technologies, you can work with content from SharePoint lists in Access just as you can other content.

You can bring a list into Access in either of two ways—by importing from or by linking to a SharePoint list.

Importing a SharePoint list creates a copy of the list in the destination Access database. During the import operation, you can specify the lists that you want to copy, and, for each selected list, you can specify whether you want to import the entire list or only a specific view. The import operation creates a table in Access, and then copies the columns and items from the source list (or view) into that table as fields and records. Changes made to the imported data in either Access or SharePoint will not be replicated.

If you're likely to import the list again—for example, to update the data stored in Access—you can save the import parameters. To repeat the saved import process, click the Saved Imports button in the Import group on the External Data tab, select the import specification you want, and then click Run.

If you want to work with data from a SharePoint list in Access but keep the information in both locations current, create a linked table. The process is the same for both operations. Linked tables are indicated in the Access Navigation Pane by a blue arrow pointing to a yellow table. Information you update in Access is reflected in the SharePoint list when you refresh the view, and vice versa.

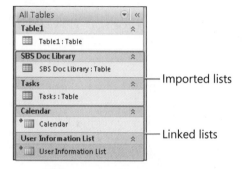 — Imported lists

— Linked lists

In this topic, we demonstrate the process of importing a SharePoint list from a collaboration site.

1. Locate the SharePoint site containing the lists you want to import, and make a note of the site address.

    A valid site address starts with *http://* followed by the name of the server, and ends with the path to the specific site on the server. For example, *http://sbsteam* or *http://sbs/sales/quarterly/*.

2. On the SharePoint site, identify the lists you want to copy to the database, and then decide whether you want the entire list or just a particular view.

    You can import multiple lists in a single import operation, but you can import only one view of each list. If one of the standard views doesn't fit your needs, create a custom view containing only the fields and list items you want, before proceeding.

3. Review the columns in the source list or view, and identify the database into which you want to import the lists.

    When you import a SharePoint list, Access creates a table with the same name as the source list. If that name is already in use, Access appends a number to the new table name—for example, Contacts1. (If Contacts1 is also already in use, Access creates Contacts2, and so on.)

> **Tip** Access will never overwrite a table in the destination database or append the contents of a list or view to an existing table.

4. On the **External Data** tab, in the **Import** group, click the **SharePoint List** button.

   The Get External Data wizard starts, displaying a list of known sites. You are not limited to this list.

5. On the **Select the source and destination of the data** page, under Specify a SharePoint site, click the address of the site you want to connect to, or type it in the box below.

6. Select the **Import the source data** or **Link to the data source** option, and click **Next**. Then, if prompted to do so, enter your site credentials.

   The Import Data From List page displays all the lists available on the selected SharePoint site.

> **Troubleshooting** While testing the prerelease version of this software, the Items To Import list did not update to include a list box for each of the SharePoint lists until step 8. This might have been fixed in a the release version of the software.

7. In the **Import** column, select the check box of each list you want to import into the database.

8. In the **Items to Import** column, for each of the selected lists, select the view (arrangement of data) that you want to import into the database.

> **Troubleshooting** If the Items To Import list does not include a list box for the SharePoint list you are importing, click in the column where the list box should be, and it will appear. This might have been fixed in a later version of the software.

9. With the **Import display values instead of IDs for fields that look up values stored in another list** check box selected, click **OK**.

   This option controls which data is imported for lookup columns in the selected lists.

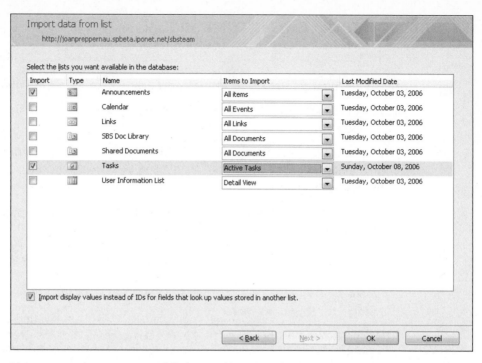

No progress bar appears while Access imports the lists, and this process could take some time. Resist clicking the OK button more than once. When the import process completes, the last page of the wizard appears.

10. If you want to save the import parameters for reuse, select the **Save import steps** check box. On the **Save Import Steps** page, enter a name and description for the specification, and then click **Save Import**.

> **Tip** If you use Microsoft Office Outlook 2007, you can opt to place a task corresponding to the saved import specification on your calendar by selecting the Create Outlook Task check box.

After you import or link to a list, open the resulting table in Datasheet view. Ensure that all of the fields and records were imported, and that there are no errors. You can review the data type and other field properties by switching to Design view.

Collecting Data Through E-Mail

If you're running Microsoft Office Outlook 2007, you can create forms that you can send to other people in e-mail, and then automatically add the responses to a database table. You might use this to process surveys, status reports, orders, or bugs via e-mail. With a little imagination, the uses for this feature are practically unlimited.

For this process to work, the survey recipients need to have an e-mail client that supports e-mail formatted as HTML; most major e-mail clients support this.

See Also For information about additional options and refinements you can make to e-mail surveys, see the Access Help file.

The Collect Data Through E-mail Messages wizard guides you through the process of creating an e-mail survey form. You can create different types of surveys depending on the applications that are installed on your computer.

1. Create a database table containing the fields you want to include in your survey. Position the insertion point in the first empty record.

2. On the **External Data** tab, in the **Collect Data** group, click the **Create E-mail** button.

3. Follow the steps in the wizard to create the form, add and reorder the fields from the table, change field labels, specify the Outlook folder to which the survey results will be delivered, elect to have Outlook automatically add replies to the original Access database table, and specify the survey recipients.

   If you do not have Outlook add the survey responses to the database, this option, you can manually add individual survey replies to the table by right-clicking each in Outlook, and then clicking Export Data To Microsoft Office Access.

4. Customize the text of the e-mail message that will be created, and then on the **Create the e-mail message** page, click **Create**.

   > **Troubleshooting** You might see a warning that you have the database open in an exclusive locked state. Don't worry about this. You can close the database after sending the e-mail and then re-open it without the lock.

   Outlook starts (if it wasn't already running) and displays a generic message along with a form based on the selected table.

5. Make any changes to the message you want, address it to the survey recipients, and then send it.

When sending a data collection e-mail message to more than one person, it is good e-mail etiquette to put your own e-mail address in the To box and other people's addresses in the Bcc box. That way, if a message recipient clicks Reply All, his or her response will go only to you, rather than to all the original recipients.

Message recipients respond to the survey by replying to your message. Outlook delivers survey responses to the Access Data Collection Replies folder (which it creates the first time you need it). You can view individual survey responses and the status of the data collection process for each in this folder, and view the survey data in the original table.

To change the way Access processes message replies, and resend or delete messages, display the table and then click the Manage Replies button in the Collect Data group.

Importing Information from a Text File

Text files are the common denominator of all document types. Almost every program that works with words and numbers can generate some kind of a text file. Access can import tabular data (tables and lists) from delimited and fixed-width text files.

In a *delimited text file*, each record ends in a carriage return, and each field is separated from the next by a comma or some other special character, called a *delimiter*. If a field contains one of these special characters, you must enclose the entire field in quotation marks. (Some people enclose all fields in quotation marks to avoid having to locate and enclose the special cases.)

In a *fixed-width text file*, the same field in every record contains the same number of characters. If the actual data doesn't fill a field, the field is padded with spaces so that the starting point of the data in the next field is the same number of characters from the beginning of every record. For example, if the first field contains 12 characters, the second field always starts 13 characters from the beginning of the record, even if the actual data in the first field is only 4 characters.

Fixed-width text files used to be difficult to import into databases because you had to carefully count the number of characters in each field and then specify the field sizes in the database or in the import program. If the length of any field was even one character off, all records from that point on would be jumbled. That is no longer a problem with Access because the Import Text wizard makes importing a fixed-width text file simple. The only way to get the data of many older programs into Access is to export the data to a fixed-width text file and then import that file into Access.

In this exercise, you will import information from a *comma-delimited text file* into an existing table in an Access database.

> **USE** the *ImportText* database and the *Employees* text file. These practice files are located in the *Documents\Microsoft Press\Access2007SBS\Populating* folder.
>
> **OPEN** the *ImportText* database.

1. On the **External Data** tab, in the **Import** group, click the **Text File** button.

   > **Tip** Text files typically have a *.txt* extension. However, some programs save delimited text files with a *.csv* or *.tab* extension. You will also occasionally see text files with an *.asc* (for *ASCII*) extension. Fixed-width text files are sometimes stored with a *.prn* (for *printer*) extension, but Access doesn't recognize this extension, so you would have to rename it with one it does recognize. Access treats files with all acceptable extensions the same way.

   The Get External Data wizard starts.

2. On the **Select the source and destination of the data** page, click **Browse**.

3. In the **File Open** dialog box, navigate to the *Documents\Microsoft Press\ Access2007SBS\Populating* folder, click the *Employees* text file, and then click **Open**.

4. Select the **Append a copy of the records to the table** option, and in the list, click **Employees**. Then click **OK**.

   The Import Text wizard starts, displaying the content of the selected delimited text file.

Each information field is enclosed in quotation marks, and the fields are separated by commas.

5. Click the **Advanced** button.

   The Employees Import Specification dialog box opens. You can make changes to the default settings.

   > **Tip** If you want to import several files that deviate in some way from the default settings, you can specify the new settings and save them. Then as you open each of the other files, you can display this dialog box and click the Specs button to select and load the saved specifications.

6. In the **Import Specification** dialog box, click **Cancel**. Then in the Import Text wizard, click **Next**.

   The wizard separates the file into fields, based on its assumption that items are separated by commas. From the neat columns you see here, this assumption is obviously a good one. If the columns were jumbled, you could choose a different delimiter from the options at the top of this page.

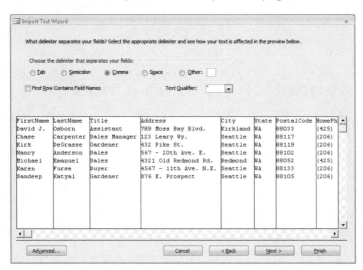

7. Select the **First Row Contains Field Names** check box, and click **Next**. Then click **Finish**.

   Access imports the text file into the Employees table.

8. On the **Save Import Steps** page, click **Close**.

9. Open the **Employees** table to confirm that Access imported seven records from the text file.

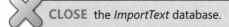

CLOSE the *ImportText* database.

Importing Information from Other Sources

Access 2007 groups the less-common types of files you can import on the More list in the Import group on the External Data tab. These additional file types include:

- ODBC Database (includes a variety of file types, such as Access and Microsoft SQL Server)

- HTML Document

- Outlook Folder

- dBASE File

- Paradox File

- Lotus 1-2-3 File

The process of importing data from any of these file types follows the same general pattern. The Get External Data wizard guides you through the process. In the next three exercises, you will experiment with this by importing data from several of these file types.

Importing Information from an XML File

Extensible Markup Language (XML) files are often used for exchanging information between programs, both on and off the Web. XML files are similar to HTML files in two ways: both are plain text files that indicate formatting within *tags*, and both use start and end tags. However, HTML tags describe how elements should look, whereas XML tags specify the structure of the elements in a document. Also, as its name implies, the XML tag set is extensible—there are ways to add your own tags. Here is an example of a simple XML file:

```
<?xml version="1.0"?>
<ORDER>
    <CUSTOMER>Mindy Martin</CUSTOMER>
    <PRODUCT>
        <ITEM>Sterilized Soil</ITEM>
        <PRICE>$8.65</PRICE>
        <QUANTITY>1 bag</QUANTITY>
    </PRODUCT>
</ORDER>
```

This simple file describes an order that Mindy Martin (the customer) placed for one bag (the quantity) of Sterilized Soil (the item) at a cost of $8.65 (the price). As you can see, when the data's *structure* is tagged rather than its *appearance*, you can easily import the data into a database table. An actual file created for this purpose would contain many instances of the <order> through </order> block, one for each order.

The information in an Access table consists of data and structure. When a table is exported to XML, the data and structure can be exported to separate files, in which case the data is placed in an *.xml* file, and the structure is placed in an *.xsd* file, which is referred to as a *schema*. (The structure can also be embedded in the *.xml* file.) In the following exercise, the *Orders* file contains both data and structure, and the *Order Details* files store the data in one file and the structure in another. If the structure is stored in an *.xsd* file, make sure it is in the same folder as the matching *.xml* file, otherwise Access will import the data and assign default properties to all fields.

In this exercise, you will import XML documents into an Access database.

USE the *ImportXML* database, the *Orders* XML file, and the *OrderDetails* XML and schema files. These practice files are located in the *Documents\Microsoft Press\Access2007SBS\ Populating* folder.

OPEN the *ImportXML* database.

1. On the **External Data** tab, in the **Import** group, click the **XML File** button.

   The Get External Data wizard starts.

2. On the **Select the source and destination of the data** page, click **Browse**.

3. In the **File Open** dialog box, navigate to the *Documents\Microsoft Press\ Access2007SBS\Populating* folder.

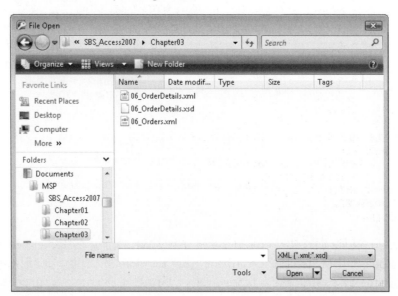

4. Click the *Orders* XML data file, and then click **Open**.

You won't see the extensions if your computer is set to hide extensions for known file types, but you can display them in a ScreenTip by pointing to each file name.

5. On the **Select the source and destination of the data** page, click **OK**.

The Import XML dialog box opens.

> **Tip** Access 2007 can apply a transform script to XML data as you import or export it. *Transforms* are a type of template used to convert XML data to other formats. When you apply a transform during import, the data is transformed before it enters the table, so you can adapt an XML file to a different table structure. For more information about using transforms, search for *transforms* in the Access Help file.

6. With the **Structure and Data** import option selected, click **OK**.

Access imports the *Orders* file and creates the Orders table with the imported data.

7. On the **Save Import Steps** page, click **Close**.

8. Repeat Steps 1 through 7 to import the *OrderDetails* XML data file (the file with the *.xml* extension, not the file with the *.xsd* extension).

9. Open the **Orders** and **OrderDetails** tables to confirm that Access imported the data and structure.

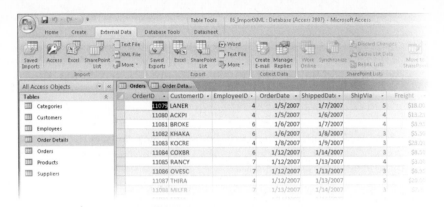

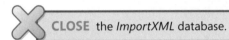 **CLOSE** the *ImportXML* database.

Importing Information from an HTML File

You might be familiar with *Hypertext Markup Language (HTML)*, which is used to create Web pages. HTML uses tags to control the appearance and alignment of text when it is displayed in a Web browser. To display a table on a Web page, the table's elements—rows and cells—are enclosed in appropriate *HTML tags*. For example, a simple HTML table might look like this:

```
    .
    .
    .
<table>
<tr>
    <td>LastName</td><td>FirstName</td>
</tr>
    <td>Anderson</td><td>Nancy</td>
</tr>
</table>
    .
    .
    .
```

Of course, a lot of other tags and text would appear above and below the table, and few tables are this simple, but the example conveys the general idea. With an HTML document, it is the <table>, <tr> (table row), and <td> (table data) tags that make the data look like a table when viewed in a Web browser.

All the 2007 Office programs can save a document in HTML format, and to a limited extent, they can read or import a document that was saved in HTML format by another program. If you attempt to import an HTML document into Access, it will *parse* the document and identify anything that looks like structured data. You can then look at what Access has found and decide whether to import it.

> **Important** If you want to import data into an existing table but the data structure isn't the same as the table structure, it is often easier to import the data into Excel, manipulate it there, and then import it into Access.

In this exercise, you will import information from an HTML document into an existing table in an Access database.

> **USE** the *ImportHTML* database and the *NewCust* HTML file. These practice files are located in the *Documents\Microsoft Press\Access2007SBS\Populating* folder.
> **OPEN** the *ImportHTML* database.

1. Open the **Customers** table, and notice that it contains 107 records. Then close the table.

2. On the **External Data** tab, in the **Import** group, click the **More** button, and then in the list, click **HTML Document**.

   The Get External Data wizard starts.

3. On the **Select the source and destination of the data** page, click the **Browse** button.

4. In the **File Open** dialog box, navigate to your the *Documents\Microsoft Press\ Access2007SBS\Populating* folder, click the *NewCust* HTML file, and then click **Open**.

5. Select the **Append a copy of the records to the table** option, click **Customers** in the list, and then click **OK**.

   The Import HTML wizard starts.

   The wizard displays the contents of the *NewCust* file, divided into rows and columns. If a file contains multiple tables or lists, the wizard shows them here, and you can select the one you want to import.

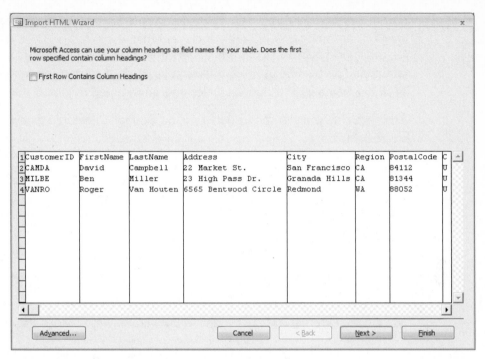

6. Select the **First Row Contains Column Headings** check box, and then click **Finish**.

   Access imports the information into the Customers table.

   > **Tip** You can click an active Finish button in a wizard at any time to accept the default setting for the remaining wizard pages.

7. On the **Save Import Steps** page, click **Close**.

8. Open the **Customers** table to verify that it contains 110 records (the original records plus three imported from the HTML file).

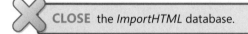

CLOSE the *ImportHTML* database.

Importing Information from an Outlook Folder

You can import address books and folders from Microsoft Office Outlook into an Access database. This could be useful if, for example, you had contact information in Outlook for all the members of a club you belong to, and wanted to import that into a database.

In this exercise, you will import data from an Outlook folder into a new table in an Access database.

USE your Outlook Contacts folder for this exercise. If your Contacts folder is empty, create some contact records at this time or substitute another folder in the exercise.
BE SURE TO install and configure Outlook before beginning this exercise.
OPEN a blank database.

1. Save the blank database in your the *Documents\Microsoft Press\Access2007SBS\ Populating* folder as ImportOutlook.

2. On the **External Data** tab, in the **Import** group, in the **More** list, click **Outlook Folder**.

   The Get External Data wizard starts.

3. With the **Import the source data into a new table in the current database** option selected, click **OK**.

   Outlook starts, if it isn't already running, and then the Import Exchange/Outlook wizard starts.

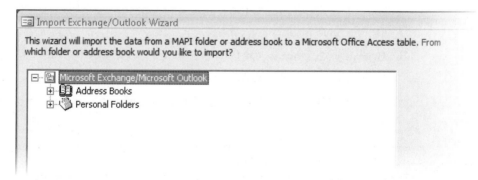

The wizard displays a list of all the address books and folders in your version of Outlook. You can click the Expand (+) or Collapse (–) button next to a folder if necessary to locate the folder you want.

4. Expand your primary mailbox folder, click the **Contacts** folder, and then click **Next**.

The wizard displays all the possible fields in the Contacts folder. You can display information about a field by clicking it. You can edit the field name and data type of the currently selected field and specify whether to index or import the field.

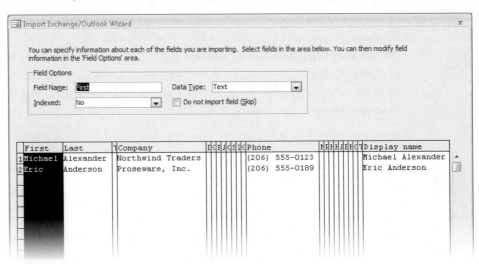

5. On the **Field Options** page, click an empty field, and select the **Do not import field** check box to instruct Access to skip that field. Then click **Next**.

The wizard presents the primary key options. You can let Access create the key, create your own key, or have no key.

6. On the **Primary Key** page, with the **Let Access add primary key** option selected, click **Next**. Then click **Finish** to import the contents of the folder.

The wizard offers you the option of saving the import steps. If you were going to repeat this process in the future, you could save time by selecting this option.

7. On the **Save Import Steps** page, click **Close**.

8. Open the **Contacts** table, to confirm that all the fields are there other than the field you chose to not import.

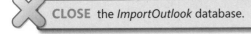

CLOSE the *ImportOutlook* database.

Importing Information from a dBASE File

Importing information from databases created in programs other than Access is usually an all-or-nothing situation, and quite often, what you get isn't in the exact format you need. You might find, for example, that *transaction records* include redundant information, such as the name of the product or purchaser, in every record. A database containing information about people might include the full name and address in one field, when you would prefer to have separate fields for the first name, last name, street address, and so on. You can choose to import information as it is and manipulate it in Access, or you can move it into some other program, such as Excel or Microsoft Office Word, and manipulate it there before importing it into Access.

Access can import data from the following versions of dBASE, Paradox, and Lotus 1-2-3:

Program	Versions
dBASE	III, IV, 5, and 7
Paradox	3, 4, 5, 8
Lotus 1-2-3	WKS, WK1, WK3, WK4

In this exercise, you will import information from a dBASE file into an existing table in an Access database. The process of importing the other file types is essentially the same.

USE the *ImportDbase* database and the *Ship* dBase file. These practice files are located in the *Documents\Microsoft Press\Access2007SBS\Populating* folder.

OPEN the *ImportDbase* database.

1. On the **External Data** tab, in the **Import** group, in the **More** list, click **dBASE File**.

   The Get External Data wizard starts.

2. On the **Select the source and destination of the data** page, click the **Browse** button.

3. In the **File Open** dialog box, navigate to the *Documents\Microsoft Press\ Access2007SBS\Populating* folder, click the *Ship* file, and then click **Open**.

4. Select the **Import the source data into a new table in the current database** option, and then click **OK**.

   Access imports the data and creates the Ship table.

5. On the **Save Import Steps** page, click **Close**.

6. Open the **Ship** table to confirm that five records were imported properly.

CLOSE the *ImportDbase* database.

Key Points

- Importing information into Access 2007 from numerous other programs is easy. If the information is still being actively maintained in another program and you want to bring it into Access to work with it, you can link your Access database to the existing data file.

- You can import entire Excel worksheets, or a named range from a worksheet, into a new table or an existing table. You can also import specific fields from a worksheet or range.

- You can import single or multiple SharePoint lists into an Access database, and even limit the data imported to a specific view of the SharePoint list.

- You can create forms to send in Outlook e-mail, and automatically update an Access database with the responses.

- You can use the Import wizard to import delimited and fixed-width text files into your Access database.

- You can easily import one or more of the standard Access objects, such as tables, queries, forms, reports, pages, macros, and modules.

- You can import data from certain versions of dBASE, Lotus 1-2-3, and Paradox into Access. You can choose to import information as it is and manipulate it in Access, or you can move it into some other program, such as Excel or Word, and manipulate it there before importing it into Access.

- You can import a document saved in HTML format by another program into Access. If you attempt to import an HTML document into Access, it will parse the document and identify anything that looks like structured data. You can then look at what Access has found and decide whether to import it.

- You can import XML files into Access. XML consists of data and a schema, which describes the structure of the data. Programs that export to XML might combine the data and schema in one file, or might create two files. If the program exports two separate files, you will need both files to import both the data and the structure into Access.

- You can link your database to data in other programs, without actually importing the data into your database. This option can be useful if someone else maintains the other data, and you want to have the current information whenever it changes.

Chapter at a Glance

Export information to a text file, **page 90**

Export information to an HTML file, **page 94**

Export information to Excel, **page 82**

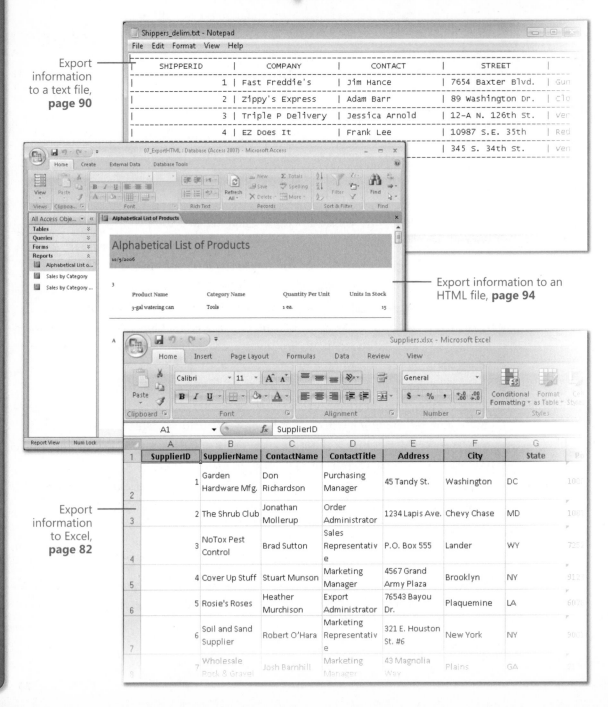

4 Sharing and Reusing Information

In this chapter, you will learn to:

✔ Export information to another Access database.

✔ Export information to Excel.

✔ Export information to a SharePoint list.

✔ Export information to Word.

✔ Export information to a text file, an XML file, or an HTML file.

✔ Copy information to other Office programs.

You can *export* Microsoft Office Access database objects in a variety of formats. From Access 2007, you can export database objects to all the file formats from which you can import data. By installing an add-in, you can also export information to Portable Document Format (PDF) and XML Paper Specification (XPS) files. The specific formats available depend on the object you are trying to export. Tables, for example, can be exported in pretty much the same formats in which they can be imported. Macros, on the other hand, can be exported only to another Access database.

Available export formats include:

Database object	Valid export formats
Table	ACCDB, XLS, XLSB, XLSX, SharePoint List, PDF, XPS, RTF, TXT, XML, ODBC, HTML, dBASE, Paradox, Lotus 1-2-3, Word Merge
Query	ACCDB, XLS, XLSB, XLSX, SharePoint List, PDF, XPS, RTF, TXT, XML, ODBC , HTML, dBASE, Paradox, Lotus 1-2-3, Word Merge
Form	ACCDB, XLS, XLSB, XLSX, PDF, XPS, RTF, TXT, XML, HTML
Report	ACCDB, PDF, XPS, RTF, TXT, XML, Snapshot, HTML
Macro	ACCDB
Module	ACCDB, TXT

> **Tip** To display a list of valid export file formats for a specific Access object, right-click the object in the Navigation Pane, and then point to Export.

When you import information to an Access database, the data being imported usually needs to match certain patterns, or the import process will fail. There aren't any such restrictions when exporting data from an Access database, and the process rarely fails. However, some exported database objects aren't very useful in certain formats.

In this chapter, you will export a variety of objects from an Access database to other 2007 Microsoft Office system applications, as well as to PDF, XPS, XML, HTML, and text file formats. You will also copy and paste data directly from an Access database into a Microsoft Office Word document and a Microsoft Office Excel spreadsheet.

See Also Do you need only a quick refresher on the topics in this chapter? See the Quick Reference section at the beginning of this book.

> **Important** Before you can use the practice files in this chapter, you need to install them from the book's companion CD to their default location. See "Using the Companion CD" at the beginning of this book for more information.

> **Troubleshooting** Graphics and operating system–related instructions in this book reflect the Windows Vista user interface. If your computer is running Windows XP and you experience trouble following the instructions as written, please refer to the "Information for Readers Running Windows XP" section at the beginning of this book.

Exporting Information to Another Access Database

It is very simple to export any single object from one Access 2007 database to either another Access 2007 database or to an Access 2003 database. You can't, however, export multiple objects in one operation.

> **Tip** Data types that are new in Access 2007, such as Attachment or Rich Text, will not export properly to Access 2003. Rich text is exported as tagged HTML, and attachments are exported as the filename of the attachment.

In this exercise, you will export a table from one Access database to another.

USE the *ExportAccess* and *Exported* databases. These practice files are located in the *Documents\Microsoft Press\Access2007SBS\Sharing* folder.

BE SURE TO start Access before beginning this exercise.

OPEN the *ExportAccess* database.

1. In the **Navigation Pane,** under **Tables,** click **Suppliers**.

   Because you will export the entire table, there is no need to open it first. You only need to select it in the Navigation Pane.

2. On the **External Data** tab, in the **Export** group, click the **More** button, and then in the list, click **Access Database**.

3. In the **Export – Access Database** wizard, click the **Browse** button.

4. In the **File Save** dialog box, navigate to the *Documents\Microsoft Press\ Access2007SBS\Sharing* folder, click *Exported.accdb*, and then click **Save**.

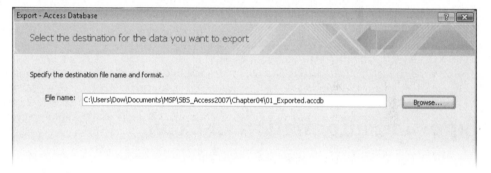

5. In the **Export – Access Database** wizard, click **OK**.

   The Export dialog box opens.

6. In the **Export** dialog box, with *Suppliers* showing in the **Export Suppliers to**: box and **Definition and Data** selected under **Export Tables**, click **OK**.

    Access exports the selected table.

7. In the **Save Export Steps** dialog box, click **Close**.

> **Tip** You can open only one database at a time in a single instance of Access. If you open a second database without first closing the one you are working in, Access prompts you to save recent changes and then closes the first database before opening the second. To open two databases at the same time, launch a second instance of Access from the Start menu, and then open the second database from the File menu; or launch Access and open the database by double-clicking the database file in Windows.

8. In Windows Explorer, navigate to the *Documents\Microsoft Press\Access2007SBS\ Sharing* folder and double-click *Exported.accdb*.

    The *Exported* database opens in a separate instance of Access 2007.

9. In the **Navigation Pane**, under **Tables**, double-click **Suppliers** and verify that the table exported correctly, then close this instance of Access.

 CLOSE the *ExportAccess* database.

Exporting Information to Excel

You can export a single table, form, or query from an Access 2007 database to an Excel 2007 workbook, and to earlier versions of Excel clear back to Microsoft Excel 5.0/95. You cannot, however, export macros, modules, or reports. When you export a form or table that contains a subform or subdatasheet, Access exports only the main form or datasheet. To export a subform or subdatasheet you must perform another export operation on each object. To combine multiple Access objects into a single Excel workbook, you first export the individual objects to different workbooks, then merge all the worksheets from within Excel.

In this exercise, you will export a table from a database to an Excel workbook.

USE the *ExportExcel* database. This practice file is located in the *Documents\Microsoft Press\Access2007SBS\Sharing* folder.

OPEN the *ExportExcel* database, then open the Suppliers table in Datasheet view.

Excel

Export to Excel
spreadsheet

1. On the **External Data** tab, in the **Export** group, click the **Export to Excel spreadsheet** button.

2. In the **Export – Excel Spreadsheet** wizard, click the **Browse** button. In the **File Save** dialog box, navigate to the *Documents\Microsoft Press\Access2007SBS\Sharing* folder, and then click **Save**.

   By default, the spreadsheet has the same name as the table it's based on. You can change the spreadsheet name in the File Save dialog box.

3. In the **Export – Excel Spreadsheet** wizard, select the **Export data with formatting and layout** check box. Then select the **Open the destination file after the export operation is complete** check box.

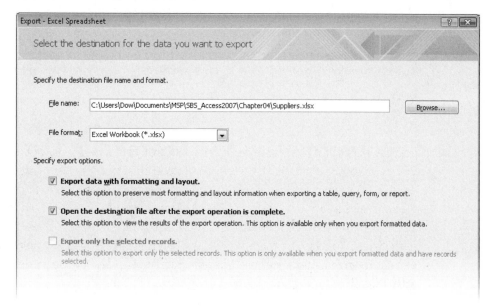

4. With **Excel Workbook** selected in the **File format** list, click **OK**.

   Access exports the table to an Excel workbook. Excel starts, and the workbook opens.

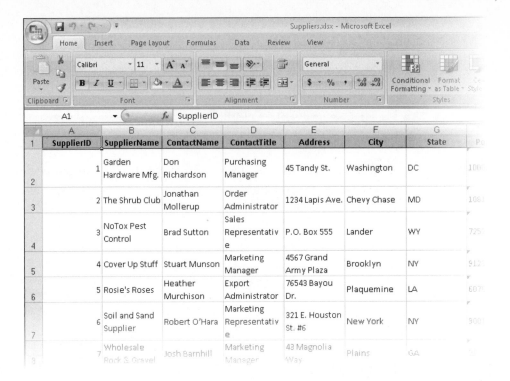

 CLOSE the *Suppliers* workbook and quit Excel. Then close the Export – Excel Spreadsheet wizard and the *ExportExcel* database.

Exporting Information to a SharePoint List

Access 2007 can export a table or the results of a query directly to a SharePoint site. If you have permission to create content on a SharePoint site, you can export data to a SharePoint list; when you do so, Access creates a copy of the selected table or query database object, and stores the copy as a list.

The list content is static and will not reflect changes made to the source table or query after the export operation. You can't overwrite or add data to an existing list.

In this topic, we demonstrate the process of exporting the contents of a table to a SharePoint site.

1. In the **Navigation Pane**, select (but don't open) the object you want to export.

> **Tip** You can export only one object at a time. However, when exporting a table, Access also exports all related tables.

2. On the **External Data** tab, in the **Export** group, click the **SharePoint List** button.

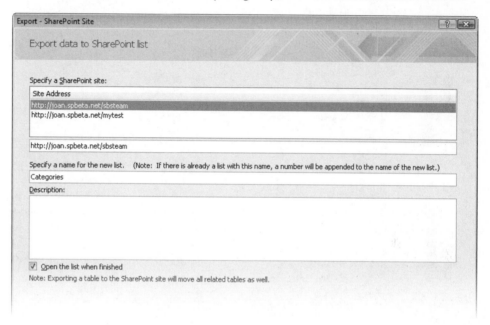

3. In the **Export – SharePoint Site** wizard, specify the SharePoint site where you want to create the list, change the list name and type a description if you want, and then click **OK**. Enter your SharePoint site credentials if prompted to do so.

    Access creates and opens the list on the SharePoint site. If the SharePoint site already includes a list of the same name as the one you are exporting, you are prompted to specify a different name for the new list.

Troubleshooting You might need to switch to the SharePoint site by clicking its taskbar button.

In the resultant SharePoint list, the data type selected for each column is based on the corresponding source field. Any errors or explanations about limited functionality appear at the bottom of the list.

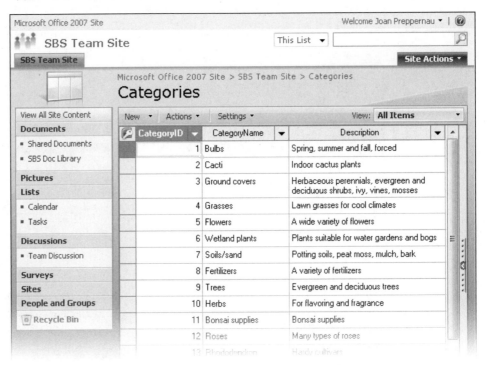

4. In the **Export – SharePoint Site** wizard, if you plan to repeat the export operation in the future, select the **Save export steps** check box.

5. If you want to be reminded to perform the operation at fixed intervals, such as weekly or monthly, select the **Create Outlook Task** check box.

   Saved export operations appear in the Navigation Pane.

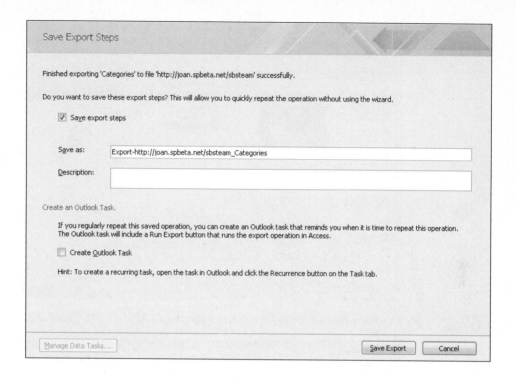

Exporting Information to Word

All Microsoft Office products can share information in various ways. If you need to move a table or the results of a query to an existing Word document, it is often easiest to simply copy and paste the records from the datasheet. But if you want to work with the contents of the Invoice report in Word, then you need to export the Invoice report.

When you export information from Access 2007 to Word, Access creates a Rich Text Format (RTF) document, which can be opened by Word and various other applications.

In this exercise, you will export a form from a database to an RTF document.

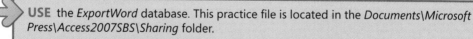

USE the *ExportWord* database. This practice file is located in the *Documents\Microsoft Press\Access2007SBS\Sharing* folder.
OPEN the *ExportWord* database.

1. In the **Navigation Pane**, under **Forms**, double-click **Customers**.

   The Customers form opens in Form view.

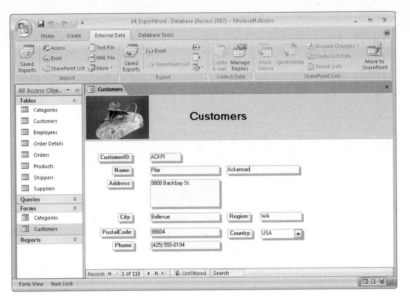

 Word

2. On the **External Data** tab, in the **Export** group, click the **Word** button.

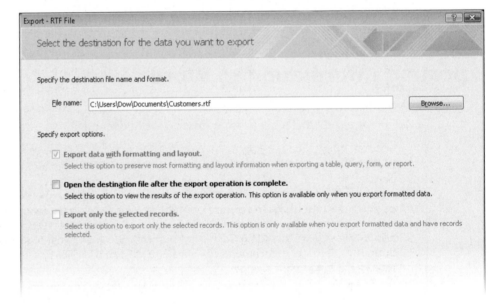

3. In the **Export – RTF File** wizard, click **Browse**. In the **File Save** dialog box, navigate to the *Documents\Microsoft Press\Access2007SBS\Sharing* folder, and then click **Save**.

4. In the **Export – RTF File** wizard, select the **Open the destination file after the export operation is complete** check box, and then click **OK**.

Access exports the table to a Word document. Word starts and the document opens. Notice that Word presents the information in a different format than Access, where only one record is displayed at a time. To see all fields on one page in Word, select the header row, then right-click the selection, point to Auto-fit, and click AutoFit to Window.

 CLOSE the Customers document and quit Word. Then close the Export – RTF File wizard and the *ExportWord* database.

Exporting Information to PDF and XPS Files

You can download an add-in from Microsoft that enables you to export information from 2007 Microsoft Office system applications to Portable Document Format (PDF) and XML Paper Specification (XPS) files. The export process follows the same steps as exporting to other formats.

You are probably familiar with the PDF format developed by Adobe Systems, as it has been around for many years. Information converted to this format should display exactly the same on any computer or operating system. The XPS format is a relatively new one developed by Microsoft to serve a similar purpose. It doesn't yet have the broad support of PDF, but is worth exploring. Because the primary purpose of both formats is to maintain the appearance of the content as it is displayed by various systems, they are good formats to use when publishing reports.

> **Tip** The XML Paper Specification describes the XPS Document format. A document in XPS Document format (XPS Document) is a paginated representation of electronic paper described in an XML-based format. The XPS Document format is an open, cross-platform document format that allows customers to effortlessly create, share, print, and archive paginated documents. XPS Documents use a file container that conforms to the Open Packaging Conventions. The 2007 Microsoft Office system also uses the Open Packaging Conventions for organizing data into files, allowing businesses to manage documents from the 2007 Microsoft Office system and XPS Documents in the same manner.

You can learn more about XPS and download several XPS viewers by visiting

www.microsoft.com/whdc/xps/.

To view a PDF document, install Adobe Reader from

www.adobe.com/products/acrobat/readstep2.html.

Exporting Information to a Text File

Text files are the lowest common denominator file format. Most applications can open, display, and save information in text format. The downside to text files is that they don't contain any formatting information, so they look consistently plain in all applications.

Depending on what type of content you are trying to export from a database, you may have the option to export the formatting and layout along with the data. If you select this option, the unformatted text will be arranged in the text file much as it is in the Access object. If you don't choose this option, the information will be saved as either delimited or fixed-length lines.

In this exercise, you will export a table from a database first as a formatted text file, and then as an unformatted text file.

USE the *ExportText* database. This practice file is located in the *Documents\Microsoft Press\Access2007SBS\Sharing* folder.

OPEN the *ExportText* database, then open the Shippers table in Datasheet view.

1. On the **External Data** tab, in the **Export** group, click the **Text File** button.

2. In the **Export – Text File** wizard, click **Browse**. In the **File Save** dialog box, navigate to the *Documents\Microsoft Press\Access2007SBS\Sharing* folder, change the default file name from *Shippers.txt* to *Shippers_delim.txt*, and then click **Save**.

3. Select the **Export data with formatting and layout** check box. Then select the **Open the destination file after the export operation is complete** check box.

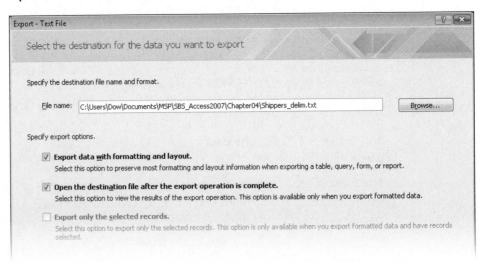

4. In the **Export – Text File** wizard, click **OK**.

The Encode As dialog box opens. From here you can select the encoding format options you want.

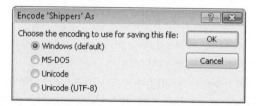

5. With the **Windows** option selected, click **OK**.

Access exports the table as a formatted text file. Your default text editor displays the *Shippers_delim* text file.

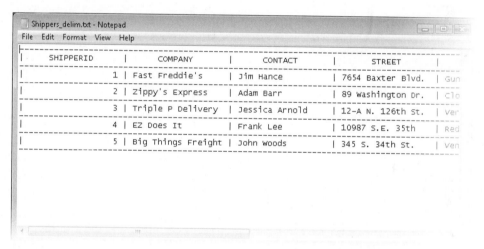

Notice that ASCII characters have been used to separate the rows and columns in the table.

6. Close the text file and the **Export – Text File** wizard.

7. Repeat Steps 1 through 4 to export the table again, but this time change the name to *Shippers_fixed.txt*, and don't select the **Export data with formatting and layout** and **Open the destination file after the export operation is complete** check boxes.

The Export Text wizard starts. This will guide you through the process of setting various options. At any point in the wizard, you can click Finish to accept the default selection for all remaining options.

> **Tip** You can move forward and backward through this wizard by clicking the Next and Back buttons. You can experiment with different options and move along as far as the last page before backing up and trying a different option.

8. With the **Delimited** option selected, click **Next**.

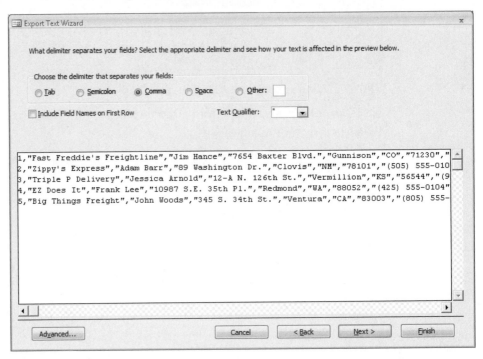

The options on this page are different depending on whether you are exporting a delimited or fixed-width file.

9. With the **Comma** option selected, click **Finish**.

Access exports the table as an unformatted text file. You can use Windows Explorer to navigate to where you saved the *Shippers_fixed* text file and double-click it to open it in your default text editor.

 CLOSE the two *Shippers* text files, the Export Text wizard, and the *ExportText* database.

Exporting Information to an XML File

Access complies with the 2001 XML Schema recommendation described at *www.w3.org/ 2001/XMLSchema/.* You can therefore export data from Access in an XML format that can be used by other applications that are also in compliance. This makes it possible for you to output XML data that can be used by Microsoft Visual Studio .NET programs.

Access 2007 supports exporting tables, queries, forms, and reports to an XML format. You can export the data (.xml file) and schema (.xsd file) files separately, or you can embed the schema in the exported XML data document. You can also export an XLS Stylesheet for use in HTML or ASP presentations of the data.

In this exercise, you will export a table from a database to an XML file.

USE the *ExportXML* database. This practice file is located in the *Documents\Microsoft Press\Access2007SBS\Sharing* folder.

OPEN the *ExportXML* database, then open the Customers table in Datasheet view.

 More ▾

1. On the **External Data** tab, in the **Export** group, click the **More** button, and then in the list, click **XML File**.

2. In the **Export – XML File** wizard, click **Browse**. In the **File Save** dialog box, navigate to the *Documents\Microsoft Press\Access2007SBS\Sharing* folder, and click **Save**.

3. In the **Export – XML File** wizard, click **OK**.

   The Export XML dialog box opens.

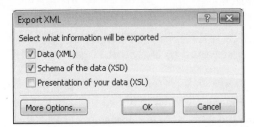

4. With the **Data (XML)** and **Schema of the data (XSD)** check boxes selected, click **OK**.

5. In the **Export – XML File** wizard, click **Close**.

6. In Windows Explorer, navigate to the *Documents\Microsoft Press\Access2007SBS\ Sharing* folder.

   Notice that Access created a data file named *Customers.xml*, and a schema file named *Customers.xsd* file from the exported Customers table. You can view the XML file in Windows Internet Explorer and the XSD file in any text editor.

> **Tip** To export a table as a combined data/schema file, in the Export XML dialog box, click More Options. On the Schema tab that appears, select the Embed Schema In Exported XML Data Document option, and then click OK.

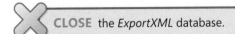
CLOSE the *ExportXML* database.

Exporting Information to an HTML File

Many organizations that store accounting, manufacturing, marketing, sales, and other information on their computers have discovered the advantages of sharing this informa-tion within the company through an *intranet*, or with the rest of the world through the Internet. With Access, you can speed up this process by exporting the information stored in a database as Hypertext Markup Language (HTML) pages.

You can export tables, queries, forms, and reports to an HTML file. Access converts a table, query, or form to an HTML table when you export it, and converts a report to a series of linked HTML files (one for each page of the report).

> **Tip** If you export to an HTML file, you can view the table in a browser, such as Internet Explorer. To see the tags that define the structure of the table, either view the source in the browser or open the file in a text editor.

In this exercise, you will export a report from a database to an HTML file.

> **USE** the *ExportHtml* database. This practice file is located in the *Documents\Microsoft Press\Access2007SBS\Sharing* folder.
>
> **OPEN** the *ExportHtml* database.

1. In the **Navigation Pane**, under **Reports**, double-click **Alphabetical List of Products**.

The Alphabetical List of Products report opens in Report view.

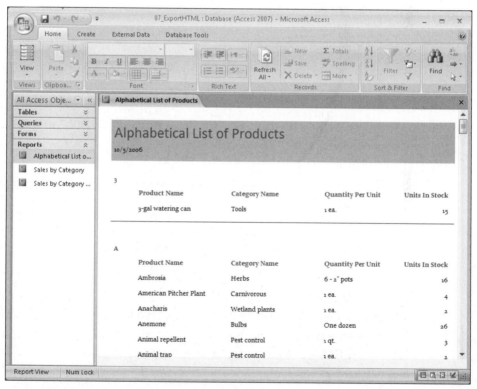

  2. On the **External Data** tab, in the **Export** group, click the **More** button, and then in the list, click **HTML Document**.

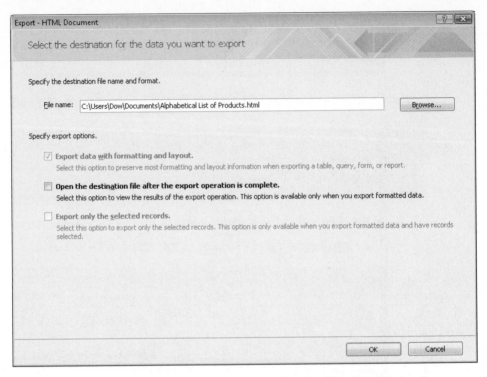

3. In the **Export – HTML File** wizard, click **Browse**. In the **File Save** dialog box, navigate to the *Documents\Microsoft Press\Access2007SBS\Sharing* folder, and then click **Save**.

4. Select the **Open the destination file after the export operation is complete** check box, and then click **OK**.

   The HTML Output Options dialog box opens. You can select the encoding you want to use for saving the file from this dialog box.

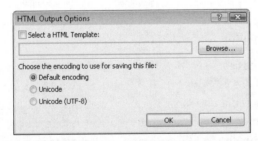

5. With the **Default encoding** option selected, click **OK**.

   For each page of the report, Access creates an HTML file with navigation links at the bottom. The report opens in your default Web browser.

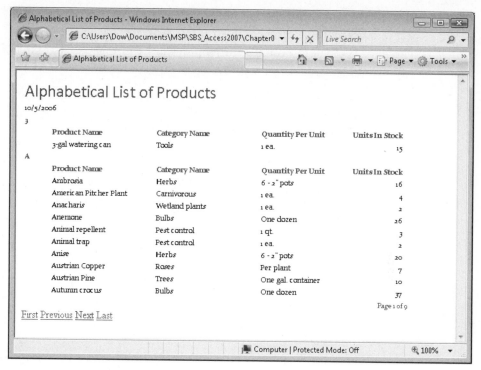

6. Browse the HTML files, comparing them to the report in Access.

 CLOSE your Web browser, the Export – HTML Document wizard, and the *ExportHtml* database.

Copying Information to Other Office Programs

All the methods of exporting data described in this chapter work well, but they aren't the only ways to share information with other programs.

Sometimes the quickest and easiest way to get information into or out of a database is to just copy it and paste it where you want it. This technique works particularly well for getting data out of an Access table and into Word or Excel. Information that you paste into a Word document becomes a Word table, complete with a header row containing the field captions as column headings. Information that you paste into an Excel worksheet appears in the normal row-and-column format.

Getting data into an Access table by using this technique is a little more complicated. The data you are pasting must meet all the criteria for entering it by hand (input mask, validation rules, field size, and so on), and you must have the correct cells selected when you use the Paste command. If Access encounters a problem when you attempt to paste a group of records, it displays an error message and pastes the problem records into a Paste Errors table. You can then troubleshoot the problem in that table, fix whatever is wrong, and try copying and pasting again.

> **Tip** To paste an entire table from one Access database to another, open both databases, copy the table from the source database to the Clipboard, and then paste it in the destination database. You can paste the table data and/or table structure as a new table or append the data to an existing table.

In this exercise, you will copy and paste records between an Access database table, an Excel worksheet, and a Word document.

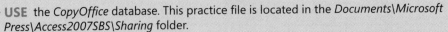

> **USE** the *CopyOffice* database. This practice file is located in the *Documents\Microsoft Press\Access2007SBS\Sharing* folder.
>
> **OPEN** the *CopyOffice* database, then open the Customers table in Datasheet view.

1. Select about six records by pointing to the row selector of the first record you want to select (the pointer changes to a right arrow), holding down the primary mouse button, and dragging to the last record you want to select.

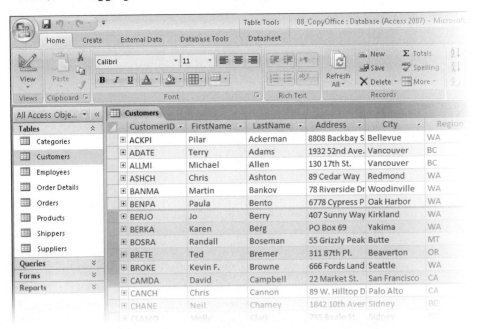

Copy

Paste

2. On the **Home** tab, in the **Clipboard** group, click the **Copy** button.

3. Start **Excel**, open a blank worksheet, and then click cell **A1**.

4. On the **Home** tab, in the **Clipboard** group, click the **Paste** button.

Excel pastes the records into the worksheet, complete with the same column headings. (You will have to widen the columns to see all the data.)

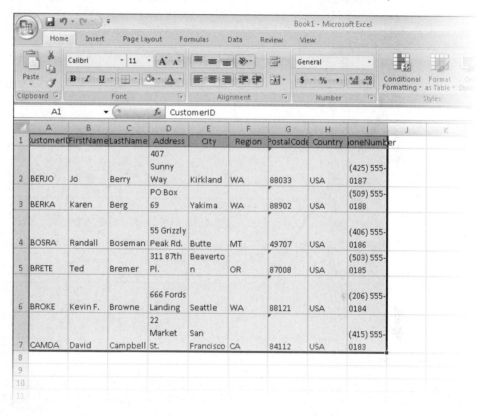

5. Press Alt + Tab to switch back to Access.

6. Select a block of cells in the middle of the table by pointing to the left edge of the first cell you want to select (the pointer changes to a thick cross) and then dragging until you have selected all the desired cells. Then in the **Clipboard** group, click the **Copy** button.

7. Press Alt + Tab to switch back to Excel, click a cell below the records you inserted in step 4, and then click the **Paste** button.

Excel pastes in the new selection, again with column headings. The copied data remains on the Office Clipboard

8. Start **Word** and open a blank document.

9. On the **Home** tab, in the **Clipboard** group, click the **Paste** button.

Word pastes the selection as a nicely formatted table with the title *Customers*, reflecting the name of the table from which this data came.

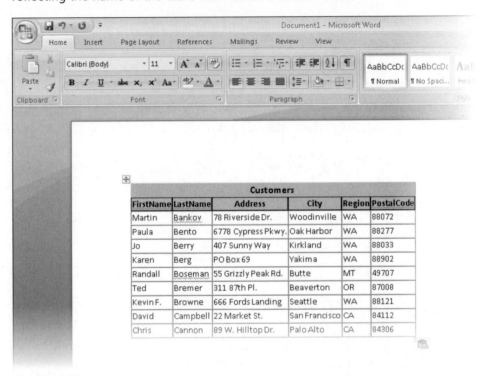

FirstName	LastName	Address	City	Region	PostalCode
Martin	Bankov	78 Riverside Dr.	Woodinville	WA	88072
Paula	Bento	6778 Cypress Pkwy.	Oak Harbor	WA	88277
Jo	Berry	407 Sunny Way	Kirkland	WA	88033
Karen	Berg	PO Box 69	Yakima	WA	88902
Randall	Boseman	55 Grizzly Peak Rd.	Butte	MT	49707
Ted	Bremer	311 87th Pl.	Beaverton	OR	87008
Kevin F.	Browne	666 Fords Landing	Seattle	WA	88121
David	Campbell	22 Market St.	San Francisco	CA	84112
Chris	Cannon	89 W. Hilltop Dr.	Palo Alto	CA	84306

10. Quit Word and Excel without saving your changes.

CLOSE the Customers table and the *CopyOffice* database. If you are not continuing directly on to the next chapter, exit Access.

Key Points

- You can export information from an Access database in a variety of formats, depending on the object you are trying to export.

- You can export any table, query, form, or report to another Access database. You can also export some of these objects to Excel, Word, PDF, XPS, XML, HTML, and text file formats.

- You can merge the information in an Access table with a Word mail merge document, publish the table in a Word document, or export the table to an Excel worksheet.

- You can copy and paste information from your database into other programs.

Chapter at a Glance

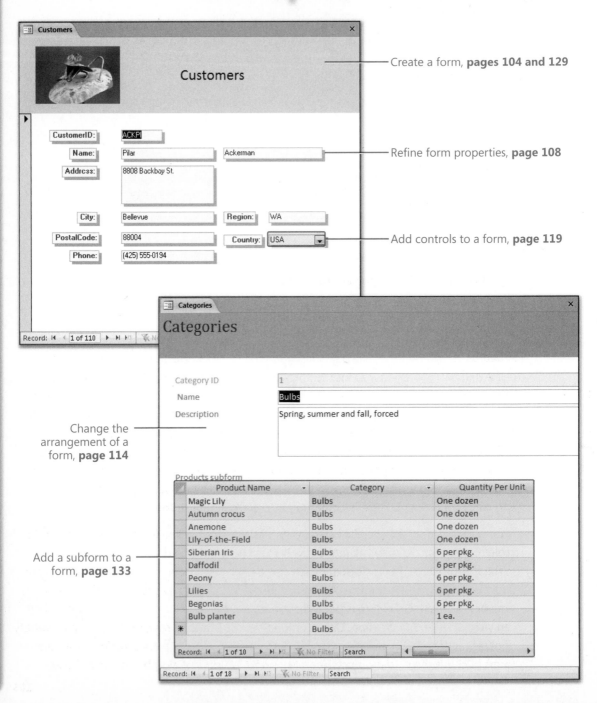

Create a form, **pages 104 and 129**

Refine form properties, **page 108**

Add controls to a form, **page 119**

Change the arrangement of a form, **page 114**

Add a subform to a form, **page 133**

5 Simplifying Data Entry by Using Forms

In this chapter, you will learn to:

✔ Create a form by using the Form tool.
✔ Refine form properties.
✔ Change the arrangement of a form.
✔ Add controls to a form.
✔ Enter data in a form by using VBA.
✔ Create a form by using an AutoForm.
✔ Add a subform to a form.

A database that contains the day-to-day records of an active company is useful only if it is kept current and if the information stored in it can be found quickly. Although Microsoft Office Access 2007 is fairly easy to use, entering, editing, and retrieving information in Datasheet view is not a task you would want to assign to someone who's not familiar with Access. Not only would these tasks be tedious and inefficient, but working in Datasheet view leaves far too much room for error, especially if details of complex transactions have to be entered into several related tables. The solution to this problem, and the first step in the conversion of this database to a database application in which you can efficiently manage information, is to create and use forms.

A form is an organized and formatted view of some or all of the fields from one or more tables or queries. Forms work interactively with the tables in a database. You use controls in the form to enter new information, to edit or remove existing information, or to locate information. Like printed forms, Access forms can include label controls that tell users what type of information they are expected to enter, as well as *text box controls* in which they can view or enter information. Unlike printed forms, Access forms can also include a variety of other controls, such as *option buttons* and *command buttons* that transform Access forms into something very much like a Microsoft Windows dialog box or wizard page.

> **Tip**   You can also create forms to navigate among the features and functions of a database application and have little or no connection with its actual data. A *switchboard* is an example of this type of form.

As with other Access objects, you can create forms manually or with the help of a wizard. It is best to create navigational and housekeeping forms, such as switchboards, manually in Design view. However, you should always create forms that are based on tables by using a wizard, and then refine the form manually—not because it is difficult to drag the necessary controls onto a form, but because there is simply no point in doing it manually.

See Also   For more information about switchboards, see "Creating a Switchboard" in Chapter 9, "Making Your Database Easy to Use."

In this chapter, you will discover how easy it is to create forms—either by using the Form tool or by using the Form wizard—that you can modify to suit your needs, and how to present information from multiple tables in one form by using subforms. You will control a form's function and appearance by inserting controls and modifying the form and control properties. Then you will learn how to automatically enter data in a form by using Microsoft Visual Basic for Applications (VBA) when a user performs an action in the control, such as clicking or entering text.

See Also   Do you need only a quick refresher on the topics in this chapter? See the Quick Reference section at the beginning of this book.

> **Important**   Before you can use the practice files in this chapter, you need to install them from the book's companion CD to their default location. See "Using the Companion CD" at the beginning of this book for more information.

> **Troubleshooting**   Graphics and operating system–related instructions in this book reflect the Windows Vista user interface. If your computer is running Windows XP and you experience trouble following the instructions as written, please refer to the "Information for Readers Running Windows XP" section at the beginning of this book.

Creating a Form by Using the Form Tool

Before you begin creating a form, you need to know which database query or table to base it on, and have an idea of how the form will be used. After making these decisions, you can create a form in many ways. Remember that like almost any other object in Access, after you create the form, you can customize it in Design view if it does not quite meet your needs.

The quickest way is to select a table or query in the Navigation Pane, and then click the Form button in the Forms group on the Create tab. This creates a simple form using all the fields in the table or query, and opens it in Layout view.

If there is one (and only one) other table in the database that has a one-to-many relationship with the table on which your form is based, then the Form tool adds a datasheet (called a subform) which displays all the records in the related table that pertain to the current record in the main form.

In this exercise, you will use the Form tool to create a form based on a table.

USE the *CreateFormTool* database. This practice file is located in the *Documents\Microsoft Press\Access2007SBS\Simplifying* folder.

BE SURE TO start Access before beginning this exercise.

OPEN the *CreateFormTool* database.

1. In the **Navigation Pane**, under **Tables**, double-click **Customers**.

The Customers table opens in Datasheet view.

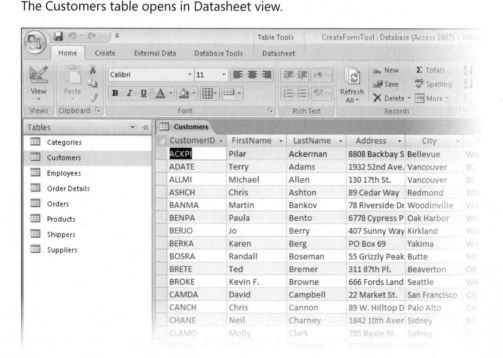

Form

2. On the **Create** tab, in the **Forms** group, click the **Form** button.

Access creates and displays a simple form based on the active table.

> **Tip** You don't have to open a table to create a form based on it. You can simply click the table in the Navigation Pane to select it, then click the Form button on the Create tab in the Forms group. But it is sometimes useful to have the table open behind the form in order to verify the form contents against the table contents.

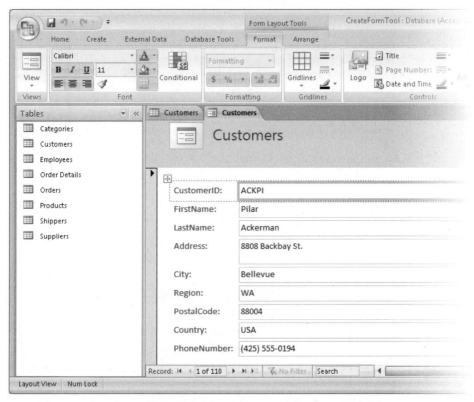

The Form tool automatically added a title (Customers) and a placeholder for a logo in the form header.

3. Scroll through a few of the records by using the navigation controls at the bottom of the form.

You can compare the information shown in the form to that in the datasheet view of the table by alternately clicking the Customers table tab and the Customers form tab in the database window to easily switch back and forth between views.

CLOSE the Customers form (without saving your changes) and the *CreateFormTool* database.

Relationships

In Access, a *relationship* is an association between common fields in two tables. You can use this association to link information in one table to information in another table. For example, you can establish a relationship based on the CategoryID field between the Categories table and the Products table. Each product is in only one category, but each category can contain many products, so this type of relationship—the most common—is known as a *one-to-many relationship*.

Less common relationships include:

- *One-to-one relationships*, in which each record in one table can have one and only one related record in the other table.

  This type of relationship isn't commonly used because it is easier to put all the fields in one table. However, you might use two related tables instead of one to break up a table with many fields, or to track information that applies to only some of the records in the first table.

- *Many-to-many relationships*, which are really two one-to-many relationships tied together through a third table.

  You could see this relationship in a database that contains Products, Orders, and Order Details tables. The Products table has one record for each product, and each product has a unique ProductID. The Orders table has one record for each order placed, and each record in it has a unique OrderID. However, the Orders table doesn't specify which products were included in each order; that information is in the Order Details table—the table in the middle that ties the other two tables together. Products and Orders each have a one-to-many relationship with Order Details. Products and Orders therefore have a many-to-many relationship with each other. In plain language, this means that every product can appear in many orders, and every order can include many products.

If there is a one-to-many relationship between two tables in a database, an excellent way to display this is through the use of a form containing a *subform*. The main, or primary, form displays one record from the "one" side of the one-to-many relationship, and the subform lists all the pertinent records from the "many" side of the relationship.

Refining Form Properties

As with tables, you can work with forms in multiple views. The two most common views are Form view, in which you view or enter data, and Design view, in which you add controls to the form or change the form's properties or layout.

When you create a form by using the Form tool or the Form wizard, every field included on the form is represented by a text box control and its associated label control. A form like the one you created earlier in this chapter is linked, or *bound*, to the table it's based on. Each text box is bound to a specific field in the table. The table is the *record source*, and the field is the *control source*. Each control has a number of *properties*, such as font, font size, alignment, fill color, and border. You can change the default values of these properties to improve the form's appearance.

A form inherits some of its properties from the table on which it is based. For instance, text box names on the form match field names in the source table, text box labels match the Caption property of each field, and the width of each text box is determined by the Field Size property. However, the properties of a form are not bound to their source. After you have created a form you can change the properties of the fields independently in the table and on the form.

In this exercise, you will edit the properties of a form.

> **USE** the *RefineProperties* database. This practice file is located in the *Documents\Microsoft Press\Access2007SBS\Simplifying* folder.
>
> **OPEN** the *RefineProperties* database.

1. In the **Navigation Pane**, under **Forms**, right-click **Customers**, and then click **Design View**.

   The Customers form opens in Design view. The form is arranged in a Stacked layout that limits the extent of changes you can make to the form.

Label   Text box

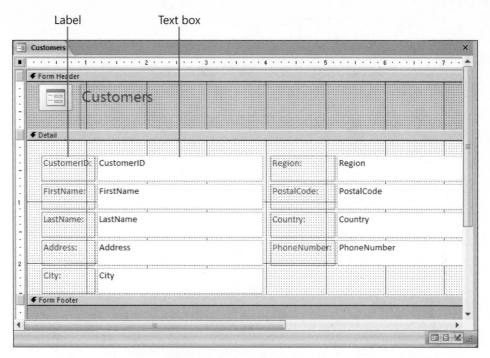

2. Click the top border of the blue **Form Footer** header and drag the Form Footer down about three inches to enlarge the Detail grid.

3. Click the **Detail** section of the form above the **Region** label, and then drag to draw a rectangle through some portion of all the controls on the right side of the form to select them.

> **Tip** You can bind a selection of controls together by clicking the Group button in the Control Layout group on the Arrange tab. Grouped controls can't be individually manipulated; to change an individual control within a group, you must first ungroup the controls.

4. Drag the selected group of controls down and to the left, positioning them just below the **City** label, then click any blank section of the grid to release the selection.

5. On the **Customers** form, click the **CustomerID** label (not its text box).

6. On the **Design** contextual tab, in the **Font** group, click the **Font** arrow, and then in the list, click **MS Sans Serif**.

7. With the label still selected, click the **Font Size** arrow, and then in the list, click **8**.

The label text becomes slightly smaller.

8. If the **Property Sheet** pane is not visible, right-click the **CustomerID** text box (not its label), and then click **Properties**.

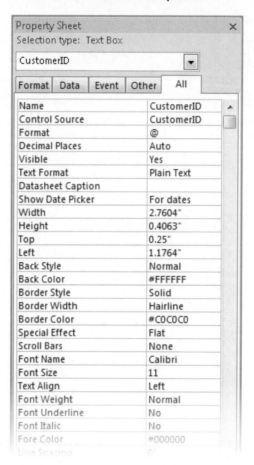

Property Sheet	✕
Selection type: Text Box	

CustomerID ▼

Format	Data	Event	Other	All

Name	CustomerID
Control Source	CustomerID
Format	@
Decimal Places	Auto
Visible	Yes
Text Format	Plain Text
Datasheet Caption	
Show Date Picker	For dates
Width	2.7604"
Height	0.4063"
Top	0.25"
Left	1.1764"
Back Style	Normal
Back Color	#FFFFFF
Border Style	Solid
Border Width	Hairline
Border Color	#C0C0C0
Special Effect	Flat
Scroll Bars	None
Font Name	Calibri
Font Size	11
Text Align	Left
Font Weight	Normal
Font Underline	No
Font Italic	No
Fore Color	#000000
Line Spacing	0"

All the settings available in the Font group (plus a few more) are available in the Property Sheet pane associated with each control. From this pane, you can display the properties of any object on the form, including the form itself.

You can display related types of properties by clicking the appropriate tab: Format, Data, Event, or Other, or display all properties by clicking the All tab.

9. In the **Property Sheet** pane, click the **Format** tab, scroll to the **Font Name** property, and change it to **MS Sans Serif**. Then set the **Font Size** property to **8**, and the **Font Weight** property to **Bold**.

The CustomerID text in the form reflects your changes.

> **Tip** You can change the width of a task pane by dragging its edge, and you can *undock* it so it floats in the program window by dragging it by the title bar.

10. Click the arrow in the **Property Sheet** pane header, and then in the property list, click **Label3** to select the label to the left of the **FirstName** text box.

11. Repeat step 9 to change the font of the text in the **FirstName** label box.

    These different ways of selecting a control and changing its properties provide some flexibility and convenience, but it would be a bit tedious to make changes to a few dozen controls in a form. The next two steps provide a faster method.

12. Click anywhere in the **Detail** section of the form, and then drag diagonally to draw a rectangle through some portion of all the controls to select them.

    > **Tip** You can select all the controls in a form, including those in the header and footer, by pressing Ctrl+A.

    Small handles appear around the selected controls. In the Property Sheet pane, the Selection type changes to *Multiple selection*, and the Objects box is blank. Only the Format settings that are the same for all the selected controls are displayed. Because the changes you made in the previous steps are not shared by all the selected controls, the Font Name, Font Size, and Font Weight settings are now blank.

13. Repeat step 9 to set the same **Font Name**, **Font Size**, and **Font Weight** properties for all the selected controls.

14. With all the controls still selected, on the **Format** tab of the **Property Sheet** pane, set the **Back Style** property to **Normal**.

    The background of the labels is no longer transparent.

Ellipsis button

15. Click the **Back Color** property, and then click the ellipsis button that appears.

16. In the **Color Builder** gallery that opens, click the **yellow** square, and then press [Enter].

    The background of all the controls changes to a bright yellow and the hexadecimal number representing this shade (#FFF200) appears in the **Back Color** property box.

    > **Tip** If the Color Builder doesn't include a color you want to use, click More Colors at the bottom of the gallery, select a color on the Standard or Custom tab of the Colors dialog box, and then click OK to set the color and add it to the list of recent colors at the bottom of the gallery.

17. In the **Back Color** property box, replace *#FFF200* with *#FFFFCC*.

    The background color changes to a pale yellow.

18. Set the **Special Effect** property to Shadowed, and the **Border Color** property to green.

19. In the form, click away from the selected controls to release the selection (in other words, to *deselect* the controls).

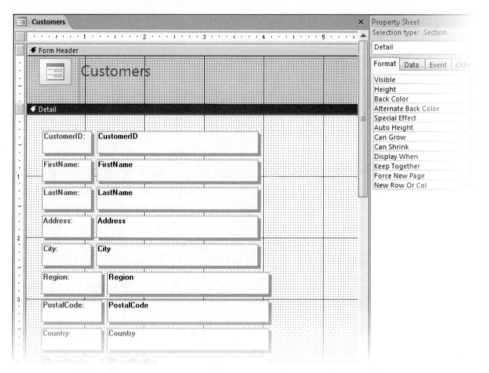

20. Click the **FirstName** label. In the **Property Sheet** pane, scroll up to the **Caption** property, change it from *FirstName* to Name, and then press `Enter`.

21. Repeat step 20 to change *Phone Number* to Phone.

> **Tip** You can edit the Caption property of a label or the Control Source property of a text box by selecting it, clicking its text, and then editing the text as you would in any other Windows program. However, take care when editing the Control Source property, which defines where the content of the text box comes from.

Remove

22. Drag through all the controls on the form to select them. On the **Arrange** tab, in the **Control Layout** group, click the **Remove** button.

Removing the Stacked layout gives you more options for arranging the controls.

23. Click away from the selected controls to release the selection.

24. Click the label to the left of **LastName**, and then press the ⟨Del⟩ key.

25. Select all the labels, but not their corresponding text boxes, by holding down the ⟨Shift⟩ key as you click each of them or by dragging through just the labels. Then in the **Property Sheet** pane, set the **Text Align** property to **Right**.

Now let's size the bottom four label boxes to match the ones above, and line up their associated text boxes.

26. Select the bottom four labels, but not their text boxes, and change their width property to 0.8847".

Size to Fit

27. Select all the labels again. On the **Arrange** contextual tab, in the **Size** group, click the **Size to Fit** button to resize the labels to fit their contents, and then click anywhere in the form (but outside the controls) to release the selection.

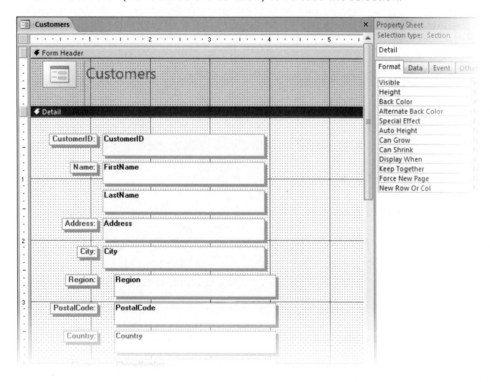

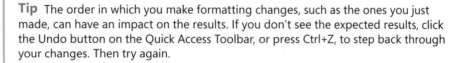
Tip The order in which you make formatting changes, such as the ones you just made, can have an impact on the results. If you don't see the expected results, click the Undo button on the Quick Access Toolbar, or press Ctrl+Z, to step back through your changes. Then try again.

28. Select all the text boxes (but not their corresponding labels), and in the **Property Sheet** pane, change the **Left** setting to 1.5" to line up the text boxes and insert space between them and the labels.

29. Change the **Font Weight** property to **Normal**, and then click anywhere in the form, but outside the controls, to deselect them.

Save

30. On the **Quick Access Toolbar**, click the **Save** button to save the design of the Customers form.

> **CLOSE** the *RefineProperties* database.

> **Tip**   Unless you close the Property Sheet pane, it remains open until you close all open forms.

Changing the Arrangement of a Form

Both automatically-generated forms and forms created by a wizard are functional, not fancy. However, it's fairly easy to customize the layout to suit your needs and preferences. You can add and delete labels, move both labels and text controls around the form, add logos and other graphics, and otherwise improve the layout of the form to make it attractive and easy to use.

While you work with a form's layout, you should pay attention to the shape of the pointer, which changes to indicate the manner in which you can change the selected item. Because a text box and its label sometimes act as a unit, you have to be aware of the pointer's shape before making any change. The shape of the pointer indicates the action to be taken:

 Four-headed arrow. Drag to move both controls together, or independently if the pointer is over a large square in the upper-left corner of the control.

 Pointing finger. Drag to move just the control.

 Vertical arrow. Drag the top or bottom border to change the height.

 Horizontal arrow. Drag the right or left border to change the width.

 Diagonal arrow. Drag the corner to change both the height and width.

In this exercise, you will rearrange the label and text box controls in a form.

USE the *RefineLayout* database. This practice file is located in the *Documents\Microsoft Press\Access2007SBS\Simplifying* folder.

OPEN the *RefineLayout* database.

1. In the **Navigation Pane**, under **Forms**, right-click **Customers**, and then click **Design View**.

    The form is divided into three sections: Form Header, Detail, and Form Footer. We are interested in only the Detail section right now.

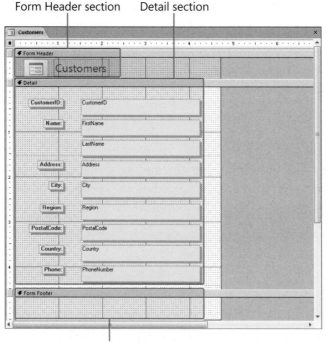

Form Header section   Detail section

Form Footer section

> **Troubleshooting**   If you can't see the Form Footer you may have to use the scroll bar to scroll down in the form until the footer appears. You can also right-click an inactive section of the Ribbon and then click Minimize The Ribbon to gain more screen space for your form. Click the minimized Ribbon and click Minimize The Ribbon again to restore the Ribbon.

2. Point to the right edge of the **Detail** grid, and when the pointer changes to a double-headed arrow, drag the edge of the background to the right until you can see about seven full grid sections.

3. Click the **LastName** text box, and then slowly move the pointer around its border, from handle to handle (there are eight handles), noticing how the pointer changes shape.

Item selector

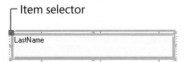

If a label or text box can be moved independently, then it will have a larger item selector in its upper-left corner.

4. Move the pointer over the **LastName** text box and when it changes to a four-headed arrow, drag it up and to the right of the **FirstName** text box.

> **Tip** If you can't move the label independently of the text box, the form is probably in Stacked layout. Drag through all the controls to select them, and then click the Remove button in the Control Layout group on the Arrange tab.

5. Resize each control, and then arrange them in logical groupings on the form.

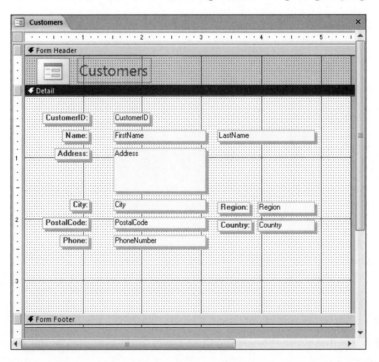

> **Tip** To fine-tune the position of a control, click it and then move the control by pressing the Up Arrow, Down Arrow, Left Arrow, or Right Arrow key. To move the control lesser distances, hold down the Ctrl key while pressing the arrow key. To fine-tune the size of a control, hold down the Shift key while pressing the arrow key.

6. On the **Arrange** contextual tab, in the **AutoFormat** group, click the **AutoFormat** button.

The AutoFormat gallery opens.

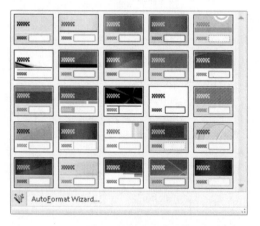

7. At the bottom of the **AutoFormat** gallery, click **AutoFormat Wizard**.

The AutoFormat wizard starts. Unlike most wizards, this one has only one page.

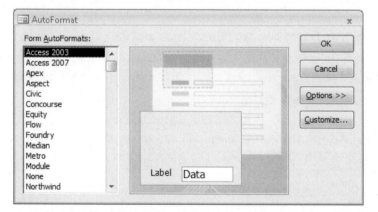

8. In the **AutoFormat** dialog box, click the **Customize** button.

The Customize AutoFormat wizard starts. Unlike most wizards, this one has only one page.

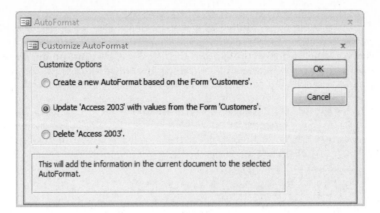

9. In the **Customize AutoFormat** dialog box, click **Create a new AutoFormat based on the Form 'Customers'**, and then click **OK**.

> **Tip** Form controls inherit whatever theme is set in the operating system. To change the theme, open Control Panel, click Appearance And Personalization, and then under Personalization, click Change The Theme. In the Theme Settings dialog box, select the theme you want, and then click OK.

The New Style Name dialog box opens.

10. In the **Style Name** box, type Customers, and then click **OK**.

In the AutoFormat wizard, the new style appears in the Form AutoFormats list. This style will now be available in any database you open on this computer.

11. In the **AutoFormat** wizard, click **OK**.

> **Tip** Access saves data automatically as you enter it, but you must manually save layout changes to any object.

12. Click the **Address** text box to select it.

13. On the **Arrange** tab, in the **Size** group, click the **Anchoring** tool.

14. In the **Anchoring** gallery, click **Stretch Across Top**.

The width of the Address text box is now set to dynamically adjust to fit the Access window.

15. Switch to Form view and resize the Access window to see how the **Address** text box adapts.

> **Tip** You can add conditional formatting to a control to identify data that meets specific criteria. To do so, select the control you want to format and then on the Design tab, in the Font group, click the Conditional button. In the Conditional Formatting dialog box, select the criteria and the formatting you want to apply when the associated content meets the criteria.

CLOSE the Customers form, saving your changes, and then close the *RefineLayout* database.

Adding Controls to a Form

Every form has three basic sections: Form Header, Detail, and Form Footer. When you use the Form tool or a wizard to create a form, they add a set of controls for each field that you select from the underlying table to the Detail section, add a logo placeholder and/or caption to the Form Header, and leave the Form Footer section blank. Because the Footer section is empty, Access collapses it, but you can resize the Footer section by dragging its *selector.* Although labels and text box controls are perhaps the most common controls found in forms, you can also enhance your forms with many other types of controls. For example, you can add groups of option buttons, check boxes, and list boxes to present people with choices instead of having them type entries in text boxes.

The controls that you can add to a form are located on the Design tab in the Controls group.

In this exercise, you will replace the logo and caption automatically placed in a form by the Form tool. You will also replace a text box control in the Detail section with a combo box control, and remove the record selector bar from the program window.

USE the *AddControls* database and the *CustomersFormLogo* graphic. These practice files are located in the *Documents\Microsoft Press\Access2007SBS\Simplifying* folder.

OPEN the *AddControls* database. Then open the Customers form in Design view.

1. In the **Customers** form, point to the horizontal line between the **Form Header** section selector and the **Detail** section selector, and when the pointer changes to a double-headed arrow, drag the **Detail** section selector down a little more than an inch.

> **Tip** Use the rulers along the top and left side of the form as guides.

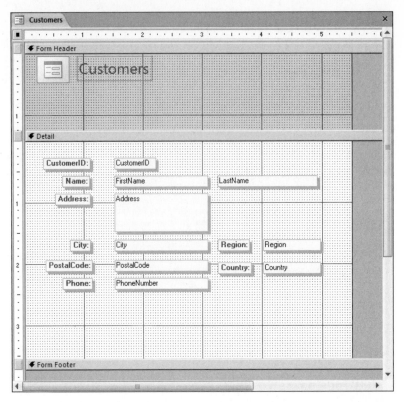

2. Select the logo and the caption in the **Form Header**, and then press `Del`.

Image

3. On the **Design** contextual tab, in the **Controls** group, click the **Image** button, and then, at the left end of the **Form Header** section, drag diagonally to draw a rectangle about 1 inch high and 1.5 inches wide.

   To view information about a control, point to its button in the Controls group. After a few seconds a ScreenTip is displayed.

   > **Tip** Access 2007 has a new Logo control that prompts you to enter a graphic name, and then automatically inserts the graphic in the form header.

4. In the **Insert Picture** dialog box, navigate to the *Documents\Microsoft Press\ Access2007SBS\Simplifying* folder, and then double-click the *CustomersFormLogo* graphic.

   > **Troubleshooting** If the practice file isn't visible, change the Files Of Type setting to Graphics Files.

   The logo appears inside the image control.

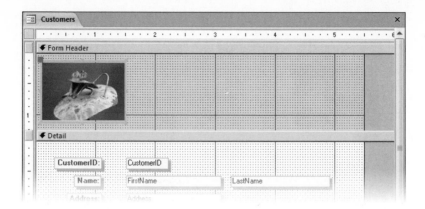

> **Tip** How an image fits into an image control is determined by the Size Mode property of the control. If the property is set to Clip and the control isn't large enough to display the entire image, the image is cropped. If the property is set to Stretch, you can enlarge the control to display the entire image. If the property is set to Zoom, the image will automatically resize to fit the control.

5. In the **Controls** group, click the **Label** button, and then drag diagonally to draw another rectangle in the header section.

Access inserts a label control containing the insertion point, ready for you to enter a caption.

6. In the active label control, type Customers. Then press Enter.

The Customers label takes on the formatting of the other labels.

> **Troubleshooting** Access displays a Smart Tag next to the control, warning you that the label is not associated with any other control. You can ignore this, or click Ignore Error to make it go away.

7. If the **Property Sheet** pane is not already open, press F4 to open it.

> **Tip** You can toggle the display of the Property Sheet pane by pressing the F4 key.

8. Change the **Font Size** property to **18**, the **Fore Color** to **Green 5**, and the **Text Align** property to **Center**. Then close the **Property Sheet** pane.

9. On the **Arrange** tab, in the **Size** group, click the Size **to Fit** button.

The size of the label control changes to fit the text.

10. Adjust the size and position of the image and label controls so that they are side-by-side.

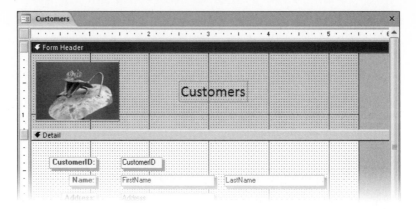

Use Control Wizards

11. On the **Design** tab, in the **Controls** group, look at the **Use Control Wizards** button. If the button is active (orange), click it to deactivate it.

Turning off the Control Wizards feature enables you to add a control with all the default settings, without having to work through the wizard's pages.

Combo Box

12. In the **Controls** group, click the **Combo Box** button. Then drag diagonally to draw a rectangle just below the **Country** text box.

When you release the mouse button, Access displays a combo box control, which is *unbound* (not attached to a field in the Customers table).

> **Troubleshooting** Access assigns a number to each control when it is created. Don't be concerned if the number displayed in your control is different from what you see in the graphics in this book.

Format Painter

13. Click the **Country** text box. In the **Font** group, click the **Format Painter** button and then click the combo box control.

Access copies the formatting of the text box to the combo box control and its label.

14. If the **Property Sheet** pane is not open, right-click the combo box, and then click **Properties**.

15. In the **Property Sheet** pane, on the **Data** tab, click the **Control Source** arrow, and then in the list, click **Country**.

> **Tip** To display the available control source options in the Expression Builder window, click the ellipsis that appears to the right of the Control Source arrow.

16. In the **Row Source** box, type

SELECT DISTINCT Customers.Country FROM Customers;

There is a period (but no space) between *Customers* and *Country*, and a semicolon at the end of the text.

This line of code is a query that extracts one example of every country in the Country field of the Customers table and displays the results as a list when you click the Country arrow.

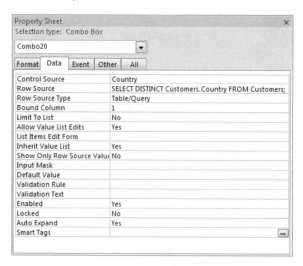

You might have to widen the Property Sheet pane to display the entire query.

> **Tip** If you need to add a customer from a country that is not in the list, you can type the country's name in the combo box. After the record is added to the database, that country shows up when the combo box list is displayed.

17. If it isn't already, set the **Row Source Type** to **Table/Query**.

18. Click the combo box label. (If you can't see the combo box label, move the **Property Sheet** pane.)

19. In the **Property Sheet** pane, on the **Format** tab, change the **Caption** to Country. Then close the **Property Sheet** pane.

20. Delete the original **Country** text box and its label, and then move the new combo box and label into their place, resizing them as needed.

View

21. On the **Other** tab of the Property Sheet pane, change the **Tab Index** from **8** to 7, to place the Country after the Postal Code in the tab order. Then on the **Home** tab, in the **Views** group, click the **View** button.

> **Tip** When a form is in Layout view or Design view, you can switch to Form view by clicking the View button.

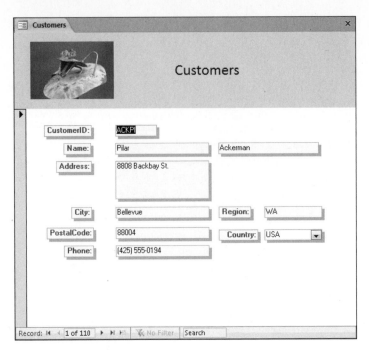

22. Scroll through a couple of records, and then click the combo box arrow to display the country list.

23. You don't need the *record selector*—the gray bar along the left edge of the form—for this exercise, so return to Design view and display the **Property Sheet** pane for the entire form by clicking the **Form** selector (the box at the junction of the horizontal and vertical rulers) and pressing [F4] (if the sheet is not already displayed). Then on the **Format** tab, change **Record Selectors** to **No**, and **Scroll Bars** to **Neither**. Then press [F4] again to close the **Property Sheet** pane.

24. Save the form's new design, and then switch to Form view for a final look.

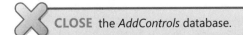 **CLOSE** the *AddControls* database.

Entering Data in a Form by Using VBA

As you might suspect by now, almost everything in Access, including the Access program itself, is an object. One of the characteristics of objects is that they can recognize and respond to *events*, which are essentially actions. Different objects recognize different events. The basic events, recognized by almost all objects, are Click, Double Click, Mouse

Down, Mouse Move, and Mouse Up. Most objects recognize quite a few other events. A text control, for example, recognizes 17 different events; a form recognizes more than 50.

> **Tip** The events recognized by an object are listed on the Event tab in the object's Property Sheet pane.

While you use a form, objects are signaling events, or *firing events*, almost constantly. However, unless you attach a macro or VBA procedure to an event, the object is really just firing blanks. By default, Access doesn't do anything obvious when it recognizes most events. So without interfering with the program's normal behavior, you can use an event to specify what action should happen. You can even use an event to trigger a macro to run or a VBA procedure to perform a set of actions.

Sound complicated? Well, it's true that events are not things most casual Access users tend to worry about. But because knowing how to handle events can greatly increase the efficiency of objects such as forms, it is helpful to have an idea of what they're all about.

For example, while looking at customer records in one of the exercise databases, you might have noticed that the CustomerID is composed of the first three letters of the customer's last name and the first two letters of his or her first name, all in capital letters. This technique usually generates a unique ID for a new customer. If you try to enter an ID that is already in use, Access won't accept the new entry, and you'll have to add a number or change the ID in some other way to make it unique. Performing trivial tasks, such as combining parts of two words and then converting the results to capital letters, is something a computer excels at. So rather than typing the ID for each new customer record that is added to the database, you can let VBA do it for you.

In this exercise, you will write a few lines of VBA code and attach the code to an event in a form. This is by no means an in-depth treatment of VBA, but this exercise will give you a taste of the power of VBA.

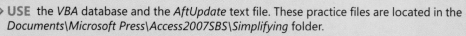

USE the *VBA* database and the *AftUpdate* text file. These practice files are located in the *Documents\Microsoft Press\Access2007SBS\Simplifying* folder.

OPEN the *VBA* database. Then open the Customers form in Design view.

1. In the **Customers** form, click the **LastName** text box, and then if the **Property Sheet** pane isn't already open, press F4 to open it.

2. Click the **Event** tab.

   This tab lists the events to which the LastName text box control can respond.

Ellipsis button

3. In the **Property Sheet** pane, click the ellipsis button to the right of the **After Update** property.

The Choose Builder dialog box opens, offering you the options of building an expression, a macro, or VBA code.

4. Click **Code Builder**, and then click **OK** to start the VBA Editor.

Project Explorer pane   Code window

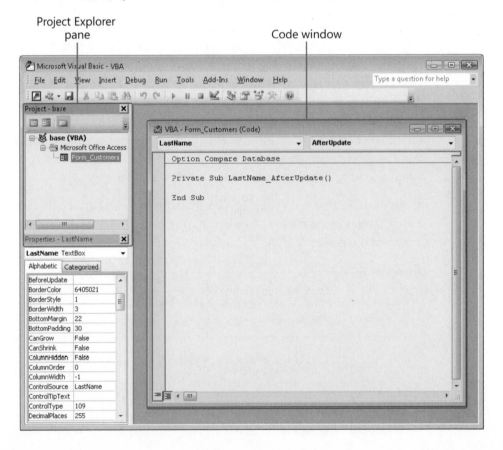

The Project Explorer pane lists any objects in the database to which you can attach code; in this case, only the Customers form (Form_Customers) appears in the list. New forms and reports appear here automatically.

The Code window displays a placeholder for the procedure that Access will use to handle the After Update event for the LastName text box control. This procedure is named *Private Sub LastName_AfterUpdate()*, and at the moment it contains only the Sub and End Sub statements that mark the beginning and end of any procedure.

5. Navigate to your *Documents\Microsoft Press\Access2007SBS\Simplifying* folder, double-click the *AftUpdate* text file to open it in your default text editor, and then copy the following lines of text to the Clipboard.

```
'Create variables to hold first and last names
' and customer ID
Dim fName As String
Dim lName As String
Dim cID As String

'Assign the text in the LastName text box to
' the lName variable.
lName = Forms!customers!LastName.Text

'You must set the focus to a text box before
' you can read its contents.
Forms!customers!FirstName.SetFocus
fName = Forms!customers!FirstName.Text

'Combine portions of the last and first names
' to create the customer ID.
cID = UCase(Left(lName, 3) & Left(fName, 2))

'Don't store the ID unless it is 5 characters long
' (which indicates both names filled in).
If Len(cID) = 5 Then
    Forms!customers!CustomerID.SetFocus

    'Don't change the ID if it has already been
    ' entered; perhaps it was changed manually.
    If Forms!customers!CustomerID.Text = "" Then
        Forms!customers!CustomerID = cID
    End If
End If

'Set the focus where it would have gone naturally.
Forms!customers!Address.SetFocus
```

> **Important** A line of text beginning with an apostrophe is a comment that explains the purpose of the next line of code. In the VBA Editor, comments are displayed in green.

6. Switch back to the Code window, and then paste the copied text between the Private Sub LastName_AfterUpdate() and End Sub statements.

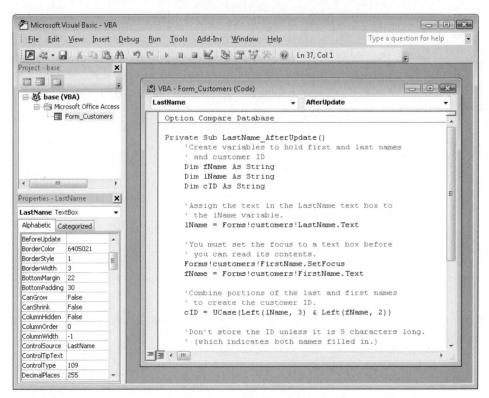

7. On the **File** menu, click **Save VBA** to save your changes.

8. On the **File** menu, click **Close and Return to Microsoft Access** to return to the Access window. Then close the **Property Sheet** pane.

New Record

9. Switch to Form view. On the **Navigation** bar, click the **New Record** button.

   A blank Customers form appears.

10. In the new record, press the Tab key to move the insertion point to the **FirstName** box, type Chris, press Tab to move to the **LastName** box, type Sells, and then press Tab again.

    If you followed the above steps correctly, *SELCH* appears in the CustomerID box.

11. Change the first name to Dana and the last name to Birkby.

Notice that the original CustomerID doesn't change, even when the names from which it was derived do.

12. Press the Esc key to remove your entry, and then try entering the last name first, followed by the first name.

Access does not create a Customer ID. The code does what it was written to do, but not necessarily what you want it to do, which is to create an ID regardless of the order in which the names are entered. There are several ways to fix this problem. For example, you could write a similar procedure to handle the After Update event in the FirstName text box, or you could write one procedure to handle both events and then jump to it when either event occurs.

13. Press Esc to clear your entries.

CLOSE the *VBA* database.

Creating a Form by Using an AutoForm

Although a form doesn't have to include all the fields from the underlying table, when it is intended as the primary method of creating new records, it usually does. The quickest way to create a form that includes all the fields from one table is to use the Form button, as you did in the first exercise in this chapter. Another method, which provides more control over the creation of the form, is to use a wizard. In either case you can easily customize the forms created.

In this exercise, you will use a wizard to create a form that displays information about each of the product categories.

USE the *CreateWizard* database. This practice file is located in the *Documents\Microsoft Press\Access2007SBS\Simplifying* folder.
OPEN the *CreateWizard* database. Then open the Categories table in Datasheet view.

1. On the **Create** tab, in the **Forms** group, click the **More Forms** button and then in the list, click **Form Wizard**.

The Form wizard starts.

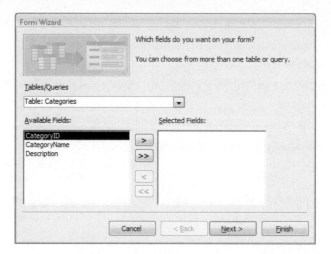

Move All

2. With the **Categories** table selected in the **Tables/Queries** list, click the **Move All** button to move all the table fields to the **Selected Fields** list, and then click **Next**.

   On the second page of the wizard, you choose the layout of the fields in the new form. When you select an option on the right side of the page, the preview area on the left side shows what the form layout will look like with that option applied.

3. With the **Columnar** option selected, click **Next**.

   On the third page of the wizard, you can select a style option to see how the style will look when applied to the form.

4. In the list of styles, click **Office**, and then click **Next**.

   Access suggests the base table name as the form's title.

5. With the **Open the form to view or enter information** option selected, click **Finish**.

   The new Categories form opens, displaying the first category record in the Categories table.

6. Scroll through a few records by using the navigation controls at the bottom of the form.

> **Tip** To change the style of a form after you create it, switch to Design view, and on the Arrange tab, in the AutoFormat group, click AutoFormat. In the list displayed, click the style you would like to use.

7. Switch to Design view so that you can make a few more changes.

8. Delete the word *Category* from the **Category Name** label.

9. You don't want to expose the CategoryID field to form users, because that value should never be changed. Click the **CategoryID** text box, and if the control's **Property Sheet** pane isn't open, press F4 to display it.

10. In the **Property Sheet** pane, on the **Data** tab, change **Enabled** to **No**. Then press F4 to close the **Property Sheet** pane.

    Disabling the CategoryID text box changes it, and the label text, to gray.

11. Switch to Form view, and then scroll through a few categories. Try to edit entries in the **CategoryID** field to confirm that you can't.

12. You don't need scroll bars or a record selector in this form, so return to Design view, and then display the form's **Property Sheet** pane by clicking the **Form selector** (the box in the upper-left corner) and pressing F4.

13. In the **Property Sheet** pane, on the **Format** tab, change **Scroll Bars** to Neither and **Record Selectors** to No. Then close the **Property Sheet** pane.

14. Switch to Form view to see the effect of your changes.

 CLOSE the Categories form, saving your changes, and then close the *CreateWizard* database.

Adding Charts to Forms and Reports

You can easily create a chart in a form or report by using the Chart Wizard. You can base the chart on an existing table or query (or both), select the specific fields you want to chart, and choose the chart type you want to best represent the data. After creating the chart, you can change the layout and format of the data to suit your needs.

To begin creating a chart, open the form or report in Design view and then in the Controls group on the Design tab, click the Chart Wizard button.

Simultaneously Creating Forms and Subforms

If you know when you create a form that you are going to add a subform, you can create the form and its subform by using the Form wizard. To do so:

1. On the **Create** tab, in the **Forms** group, click the **More Forms** button, and then in the list, click **Form Wizard**.

2. In the **Form** wizard, in the **Tables/Queries** list, click the table on which you want to base the form. Then click the **Move All** button to include all the table fields in the new form.

3. In the **Tables/Queries** list, click the table on which you want to base the subform.

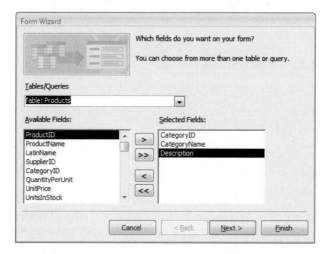

4. In the **Available Fields** list, double-click the fields you want to include in the subform to move them to the **Selected Fields** list, and then click **Next**.

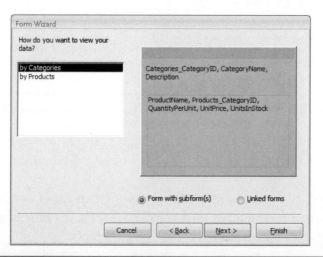

5. With your primary table and **Form with subform(s)** selected, click **Next**.

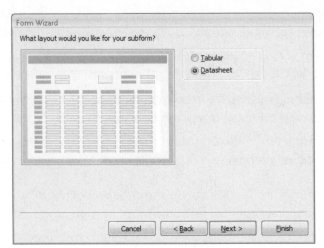

6. With **Datasheet** selected, click **Next**.

7. On the last page of the wizard, select a style, and then click **Finish**.

   The wizard creates and opens the form and subform.

You can edit the form created by the Form wizard to suit your needs.

If there is only one one-to-many relationship between the tables you want to include in the form, and that relationship has been defined in the Relationships window, the fastest way to create the form and its subform is by using the Form tool. Simply select the primary table then on the Create tab, in the Forms group, click Form.

The Form tool creates and displays a form and subform, each containing all the fields of its source table.

> **Troubleshooting** If the relationship between the selected tables has not been defined, Access displays a message containing a link to the Relationships window. If this occurs, you will need to define the relationship and then re-start the wizard.

Adding a Subform to a Form

A form can display information (fields) from one or more tables or queries. If you want to display fields from several tables or queries in one form, you have to give some thought to the relationships that must exist between those objects.

In this exercise, you will add a subform to an existing form.

> **USE** the *AddSubform* database. This practice file is located in the *Documents\Microsoft Press\Access2007SBS\Simplifying* folder.
>
> **OPEN** the *AddSubform* database. Then open the Categories form in Design view.

1. Drag the **Form Footer** section selector down about 1 inch to give yourself about 3 inches of vertical space to work in the Details section of the form.

Use Control Wizards

Subform/ Subreport

2. On the **Design** tab, in the **Controls** group, make sure the **Use Control Wizards** button is active (orange).

3. In the **Controls** group, click the **Subform/Subreport** button, and then drag diagonally to draw a rectangle in the lower portion of the **Detail** section.

A white object appears in the form, and the SubForm wizard starts.

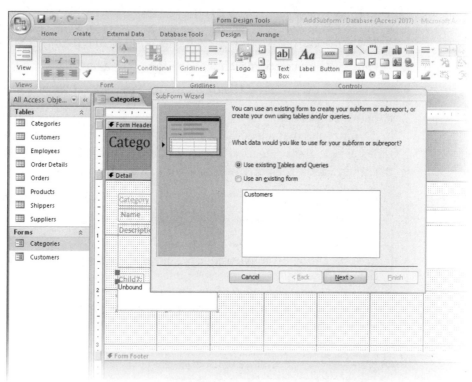

> **Tip** If prompted to do so, follow the instructions to install this wizard.

4. With the **Use existing Tables and Queries** option selected, click **Next**.

5. In the **Tables/Queries** list, click **Table: Products**.

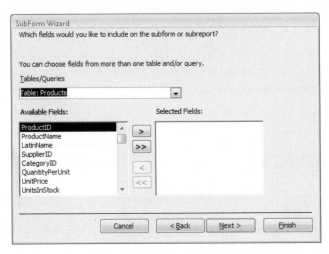

6. In the **Available Fields** list, double-click the **ProductName**, **CategoryID**, **QuantityPerUnit**, **UnitPrice**, and **UnitsInStock** fields to add them to the **Selected Fields** list. Then click **Next**.

   Because the CategoryID field in the subform is related to the CategoryID field in the main form, the wizard selects Show Products For Each Record In Categories Using CategoryID as the Choose From A List option.

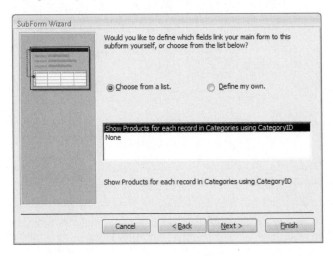

> **Tip** If the wizard can't figure out which fields are related, it selects the Define My Own option and displays list boxes in which you can specify the fields to be related.

7. With the **Define my own** option selected, click **Finish**.

   Access displays the Categories form in Design view, with an embedded Products subform. The size and location of the subform is determined by the size and location of the original rectangle you created in the form.

8. Adjust the size and location of the objects in your form as needed to view the entire subform.

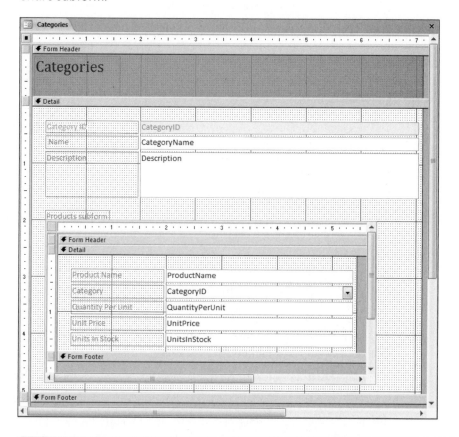

> **Tip** A new feature in Access 2007 is the ability to simultaneously view data in Form view and in Datasheet view by using a split form. This greatly simplifies the process of finding and editing records. Similarly, if you want to display more than one record at a time on a form page, you can create a multiple item form. To create a split form or multiple item form for a table, open the table in Datasheet view and then on the Create tab, in the Forms group, click Split Form or Multiple Items.

Form View

9. Notice the layout of the subform in Design view, and then on the **View** toolbar in the lower-right corner of the Access program window, click the **Form View** button to switch views.

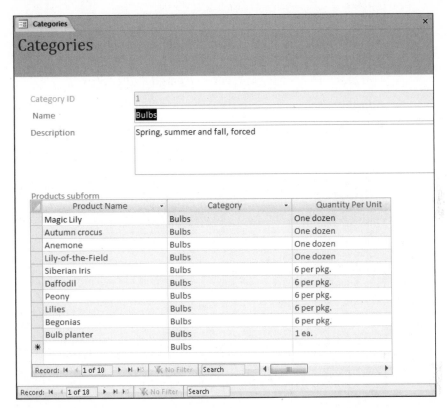

The format of the subform has totally changed. In Design view, it looks like a simple form, but in Form view, it looks like a datasheet.

10. Switch back to Design view, make any necessary size adjustments, and then open the **Property Sheet** pane if it isn't already open.

11. Click the **Form** selector in the upper-left corner of the subform twice.

The first click selects the Products subform control, and the second click selects the form. A small black square appears on the selector.

> **Tip** You can quickly adjust the width of columns to fit their data by double-clicking the double arrow between column headings.

Products subform Form selector

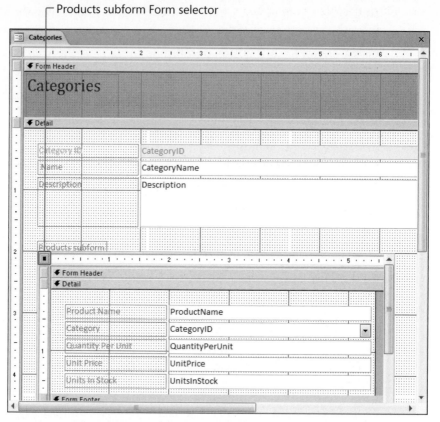

12. In the **Property Sheet** pane, on the **Format** tab, change the **Record Selectors** and **Navigation Buttons** properties to No.

13. Close the **Property Sheet** pane, switch back to Form view, and then adjust the width of the columns by dragging the column dividers, until you can see all the fields.

Product Name	Category	Quantity Per Unit	Unit Price	Units In
Magic Lily	Bulbs	One dozen	$40.00	40
Autumn crocus	Bulbs	One dozen	$18.75	37
Anemone	Bulbs	One dozen	$28.00	26
Lily-of-the-Field	Bulbs	One dozen	$38.00	34
Siberian Iris	Bulbs	6 per pkg.	$12.95	30
Daffodil	Bulbs	6 per pkg.	$12.95	24
Peony	Bulbs	6 per pkg.	$19.95	20
Lilies	Bulbs	6 per pkg.	$10.50	18
Begonias	Bulbs	6 per pkg.	$18.95	12
Bulb planter	Bulbs	1 ea.	$6.95	6
*	Bulbs		$0.00	0

14. Scroll through several categories by using the navigation buttons.

As each category appears at the top of the form, the products in that category are listed in the datasheet in the subform.

First Record

15. Click the **First Record** button to return to the first category (Bulbs). In the subform click **Bulbs** in the **Category** column to the right of the first product (Magic Lily).

The arrow at the right end of the box indicates that this is a combo box.

16. Click the arrow to display the list of categories, and then change the category to **Cacti**.

Next Record

17. Click the **Next Record** navigation button to move to the Cacti category.

Magic Lily is now included in this category.

18. Display the category list to the right of Magic Lily, and return it to the **Bulbs** category.

19. To prevent people from changing a product's category, return to Design view, click the **CategoryID** text box control in the subform, and then press ⎀Del⎀.

The CategoryID text box and its label no longer appear on the form.

> **Important** You included the CategoryID field when the wizard created this subform because it is the field that relates the Categories and Products tables. The underlying Products table uses a combo box to display the name of the category instead of its ID number, so that combo box also appears in the subform.

20. Save the form, switch back to Form view, and then adjust the width of the subform columns and the size of the Form window until you can clearly see the fields.

Product Name	Quantity Per Unit	Unit Price	Units In
Magic Lily	One dozen	$40.00	40
Autumn crocus	One dozen	$18.75	37
Anemone	One dozen	$28.00	26
Lily-of-the-Field	One dozen	$38.00	34
Siberian Iris	6 per pkg.	$12.95	30
Daffodil	6 per pkg.	$12.95	24
Peony	6 per pkg.	$19.95	20
Lilies	6 per pkg.	$10.50	18
Begonias	6 per pkg.	$18.95	12
Bulb planter	1 ea.	$6.95	6
*		$0.00	0

CLOSE the *AddSubform* database. If you are not continuing directly on to the next chapter, exit Access.

Key Points

- A form is an organized and formatted view of some or all of the fields from one or more tables or queries. Forms work interactively with the tables in a database. You use controls in the form to enter new information, to edit or remove existing information, or to locate information.

- The quickest way to create a form that includes all the fields from one table is by using the Form tool. You can easily customize the form later in Design view.

- When you know what table to base your form on, and have an idea of how the form will be used, you can use the Form wizard to quickly create a form. You can make modifications to the form in Design view.

- The two most common views to work with forms in are Form view, in which you view or enter data, and Design view, in which you add controls, change form properties, and change the form layout.

- Each text box in a form is bound to a specific field in the underlying table. The table is the record source and the field is the control source. Each control has a number of properties, such as font style, font size, and font color, which you can change to improve a form's appearance.

- You can resize the three basic sections of a form: the Form Header, Detail, and Form Footer. You can customize any section of your form's layout by adding and deleting labels, moving labels and text controls, and adding logos and other graphics. The most popular controls are available in the Controls group on the Design tab.

- The objects in your form can recognize and respond to events, which are essentially actions. But without a macro or VBA procedure attached to it, an event doesn't actually do anything. Knowing how to handle events can greatly increase the efficiency of objects, such as forms.

- If you want to display fields from several tables or queries in one form, you have to give some thought to the relationships that must exist between those objects. In Access, a relationship is an association between common fields in two tables, and you can relate the information in one table to the information in another table. There are three types of relationships that Access recognizes: one-to-one, one-to-many, and many-to-many.

- After you define a relationship between tables, you can add subforms to your forms. For example, for each category displayed in your main form, you might have a subform that displays all the products in that category.

- Split forms and multiple item forms are useful new tools for viewing and editing records.

Chapter at a Glance

Filter information by using a form, **page 153**

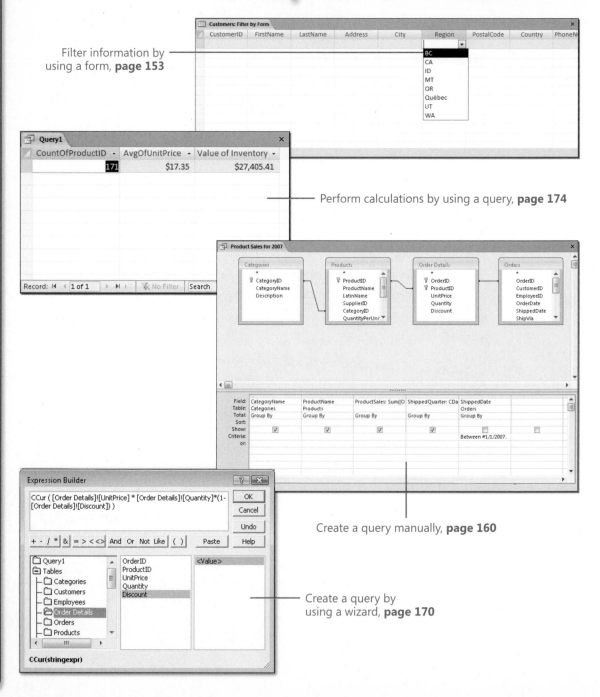

Perform calculations by using a query, **page 174**

Create a query manually, **page 160**

Create a query by using a wizard, **page 170**

6 Locating Specific Information

In this chapter, you will learn to:

✔ Sort and filter information in a table.

✔ Filter information by using a form.

✔ Locate information that matches multiple criteria.

✔ Create a query manually or by using a wizard.

✔ Perform calculations by using a query.

A database is a repository for information. It might contain only a few records or thousands of records, stored in one table or multiple tables. No matter how much information a database contains, it is useful only if you can locate the information you need when you need it. In a small database you can find information simply by scrolling through a table until you find what you are looking for. But as a database grows in size and complexity, locating and analyzing information becomes more difficult.

Microsoft Office Access 2007 provides a variety of tools you can use to organize the display of information stored in a database and to locate specific items of information. Using these tools, you can organize all the records in a table by quickly *sorting* it based on any field or combination of fields, or you can *filter* the table so that information containing some combination of characters is displayed or excluded from the display. With a little more effort, you can create queries to display specific fields from specific records from one or more tables. You can save queries and run the saved queries to generate updated results when data changes.

In this chapter, you will learn how to sort and filter information in a table, display selected information in a form; and locate information that matches multiple criteria. Then you will create queries to locate information and to perform calculations.

See Also Do you need only a quick refresher on the topics in this chapter? See the Quick Reference section at the beginning of this book.

Important Before you can use the practice files in this chapter, you need to install them from the book's companion CD to their default location. See "Using the Companion CD" at the beginning of this book for more information.

Troubleshooting Graphics and operating system–related instructions in this book reflect the Windows Vista user interface. If your computer is running Windows XP and you experience trouble following the instructions as written, please refer to the "Information for Readers Running Windows XP" section at the beginning of this book.

Sorting Information in a Table

You can sort the information stored in a table based on the values in one or more fields, in either ascending or descending order. For example, you could sort customer information alphabetically by last name and then by first name. This would result in the order found in telephone books.

Last	First
Smith	Denise
Smith	James
Smith	Jeff
Thompson	Ann
Thompson	Steve

Sorting a table groups all entries of one type together, which can be useful. For example, to qualify for a discount on postage, you might want to group customer records by postal code before printing mailing labels.

How Access Sorts

The concept of sorting seems quite intuitive, but sometimes your computer's approach to such a concept is not so intuitive. Sorting numbers is a case in point. In Access, numbers can be treated as text or as numerals. Because of the spaces, hyphens, and punctuation typically used in street addresses, postal codes, and telephone numbers, the numbers in these fields are usually treated as text, and sorting them follows the logic applied to sorting all text. Numbers in a price or quantity field, on the other hand, are typically treated as numerals.

When Access sorts text, it sorts first on the first character in the selected field in every record, then on the next character, then on the next, and so on—until it runs out of characters. When Access sorts numbers, it treats the contents of each field as a single value, and sorts the records based on that value. This tactic can result in seemingly strange sort orders. For example, sorting the list in the first column of the following table as text produces the list in the second column. Sorting the same list as numerals produces the list in the third column.

Original	Sort as text	Sort as numerals
1	1	1
1234	11	3
23	12	4
3	1234	11
11	22	12
22	23	22
12	3	23
4	4	1234

If a field with the Text data type contains numbers, you can sort the field numerically by padding the numbers with leading zeros so that all entries are the same length. For example, 001, 011, and 101 are sorted correctly even if the numbers are defined as text.

In this exercise, you will sort records first by one field, and then by multiple fields.

> **USE** the *SortTable* database. This practice file is located in the *Documents\Microsoft Press\Access2007SBS\Locating* folder.
>
> **OPEN** the *SortTable* database.

1. In the **Navigation Pane**, under **Tables**, double-click **Customers**.

   The Customers table opens in Datasheet view.

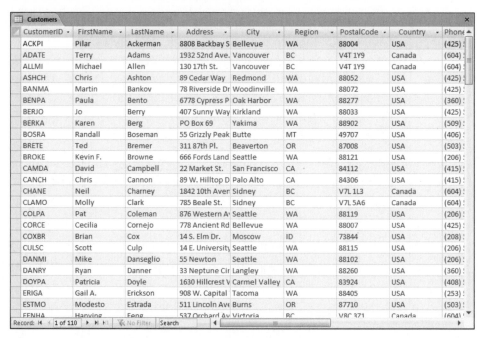

2. Click the arrow at the right side of the **Region** column header, and then click **Sort A to Z**.

   Access rearranges the records in alphabetical order by region, and displays a narrow upward-pointing arrow at the right side of the column header to indicate the sort order.

Descending

3. To reverse the sort order by using a different method, on the **Home** tab, in the **Sort & Filter** group, click the **Descending** button.

   The sort order reverses. The records for customers living in Washington (WA) are now at the top of your list. In both sorts, the region was sorted alphabetically, but the City field was left in a seemingly random order.

Suppose that you want to see the records arranged by city within each region. You can do this by sorting the City column and then the Region column, or by moving the Region column to the left of the City column, selecting both, and then sorting them together.

> **Tip** Access can sort on more than one field, but it sorts consecutively from left to right. So the fields you want to sort must be adjacent, and they must be arranged in the order in which you want to sort them.

4. To sort the cities in ascending order within the regions, first click the **City** sort order arrow, and then click **Sort A to Z**.

Access sorts the records alphabetically by city.

5. To finish the process, right-click anyplace in the **Region** column, and then click **Sort A to Z**.

The two columns are now sorted so the cities in each region are listed in ascending order.

6. To sort both columns at the same time in descending order, move the **Region** field to the left of the **City** field by clicking its header to select the column, and then dragging the column to the left until a dark line appears between **Address** and **City**. Release the mouse button to complete the move operation.

7. With the **Region** column selected, hold down the ⌗Shift⌗ key and click the **City** header to extend the selection so that both the **Region** and **City** columns are selected.

8. In the **Sort & Filter** group, click the **Descending** button to arrange the records with the regions in descending order and the city names also in descending order within each region (or in this case, each state).

9. Experiment with various ways of sorting the records to display different results.

> **Tip** You can sort records while viewing them in a form. Click the field on which you want to base the sort, and then click the Sort command you want. You can't sort by multiple fields at the same time in Form view, but you can sort on one field then the next to achieve the same results.

 CLOSE the Customers table without saving your changes, and then close the *SortTable* database.

Filtering Information in a Table

Sorting the information in a table organizes it in a logical manner, but you still have the entire table to deal with. To locate only the records containing (or not containing) specific information, filtering is more effective than sorting. For example, you could quickly create a filter to locate only customers who live in Seattle, only items that were purchased on January 13, or only orders that were not shipped by standard mail.

You can apply simple filters while viewing information in a table or form. To filter information by multiple criteria, you can apply additional filters to the results of the first one.

You can save a filter as a query so you can quickly display the filtered results at any time. To save a filter as a query:

1. On the **Home** tab, in the **Sort & Filter** group, click the **Advanced** button and then click **Save As Query**.

2. In the **Save As Query** dialog box, give the query and appropriate name, and then click **OK**.

Wildcards

If you want to locate records containing certain information but aren't sure of all the characters, or want your search to return multiple variations of a base character set, you can include *wildcard characters* in your search criteria. The most common wildcards are:

- * (asterisk) represents any number of characters For example

  LastName = Co* returns entries including Colman and Conroy

- ? (question mark) represents any single alphabetic character. For example

  FirstName = er?? returns entries including Eric and Erma

- # (number sign) represents any single numeric character. For example

  ID = 1## returns any ID from 100 through 199

> **Tip** Access supports several sets of wildcards. For more information on these, search Access Help for *wildcards* and read the topic titled "Access wildcard character reference."

When searching for information in a text field, you can also use the Contains text filter to locate records containing words or character strings.

In this exercise, you will filter records by a single criterion and then by multiple criteria.

> **Tip** The Filter commands you will use in this exercise are available in the Sort & Filter group on the Home tab, on the column menu displayed when you click a column header arrow, and on the shortcut menu displayed when you right-click a column. However, not all Filter commands are available in each of these places.

> **USE** the *FilterTable* database. This practice file is located in the *Documents\Microsoft Press\Access2007SBS\Locating* folder.
> **OPEN** the *FilterTable* database, and then open the Customers table in Datasheet view.

1. In the **City** field, click any instance of **Vancouver**.

2. On the **Home** tab, in the **Sort & Filter** group, click the **Selection** button, and then in the list, click **Equals "Vancouver"**.

   The number of customers displayed in the table (and on the status bar at the bottom of the table) changes from *110* to *6*, because only six customers live in Vancouver.

   Access displays a small filter icon at the right side of the City column header to indicate that the table is filtered by that field. The Toggle Filter button in the Sort & Filter group and the Filter status on the status bar changes to Filtered.

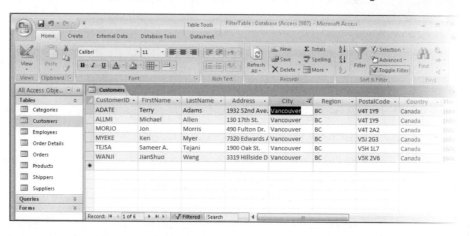

> **Important** When you filter a table, Access doesn't remove the records that don't match the filter; it simply hides them.

3. In the **Sort & Filter** group, click the **Toggle Filter** button.

Access removes the filter and displays all the records. If you click the Toggle Filter button again, the last filter used will be reapplied.

Suppose that you want a list of all customers with postal codes starting with *880*.

4. Click the **PostalCode** column header arrow, point to **Text Filters**, and then click **Begins With**.

> **Tip** The sort and filter options displayed when you click the column header arrow are determined by the field type. If this were a numeric field, then the submenu would be Number Filters and different options would be listed. U.S. Zip Codes and international postal codes are usually text fields to allow for the ZIP+4 codes.

The Custom Filter dialog box opens.

5. In the **PostalCode begins with** box, type *880*. Then click **OK**.

The filtered table includes 30 records that have postal codes starting with *880*.

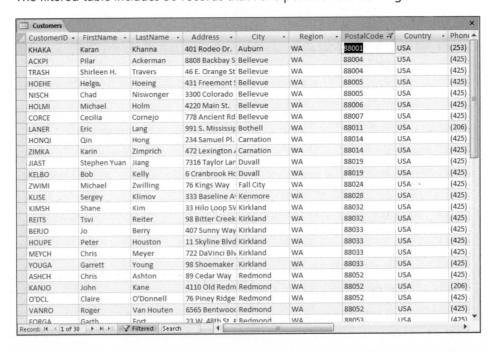

6. In the **Sort & Filter** group, click the **Toggle Filter** button to remove the filter and display all the records.

   Suppose you want to display only those customers who live outside of the United States.

7. In the **Country** column, right-click any instance of **USA**, and then click **Does Not Equal "USA"**.

   Access displays all the customers from countries other than the United States (in this case, only Canada).

8. Remove the filter, save and close the **Customers** table, and then open the **Orders** table in Datasheet view.

9. In the **EmployeeID** field, right-click **Emanuel, Michael**, and then click **Equals "Emanuel, Michael"**.

   > **Troubleshooting** If you continued with the *SortTable* database from the previous exercise, the EmployeeID field does not list employee names. To complete this exercise, you must use the *FilterTable* database.

10. In the **OrderDate** field, right-click **2/1/2007**, and then click **On or After 2/1/2007**.

    > **Tip** To see a list of the available options for date filters, right-click any cell in the OrderDate column and then point to Date Filters.

    You now have a list of orders placed with the selected employee on or after the specified date. You could continue to refine the list by filtering on another field, or you could sort the results by a field.

    > **Tip** After you locate the information you want, you can display the results in a form or report. To do so, on the Create tab, click the object you want to create.

 CLOSE the Orders table without saving changes, and then close the *FilterTable* database.

> **Tip** You can filter records while displaying them in a form by using the same commands as you do to filter forms in a table.

Expressions

In Access lingo, *expressions* are synonymous with *formulas*. An expression is a combination of *operators*, *constants*, *functions*, and *control properties* that evaluates to a single value. Access builds formulas using the format *a=b+c*, where *a* is the *result* and *=b+c* is the expression. You can use an expression to assign properties to tables or forms, to determine values in fields or reports, as part of queries, and so on.

The expressions you use in Access combine multiple criteria to define a set of conditions that a record must meet to be included in the result of a filter or query. Multiple criteria are combined using logical, comparison, and arithmetic operators. Different types of expressions use different operators.

The most common *logical operators* are:

- And. This operator selects records that meet all the specified criteria.
- Or. This operator selects records that meet at least one of the criteria.
- Not. This operator selects records that don't match the criteria.

Common *comparison operators* include:

- < (less than)
- > (greater than)
- = (equal to)

You can combine these basic operators to form:

- <= (less than or equal to)
- >= (greater than or equal to)
- <> (not equal to)

The Like operator is sometimes grouped with the comparison operators and is used to test whether or not text matches a pattern.

You use *arithmetic operators* with numerals. The most common are:

- + (add)
- - (subtract)
- * (multiply)
- / (divide)

A related operator, & (a text form of +) is used to concatenate (combine) two text strings.

Filtering Information by Using a Form

The Filter By Form command, available from the Advanced Filter Options list, provides a quick and easy way to filter a table based on the information in several fields. When you invoke this command within a table, Access displays a Look For tab containing a filtering form that looks like an empty datasheet. However, each of the blank cells is actually a combo box containing a list of all the entries in that field. You can select a filter criterion from the list, or enter a new one. Then you click the Toggle Filter button to display only the records containing your selected criteria.

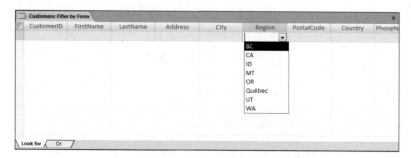

Using Filter By Form on a table that has only a few fields, such as the one shown above, is easy. But using it on a table that has a few dozen fields gets a bit cumbersome, and it is simpler to find information by using the Filter By Form command in the form version of the table. When you invoke this command within a form, Access filters the form in the same way it filters a table.

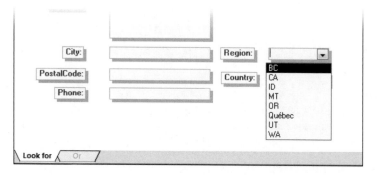

In a filtered form, you move between records by clicking the navigation buttons at the bottom of the form window.

> **Tip** Filter By Form offers the same features and techniques whether you are using it in a form or a table. Because defining the filter is sometimes easier in a form and viewing the results is sometimes easier in a table, you might consider creating a simple form based on the table, filtering the data within the form, and then switching to Datasheet view to display the results.

In this exercise, you will locate a record by using the Filter By Form command.

> **USE** the *FilterForm* database. This practice file is located in the *Documents\Microsoft Press\Access2007SBS\Locating* folder.
>
> **OPEN** the *FilterForm* database.

1. In the **Navigation Pane**, under **Forms**, double-click **Customers**.

   The Customers form opens in Form view.

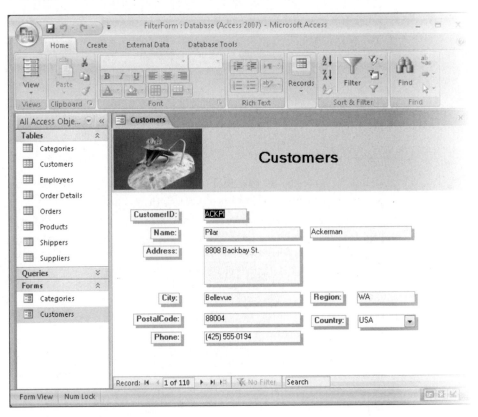

2. On the **Home** tab, in the **Sort & Filter** group, click the **Advanced** button, and then in the list, click **Filter By Form**.

   The Customers form, which displays the information from one record, is replaced by its Filter By Form version, which has a blank box for each field and the Look For and Or tabs at the bottom.

3. Click the second text box to the right of the **Name** label (the box intended to contain the surname), type s*, and then press Enter.

Access converts your entry to the proper format, or *syntax*, for this type of expression: *Like "s*"*.

4. In the **Sort & Filter** group, click the **Toggle Filter** button.

Access displays all records including last names starting with *S*.

5. Click the **Filter By Form** button again to switch back to the filter form.

Your filter criteria are still displayed. When you enter filter criteria using any method, they are saved as a form property and are available until they are replaced by other criteria.

6. Click the box to the right of **Region**, click the arrow that appears, and then in the list, click **CA**.

7. Click the **Toggle Filter** button to see only the customers living in California whose last names begin with *S*.

Access replaces the filter window with the regular Customers form, and the status bar at the bottom of the form indicates that three filtered records are available.

8. Click the **Filter By Form** button again to switch back to the filter form.

9. At the bottom of the form window, click the **Or** tab.

> **Tip** Criteria you enter on the Look For tab are joined with the And operator to reduce the number of possible hits in the underlying table. Criteria entered on the Or tabs tend to increase the number of hits.

This tab has the same blank cells as the Look For tab. You can switch between the two tabs to confirm that your criteria haven't been cleared.

> **Tip** When you display the Or tab, a second Or tab appears so that you can include a third criterion if you want.

10. Type s* in the **LastName** box, type or click WA in the **Region** box, and then click the **Toggle Filter** button.

You can scroll through the filtered Customers form to view the six records containing WA in the Region field.

 CLOSE the Customers form and the *FilterForm* database.

> **Tip** Although most forms facilitate data entry, the PivotTable form is most useful for comparing and analyzing large quantities of data. This form displays an interactive table that uses whatever calculation methods you specify to summarize the data. You can rotate the row and column headings of this multidimensional table to display different views of the data. To create a PivotTable form, click the More Forms button in the Forms group on the Create tab, and then click PivotTable.

Locating Information That Matches Multiple Criteria

The filtering methods discussed earlier in this chapter are quick and easy ways to narrow down the amount of information displayed, as long as your filter criteria are fairly simple. But suppose you need to locate something more complex, such as all the orders shipped to Midwest states between specific dates by either of two shippers. When you need to search a single table for records that meet multiple criteria, or with criteria based on complex expressions as criteria, you can use the Advanced Filter/Sort command, available from the Advanced Filter Options list.

You work with the Advanced Filter/Sort command in the *design grid*.

In this exercise, you will filter a table to display customers located in two states. Then you will experiment with the design grid to better understand its filtering capabilities.

> **USE** the *MultipleCriteria* database. This practice file is located in the *Documents\Microsoft Press\Access2007SBS\Locating* folder.
>
> **OPEN** the *MultipleCriteria* database. Then open the Customers table in Datasheet view.

  1. On the **Home** tab, in the **Sort & Filter** group, click the **Advanced Filter Options** button, and then in the list, click **Advanced Filter/Sort**.

The CustomersFilter1 query window opens, displaying the Customers field list in a floating window at the top, and the design grid at the bottom.

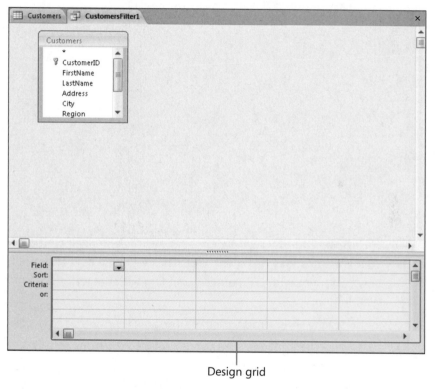

Design grid

2. In the **Customers** field list, double-click **LastName** to copy it to the **Field** cell in the first column of the design grid.

3. In the **Criteria** cell under **LastName**, type s*, and then press [Enter].

Access changes the criterion to *Like "s*"*.

4. In the **Customers** field list, double-click **Region** to copy it to the next available column of the design grid.

5. In the **Criteria** cell under **Region**, type ca or wa, and then press [Enter].

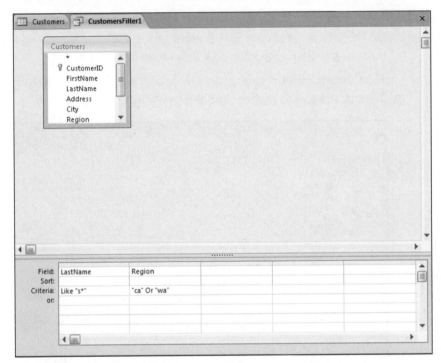

Your entry changes to *"ca" Or "wa"*. The query will now filter the table to display only customers with last names beginning with the letter *S* who live in California or Washington.

6. In the **Sort & Filter** group, click the **Toggle Filter** button to display only records that match the criteria.

Access switches to the Customers table and displays the query results. There are six customers with last names beginning with *S* who live in either California or Washington.

7. Click the **CustomersFilter1** tab to switch to the filter window. In the **or** cell under **LastName**, type b*, and then press Enter.

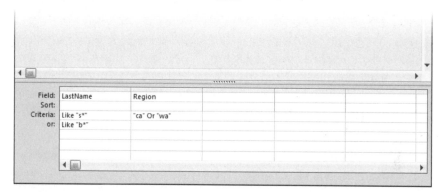

8. In the **Sort & Filter** group, click the **Toggle Filter** button.

   The result includes records for all customers with last names that begin with *s* or *b*, but some of the *b* names live in Montana and Oregon. If you look again at the design grid, you can see that the filter is formed by combining the fields in the Criteria row with the *And* operator, combining the fields in the "Or" row with the *And* operator, and then using the *Or* operator to combine the two rows. So the filter is searching for customers with names beginning with *s* who live in California or Washington, or customers with names beginning with *b*, regardless of where they live.

9. Switch to the filter window, type ca or wa in the **or** cell under **Region**, press Enter, and then apply the filter to display only customers with last names beginning with *B* or *S* located in California and Washington.

CLOSE the Customers table without saving your changes, and then close the *MultipleCriteria* database.

Creating a Query Manually

A query can do more than simply return a list of records from a table. You can use functions in a query to perform calculations on the information in a table to produce the sum, average, count, and other mathematical values.

When you want to work with more than one table, you need to move beyond filters and into the realm of queries. Common types of queries include the following:

- A *select query* retrieves data from one or more tables and displays the results in a datasheet. You can also use a select query to group records and calculate sums, counts, averages, and other types of totals. You can work with the results of a select query in Datasheet view to update records in one or more related tables at the same time. This is the most common type of query.

- A *duplicate query* is a form of select query that locates records that have the same information in one or more fields that you specify. The Find Duplicates Query wizard guides you through the process of specifying the table and fields to use in the query.

- An *unmatched query* is a form of select query that locates records in one table that don't have related records in another table. For example, you could use this to locate people in the customer table who don't have an order in the order table. The Find Unmatched Query wizard guides you through the process of specifying the tables and fields to use in the query.

- A *parameter query* prompts you for information to be used in the query—for example, a range of dates. This type of query is particularly useful when used as the basis for a report that is run periodically.

- A *crosstab query* calculates and restructures data for easier analysis. You can use a crosstab query to calculate a sum, average, count, or other type of total for data that is grouped by two types of information—one down the left side of the datasheet and one across the top. The cell at the junction of each row and column displays the results of the query's calculation.

- An *action query* updates multiple records in one operation. It is essentially a select query that performs an action on the results of the selection process. Four types of actions are available:

  - *Delete queries*, which delete records from one or more tables
  - *Update queries*, which make changes to records in one or more tables
  - *Append queries*, which add records from one or more tables to the end of one or more other tables
  - *Make-table queries*, which create a new table from all or part of the data in one or more tables

> **Tip** In addition to these, you can create Structured Query Language (SQL) queries. SQL queries are beyond the scope of this book.

Access includes wizards that guide you through the creation of the common queries, but you create less common queries by hand in Design view, using the design grid.

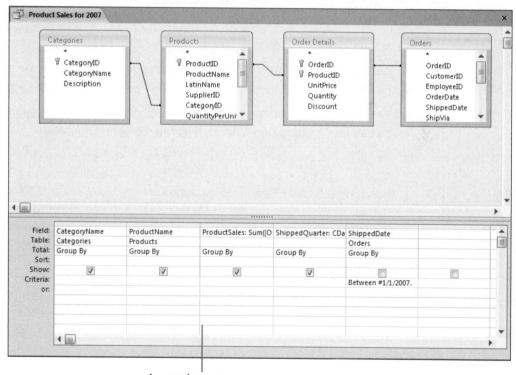

A complex query,
shown in Design view

The field lists (in the small windows at the top of the query window) list the fields in the four tables that can be included in this query. The lines connecting the tables indicate that they are related by virtue of common fields. The first row of the grid contains the names of the fields actually included in the query, and the second row shows which table each field belongs to. The third row (labeled *Total*) performs calculations on the field values, and the fourth row indicates whether the query results will be sorted on this field. A selected check box in the fifth row (labeled *Show*) means that the field will be displayed in the results datasheet. (If the check box isn't selected, the field can be used in determining the query results, but it won't be displayed.) The sixth row (labeled *Criteria*) contains criteria that determine which records will be displayed, and the seventh row (labeled *or*) sets up alternate criteria.

You can create a query by hand or by using a wizard. Regardless of what method you use to create the query, what you create is a statement describing the conditions that must be met for records to be matched in one or more tables. When you run the query, the matching records appear in a new datasheet.

> ## Filters and Sorts vs. Queries
>
> The major differences between filtering a table, sorting a table, and querying a table are:
>
> - The Filter and Sort commands are usually faster to implement than queries.
> - The Filter and Sort commands are not saved, or are saved only temporarily. You can save a query permanently and run it again at any time.
> - The Filter and Sort commands are applied only to the table or form that is currently open. A query can be based on multiple tables and on other queries, which don't have to be open.

> **Tip** It is possible to use the results of one query as a field in another query. This nesting of an SQL Select statement in a select or action query is called a *subquery*.
>
> **See Also** For more information about subqueries, see the Access Help system topic "Nest a query inside another query or in an expression by using a subquery."

In this exercise, you will create a form based on a select query that combines information from two tables into a datasheet and calculates the extended price of an item based on the unit price, quantity ordered, and discount.

Query Design

USE the *QueryDesign* database. This practice file is located in the *Documents\Microsoft Press\Access2007SBS\Locating* folder.

OPEN the *QueryDesign* database.

1. On the **Create** tab, in the **Other** group, click the **Query Design** button.

   A query window opens in Design view, and the Show Table dialog box opens. In this dialog box, you can specify which tables and saved queries to include in the current query.

2. In the **Show Table** dialog box, on the **Tables** tab, double-click **Order Details** and then **Products** to add each table to the query window. Then close the dialog box.

   Each of the selected tables is represented in the top portion of the window by a small field list window with the name of the table—in this case, Order Details and Products—in its title bar.

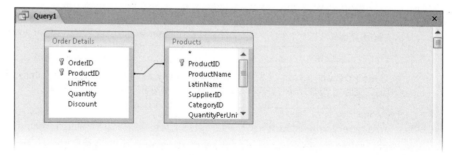

   An asterisk at the top of each list represents all the fields in the list. The primary key field in each list is indicated by a key icon. The line from ProductID in the Order Details table to ProductID in the Products table indicates that these two fields are related.

Joining Fields in a Query

In a query, relationships between fields are represented by joins. The most common joins are inner joins and outer joins:

● *Inner joins* tell a query to return only records where the values in both related table fields match. Access automatically creates inner joins when you establish a table relationship.

● *Outer joins* can be left outer joins or right outer joins—a left outer join returns all records from the first table and matching records from the second; a right outer join returns all records from the second table and matching records from the first.

Tip To add an existing table field to a query, open the query in Design view and double-click the field. To add a field from another table, drag the table from the Navigation Pane to the upper section of the design window, and double-click the field.

To delete a field from a query, select the field in the lower section of the design window, and then press the Delete key. To delete a table from a query, right-click the table in the upper section of the design window, and then click Remove Table.

The lower area of the query window contains the design grid where you will specify the query's criteria.

3. Drag the following fields from the field lists to consecutive columns in the design grid:

From this table	Drag this field
Order Details	OrderID
Products	ProductName
Order Details	UnitPrice
Order Details	Quantity
Order Details	Discount

The query will include only the fields that are in the design grid.

Tip You can quickly copy a field to the next available column in the design grid by double-clicking the field. To copy all fields to the grid, double-click the title bar above the field list to select the entire list, and then drag the selection over the grid. When you release the mouse button, Access adds the fields to the columns in order. You can drag the asterisk to a column in the grid to include all the fields in the query, but you also have to drag individual fields to the grid if you want to sort on those fields or add conditions to them.

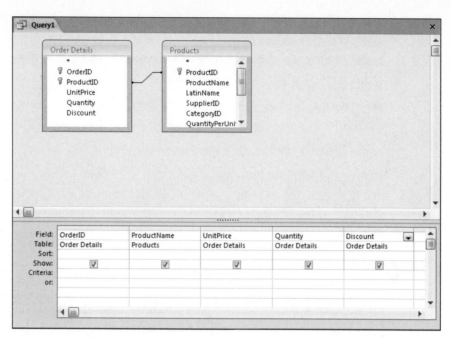

Run

4. On the **Design** contextual tab, in the **Results** group, click the **Run** button.

Access runs the query and displays the results in Datasheet view.

OrderID	Product Name	UnitPrice	Quantity	Discount
11091	Autumn crocus	$18.75	4	0
11079	Compost bin	$58.00	1	0
11083	Compost bin	$58.00	1	0
11138	Compost bin	$58.00	1	0
11152	Compost bin	$58.00	1	0
11085	Cactus sand potting mix	$4.50	2	0
11093	Cactus sand potting mix	$4.50	2	0
11121	Cactus sand potting mix	$4.50	1	0
11132	Cactus sand potting mix	$4.50	1	0
11148	Cactus sand potting mix	$4.50	1	0
11114	Weeping Forsythia	$18.00	3	0
11147	Weeping Forsythia	$18.00	1	0
11082	Bat box	$14.75	3	0
11086	Bat box	$14.75	2	0
11159	Bat box	$14.75	3	0.1
11152	Beneficial nematodes	$19.95	1	0
11089	Crown Vetch	$12.95	1	0
11110	Crown Vetch	$12.95	1	0
11089	English Ivy	$5.95	1	0
11110	English Ivy	$5.95	1	0
11137	Persian Yellow Rose	$12.95	6	0.1

Record: 1 of 213   No Filter   Search

The results show that the query is working thus far. There are two things left to do: sort the results on the OrderID field and add a field for calculating the extended price, which is the unit price times the quantity sold minus any discount.

5. Switch to Design view.

The third row in the design grid is labeled Sort. You can select Ascending, Descending, or (not sorted) in this cell for any of the query fields.

6. In the **OrderID** column, click the **Sort** arrow, and then in the list, click **Ascending**.

Neither of the tables includes an extended price field. Rather than creating the field in a table, you will use the Expression Builder to insert an expression in the design grid that computes this price from existing information.

7. Right-click the **Field** cell in the first blank column in the design grid (the sixth column), and then click **Build**.

The Expression Builder dialog box opens.

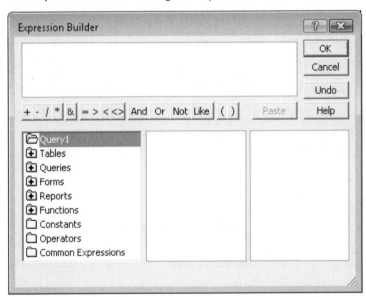

Here is the expression you will build:

```
CCur([Order Details]![UnitPrice]*[Order Details]![Quantity]*(1-[Order
Details]![Discount]))
```

The CCur function converts the results of the math inside its parentheses to currency format.

> **Tip** If you were to type this expression directly into the field, you could simplify it a bit to this:
> ExtendedPrice: CCur([Order Details]![UnitPrice]*[Quantity]*(1-[Discount]))
> The [Order Details]! part is required only with fields that appear in both tables. It tells the query which table to use.

8. In the first column of the elements area, double-click the **Functions** folder to display its contents, and then click **Built-In Functions**.

   Categories of built-in functions appear in the second column; actual functions within each category appear in the third column.

9. In the second column, click **Conversion** to limit the functions in the third column to those in that category. Then in the third column, double-click **Ccur**.

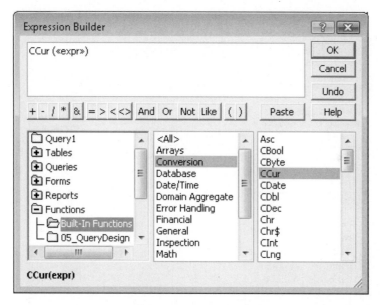

You've inserted the currency conversion function into the expression box. The *<<expr>>* inside the parentheses represents the other expressions that will eventually result in the number Access should convert to currency format.

10. In the expression box, click **<<expr>>** to select it so that the next thing you enter will replace it.

    The next element you want in the expression is the UnitPrice field from the Order Details table.

11. In the first column, double-click the **Tables** folder, and click **Order Details**. Then in the second column, double-click **UnitPrice**.

The insertion point is currently situated after UnitPrice, which is exactly where you want it. Now you want to multiply the amount in the UnitPrice field by the amount in the Quantity field.

Multiply

12. In the row of operator buttons below the expression box, click the **Multiply** button. Access inserts the multiplication sign and another *<<Expr>>* placeholder.

13. In the expression box, click **<<Expr>>** to select it, and then in the second column, double-click **Quantity**.

What you have entered so far calculates the total cost by multiplying the price of an item by the quantity ordered. However, suppose the sale price is discounted due to quantity or another factor. The discount, which is stored in the Order Details table, is expressed as the percentage to deduct. But it is easier to compute the percentage to be paid than it is to compute the discount and subtract it from the total cost.

14. In the expression box, type *(1-. In the second column, double-click **Discount**, and type). If the entire expression isn't visible in the window, widen the window by dragging its right edge.

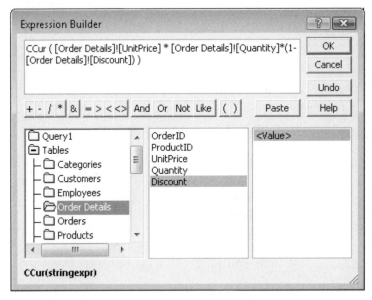

Although the discount is formatted in the datasheet as a percentage, it is actually stored in the database as a decimal number between 0 and 1. (For example, a discount displayed as 10% is stored as 0.1). So if the discount is 10%, the result of *(1-Discount) is *.9. In other words, the formula multiplies the unit price by the quantity and then multiplies that result by 0.9.

15. In the **Expression Builder** dialog box, click **OK**.

Access enters the expression in the design grid.

16. Press Enter to move the insertion point out of the field and complete the entry of the expression.

Access labels the expression Expr1, which isn't particularly meaningful.

> **Tip** You can quickly make a column in the design grid as wide as its contents by double-clicking the line in the gray selection bar that separates the column from the column to its right.

17. In the design grid, double-click **Expr1**, and then type ExtendedPrice as the label (also called the *field alias*) for the expression.

18. Switch to Datasheet view.

The orders are now sorted by the OrderID field, and the extended price is calculated in the last field.

19. Scroll down to see a few records with discounts.

If you check the math, you will see that the query calculates the extended price correctly.

20. Close the query window. In the **Microsoft Office Access** message box asking whether to save the query, click **Yes**. In the **Save As** dialog box, type Order Details Extended, and then click **OK**.

CLOSE the *QueryDesign* database.

> ## Expression Builder
>
> To create an expression as a filter or query option, you can either type the expression or use the Expression Builder. You can open the Expression Builder by clicking Build on a shortcut menu, clicking Builder in the Query Setup group, or by clicking the Build button (which resembles an ellipsis) at the right end of a box that can accept an expression.
>
> The Expression Builder isn't a wizard; it doesn't lead you through the process of building an expression. But it does provide a hierarchical list of the most common elements that you can include in an expression. You can either type your expression in the expression box, or you can select functions, operators, and other elements to copy them to the expression box.

Creating a Query by Using a Wizard

The process of creating a simple select query by using the Query wizard is almost identical to that of creating a form by using the Form wizard. Within the Query wizard, you can build a new query based on one or more fields from existing tables or queries. You can also create Crosstab, Find Duplicates, and Find Unmatched queries with the wizard.

For Access to work effectively with multiple tables, it must understand the relationships between the fields in those tables. If these relationships don't already exist.

See Also For more information about creating relationships, see the sidebar "Relationships" in Chapter 5, "Simplifying Data Entry by Using Forms."

In this exercise, you will use the Query wizard to create a query that combines information from two tables related through common fields.

> **USE** the *QueryWizard* database. This practice file is located in the *Documents\Microsoft Press\Access2007SBS\Locating* folder.
>
> **OPEN** the *QueryWizard* database.

Query Wizard

1. On the **Create** tab, in the **Other** group, click the **Query Wizard** button.

   The New Query dialog box opens.

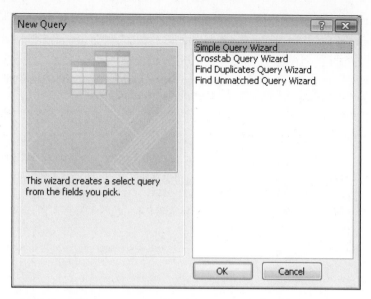

2. With **Simple Query Wizard** selected in the list, click **OK**.

The Simple Query wizard starts.

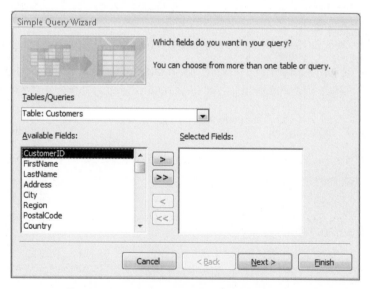

Move All

3. In the **Tables/Queries** list, click **Table: Orders**. Then click the **Move All** button to move all the fields from the **Available Fields** list to the **Selected Fields** list.

4. In the **Tables/Queries** list, click **Table: Customers.**

5. In the **Available Fields** list, double-click the **Address**, **City**, **Region**, **PostalCode**, and **Country** fields to move them to the **Selected Fields** list, and then click **Next**.

> **Tip** If the relationship between two tables hasn't already been established, you will be prompted to define it and then restart the wizard.

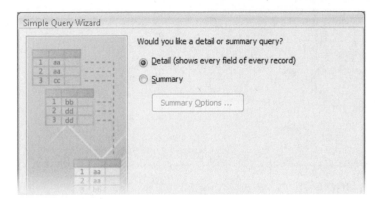

6. With the **Detail** option selected, click **Next**.

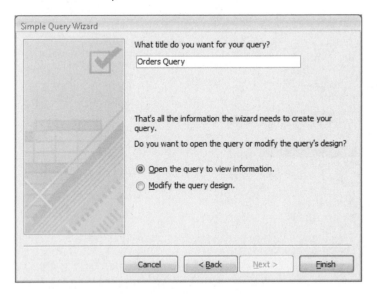

7. With the **Open the query to view information** option selected, click **Finish**.

Access runs the query and displays the results in Datasheet view. You can scroll through the results and see that information is displayed for all the orders.

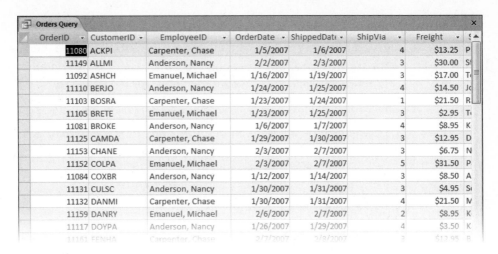

8. Switch to Design view.

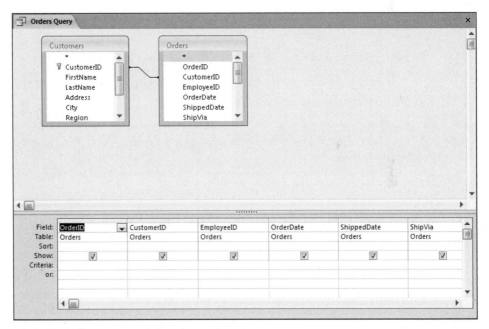

Notice that the Show check box is selected by default for each of the fields used in the query. If you want to use a field in a query—for example, to sort on, to set criteria for, or in a calculation—but don't want to see the field in the results datasheet, you can clear its Show check box.

9. Clear the **Show** check box for **OrderID**, **CustomerID**, and **EmployeeID**, and then switch back to Datasheet view.

The three fields have been removed from the results datasheet.

10. Switch to Design view.

    This query returns all records in the Orders table. To have the query match the records for a range of dates, you will convert it to a parameter query, which requests the date range each time you run it.

11. In the **OrderDate** column, type the following text in the **Criteria** cell, exactly as shown:

    Between [Type the beginning date:] And [Type the ending date:]

Run

12. On the **Design** contextual tab, in the **Results** group, click the **Run** button to run the query.

13. Enter a beginning date of 1/1/07, and then press ⏎ Enter.

14. Enter an ending date of 1/31/07, and then press ⏎ Enter.

    Access redisplays the datasheet, this time listing only orders between the specified dates.

CLOSE the datasheet, saving the changes to the query, and then close the *QueryWizard* database.

Performing Calculations by Using a Query

You typically use a query to locate all the records that meet some criteria. But sometimes you are not as interested in the details of all the records as you are in summarizing them in some way. For example, you might want to know how many orders have been placed this year or the total dollar value of all orders placed. The easiest way to get this information is by creating a query that groups the necessary fields and does the math for you. To do this, you use *aggregate functions* in the query.

> **Tip** You can easily summarize table data by adding a Totals row. To do so, display the table in Datasheet view and then on the Home tab, in the Records group, click the Totals button. Click in each cell of the Totals row that appears at the end of the table, and select the summary data you want to appear in that cell. The data types available for each column depend on the data stored in that field.

Access queries support the aggregate functions shown in the following table.

Function	Calculates
Sum	Total of the values in a field
Avg	Average of the values in a field
Count	Number of values in a field, not counting Null (blank) values
Min	Lowest value in a field
Max	Highest value in a field
StDev	Standard deviation of the values in a field
Var	Variance of the values in a field

In this exercise, you will create a query that calculates the total number of products in an inventory, the average price of all the products, and the total value of the inventory.

USE the *Calculate* database. This practice file is located in the *Documents\Microsoft Press\ Access2007SBS\Locating* folder.

OPEN the *Calculate* database.

Query
Design

1. On the **Create** tab, in the **Other** group, click the **Query Design** button.

Access opens the query window and the Show Table dialog box.

2. In the **Show Table** dialog box, double-click **Products**, and then click **Close**.

Access adds the Products table to the query window and closes the Show Table dialog box.

3. In the **Products Items** field list, double-click **ProductID** and then **UnitPrice**.

Access copies both fields to the design grid.

Totals

4. On the **Design** contextual tab, in the **Show/Hide** group, click the **Totals** button.

Access adds a row named *Total* to the design grid.

5. In the **ProductID** column, click the **Total** arrow, and then in the list, click **Count**.

Access enters the word *Count* in the Total cell. When you run the query, this function will return a count of the number of records containing a value in the ProductID field.

6. In the **UnitPrice** column, click the **Total** arrow, and then in the list, click **Avg**.

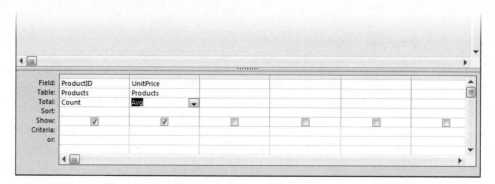

When you run the query, this function will return the average of all the UnitPrice values.

7. In the **Results** group, click the **Run** button.

The query returns a single record containing the count and the average price.

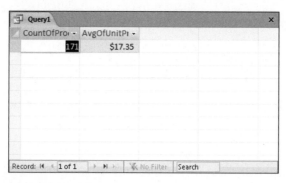

8. Switch back to Design view.

9. In the third column, in the **Field** cell, type UnitPrice*UnitsInStock, and press Enter.

Access changes the expression you typed to

Expr1: [UnitPrice][UnitsInStock]*

This expression will multiply the price of each product by the number of units in stock.

10. Select **Expr1** and type Value of Inventory to re-label the expression.

11. In the third column, click the **Total** arrow, and then in the list, click **Sum**.

Access will return the sum of all the values calculated by the expression.

12. On the **Design** tab, in the **Results group**, click the **Run** button.

 CLOSE the query window without saving your changes, and then close the *Calculate* database. If you are not continuing directly on to the next chapter, exit Access.

Key Points

- Microsoft Office Access 2007 provides a variety of tools you can use to organize the display of information in a database and to locate specific items of information. These tools make it easy to search through and find information in your database, even as it grows in size and complexity.

- You can sort a table in either ascending or descending order, based on the values in any field (or combination of fields). In Access, numbers can be treated as text or numerals.

- You can filter a table so that information containing some combination of characters is displayed (or excluded from the display). You can apply simple filters while viewing information in a table or a form. These filters are applied to the contents of a selected field, but you can apply another filter to the results of the first one to further refine your search.

- The Filter By Form command filters a table or form based on the information in several fields.

- The Advanced Filter/Sort command searches a single table for records that meet multiple criteria or that require complex expressions as criteria.

- You can create queries to display specific fields from specific records from one or more tables, even designing the query to perform calculations for you. You can then save your queries for later use.

Chapter at a Glance

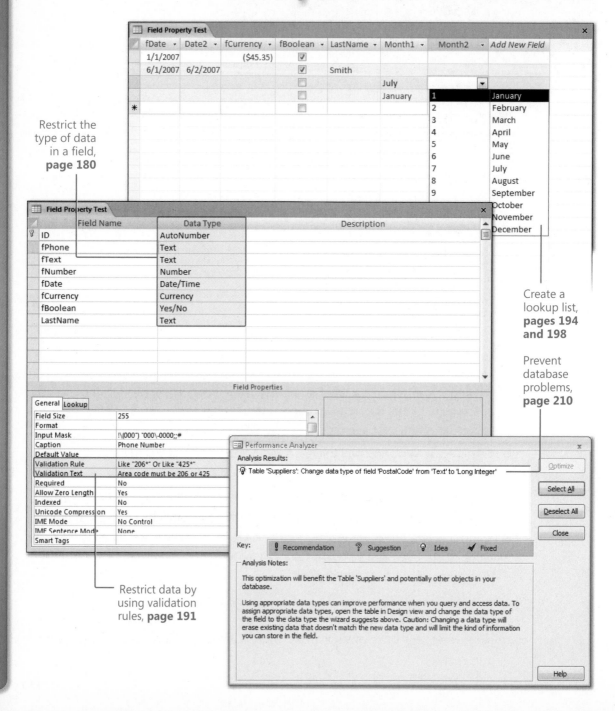

Restrict the type of data in a field, **page 180**

Create a lookup list, **pages 194 and 198**

Prevent database problems, **page 210**

Restrict data by using validation rules, **page 191**

7 Keeping Your Information Accurate

In this chapter, you will learn to:

✔ Restrict the type and amount of data in a field.

✔ Specify the format of data in a field.

✔ Restrict data by using validation rules.

✔ Create a simple or multi-column lookup list.

✔ Update information in a table.

✔ Delete information from a table.

✔ Prevent database problems.

Depending on how much information you have and how organized you are, you might compare a database to an old shoebox or to a file cabinet, into which you toss items such as photographs, bills, receipts, and a variety of other paperwork for later retrieval. However, neither a shoebox nor a file cabinet restricts anything other than the physical size of what you can place in it or imposes any order on its content. It is up to you to decide what you store there and to organize it properly so that you can find it when you next need it.

When you create a database by using Microsoft Office Access 2007, you can set properties that restrict what can be entered and impose order on the database contents, thereby helping you to keep the database organized and useful. You would not, for example, want employees to enter text into a price field, or to enter a long text description in a field when a simple "yes" or "no" answer would work best.

To ensure the ongoing accuracy of a database, you can create and run *action queries* that quickly update information or delete selected records from a table. You could, for example, increase the price of all products in one category by a certain percentage, or remove all the elements of a specific product line. This type of updating is easy to do with an action query. Not only does using a query save time, but it helps to avoid errors.

In this chapter, you will restrict the type, amount, and format of data allowed in a field, and create a list from which a database user can choose a specific option. Then you will create and run an update query and a delete query.

See Also Do you need only a quick refresher on the topics in this chapter? See the Quick Reference section at the beginning of this book.

Important Before you can use the practice files in this chapter, you need to install them from the book's companion CD to their default location. See "Using the Companion CD" at the beginning of this book for more information.

Troubleshooting Graphics and operating system–related instructions in this book reflect the Windows Vista user interface. If your computer is running Windows XP and you experience trouble following the instructions as written, please refer to the "Information for Readers Running Windows XP" section at the beginning of this book.

Restricting the Type of Data in a Field

The Data Type setting restricts entries in a field to a specific type of data, such as text, numbers, or dates. If, for example, the data type is set to Number and you attempt to enter text, Access refuses the entry and displays a warning.

The *field properties* you can set to control input are:

- Required
- Allow Zero Length
- Field Size
- Input Mask
- Validation Rule

The Required and Allow Zero Length properties are fairly obvious. If the Required property is set to *Yes*, the field can't be left blank. However, Access differentiates between a blank field (which it refers to as a Null field) and a field that looks blank, but contains an empty string. If Allow Zero Length is set to *Yes*, you can enter an *empty string* (two quotation marks with nothing in between), which looks like a blank field, but it is classified as empty rather than Null. This differentiation might seem silly, but if you are using programming code to work with an Access database, you will find that some commands produce different results for Null fields than they do for empty fields.

The Field Size, Input Mask, and Validation Rule properties are more complex, so the exercises in this chapter will focus on them.

> **Tip** Each field property has many options. For more information, search for *field property* in Access Help.

In this exercise, you will add fields of the most common data types to a table, and then use the Data Type setting and Field Size property to restrict the data that can be entered into the table.

> **USE** the *FieldTest* database. This practice file is located in the *Documents\Microsoft Press\ Access2007SBS\Accuracy* folder.
>
> **OPEN** the *FieldTest* database. Then display the Field Property Test table in Design view.

1. Click in the first available **Field Name** cell (below the automatically-generated ID field), type **fText**, and then press the ⌨Tab key to move to the **Data Type** cell.

   The data type defaults to **Text**.

2. In the second **Field Name** cell, type **fNumber**, and then press ⌨Tab.

3. Click the **Data Type** arrow, and in the list, click **Number**.

> **Tip** You can scroll the list to the data type you want by typing the first letter of its name in the cell.

4. Repeat Steps 2 and 3 to add the following fields:

Field	Data type
fDate	Date/Time
fCurrency	Currency
fBoolean	Yes/No

> **Tip** The data type referred to as *Yes/No* in Access is more commonly called *Boolean* (in honor of George Boole, an early mathematician and logistician). This data type can hold either of two mutually exclusive values, often expressed as *yes/no, 1/0, on/off*, or *true/false*.

5. Click the **fText** field name to select it.

Access displays the properties of the selected field in the lower portion of the dialog box.

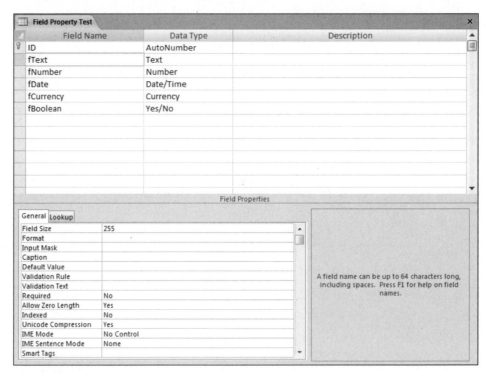

Save

6. Repeat step 5 to review the properties of each field, and then on the **Quick Access Toolbar**, click the **Save** button.

7. On the **View** toolbar, click the **Datasheet View** button.

Datasheet View

8. In the **fText** cell, type This entry is 32 characters long.

9. In the **fNumber** cell, type Five hundred.

The data type for this field is Number. Access does not accept your text entry, and displays a warning offering you several options.

> The value you entered does not match the Number data type in this column.
>
> Enter new value.
>
> Convert the data in this column to the Text data type.
>
> Help with data types and formats.

10. In the **Microsoft Office Access** message box, click **Enter new value**. Then replace *Five Hundred* with 500.

11. In the **fDate** cell, type date, and then press [Tab].

Access does not accept the unexpected data format.

12. In the **Microsoft Office Access** message box that appears, click **Enter new value**, type Jan 1, and then press [Tab].

The fDate field accepts almost any entry that can be recognized as a date, and displays it in the default date format. Depending on the default format on your computer, Jan 1 might be displayed as *1/1/2007, 1/1/07*, or in some other format.

> **Tip** If you enter a month and day but no year in a date field, Access assumes the date is in the current year. If you enter a month, day, and two-digit year from 00 through 30, Access assumes the year is 2000 through 2030. If you enter a two-digit year that is greater than 30, Access assumes you mean 1931 through 1999.

13. In the **fCurrency** field, type the word currency, and then press [Tab].

Access does not accept the unexpected data format.

14. In the **Microsoft Office Access** message box that appears, click **Enter new value**, type −45.3456, and then press [Tab].

Access stores the number you entered but displays *($45.35)*, the default format for negative currency numbers.

> **Tip** Access uses the regional settings in the Windows Control Panel to determine the display format for date, time, currency, and other numbers. You can create custom formats to ensure that the correct currency symbol is always displayed with your values. Otherwise, the numbers won't change, but the currency symbol might, for instance from dollars to pounds, pesos, or euros.

15. In the **fBoolean** field, enter 123. Then click anywhere in the field to toggle the check box between **No** (not checked) and **Yes** (checked), finishing with the field in the checked state.

This field won't accept anything you type; you can switch only between two predefined values.

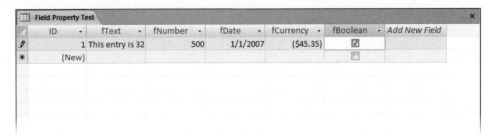

> **Tip** In Design view, you can open the Properties dialog box, and on the Lookup tab, set the Boolean field to display as a check box, text box, or combo box. You can set the Format property on the General tab to use True/False, Yes/No, or On/Off as the displayed values in this field (though the stored values will always be -1 and 0).

 CLOSE the table without saving your changes, and then close the *FieldTest* database.

Restricting the Amount of Data in a Field

The Field Size property, which is valid for the Text, Number, and AutoNumber data types, restricts the number of characters that can be entered in a text field (from 0 to 255) and the number of digits that can be entered in a number or AutoNumber field. You can set number fields to any of the following values:

Setting	Description
Byte	Stores whole numbers from 0 to 255
Integer	Stores whole numbers from −32,768 to 32,767
Long Integer	(The default.) Stores whole numbers from −2,147,483,648 to 2,147,483,647
Single	Stores negative numbers from −3.402823E38 to −1.401298E−45 and positive numbers from 1.401298E−45 to 3.402823E38
Double	Stores negative numbers from −1.79769313486231E308 to −4.94065645841247E−324 and positive numbers from 1.79769313486231E308 to 4.94065645841247E−324
Decimal	Stores numbers from -10^28 -1 through 10^28 -1

AutoNumber fields are automatically set to Long Integer.

By setting the Field Size property to a value that allows the largest valid entry, you prevent the user from entering certain types of invalid information. If you try to type more characters in a text field than the number allowed by the Field Size setting, an audio alert sounds, and Access refuses to accept the entry. Likewise, Access rejects any value that is below or above the limits of a number field when you try to move out of the field.

See Also For more information about data restrictions, see the Access Help system topic "Introduction to data types and field properties."

In this exercise, you will change the Field Size property for several fields to see the impact this has on data already in the table and on new data that you enter.

USE the *Size* database. This practice file is located in the *Documents\Microsoft Press\ Access2007SBS\Accuracy* folder.

OPEN the *Size* database. Then open the Field Property Test table in Datasheet view.

1. Review the contents of the one record.

Design View

2. On the **View** toolbar, click the **Design View** button.

3. Click any cell in the **fText** row, and then in the **Field Properties** area, change the **Field Size** property from *255* to *12*.

4. Click any cell in the **fNumber** row, click the **Field Size** arrow, and then in the list, click **Byte**.

   Access restricts the number of characters that can be entered in the text field to 12, and the values that can be entered in the number field to the range from 0 to 255 (inclusive).

5. Switch to Datasheet view, clicking **Yes** when prompted to save the table.

   The table contains data that doesn't fit these new property settings, so Access displays a warning that some data might be lost.

6. Click **Yes** to acknowledge the risk, and click **Yes** again to accept the deletion of the contents of one field.

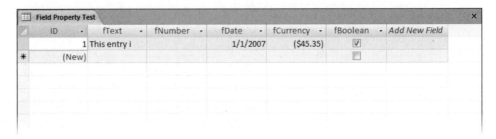

fText now contains only 12 characters, rather than the 32 you entered. The other 20 characters have been permanently deleted. fNumber is empty because it is now limited to whole numbers from 0 through 255, and the value of 500 that you entered was deleted.

7. In the **fNumber** field, type 2.5, and then press the ⏎ Enter key.

Access rounds the entered value to the nearest whole number.

CLOSE the Field Property Test table and the *Size* database.

Specifying the Format of Data in a Field

When you use *masks* in tables or forms, people entering information can see at a glance the format in which they should make entries and how long they should be. You can use the InputMask property to control how data is entered in text, number, date/time, and currency fields. This property has three sections, separated by semicolons, like the mask for a telephone number, shown here:

!\(000") "000\-0000;1;#

The first section contains characters that are used as placeholders for the information to be typed, as well as characters such as parentheses and hyphens. Together, all these characters control the appearance of the entry. The following table explains the purpose of the most common input mask characters:

Character	Description
0	Required digit (0 through 9).
9	Optional digit or space.
#	Optional digit or space; blank positions are converted to spaces; plus and minus signs are allowed.
L	Required letter (A through Z).
?	Optional letter (A through Z).
A	Required letter or digit.
a	Optional letter or digit.
&	Required character (any kind) or a space.
C	Optional character (any kind) or a space.
<	All characters that follow are converted to lowercase.
>	All characters that follow are converted to uppercase.
!	Characters typed into the mask fill it from left to right. You can include the exclamation point anywhere in the input mask.
\	Character that follows is displayed as a literal character.
"any text"	Access treats the string enclosed in double quotation marks as a literal string.
Password	Creates a password entry box. Any character typed in the box is stored as the character but displayed as an asterisk (*).

Any characters not included in this list are displayed as literal characters. If you want to use one of the special characters in this list as a literal character, precede it with the \ (backslash) character.

The second and third sections of the input mask are optional. Including a 1 in the second section or leaving it blank tells Access to store only the characters entered; including a 0 tells it to store both the characters entered and the mask characters. Entering a character in the third section causes Access to display that character as a placeholder for each of the characters to be typed; leaving it blank displays an underscore as the placeholder.

The input mask !\(000") "000\-0000;1;# creates this display in a field in either a table or a form:

(###) ###-####

In this example, you are restricting the entry to ten digits—no more and no less. The database user does not enter the parentheses, space, or dash, nor does Access store those characters (although you could display them in your table, form, or report if you set the correct format property). Access stores only the ten digits.

In this exercise, you will use the Input Mask wizard to apply a predefined telephone number input mask to a text field, forcing entered numbers into the (XXX) XXX-XXXX format. You will then create a custom mask to force the first letter entered in another text field to be uppercase (a capital letter).

> **USE** the *Accurate* database. This practice file is located in the *Documents\Microsoft Press\ Access2007SBS\Accuracy* folder.
>
> **OPEN** the *Accurate* database. Then display the Field Property Test table in Design view.

1. In the first blank **Field Name** cell, type fPhone, and leave the data type set to *Text*.

2. Click the row selector to select the row, and then drag the selected field up to place it just below the ID field.

3. Save the table design, and with **fPhone** still selected, click **Input Mask** in the **Field Properties** area.

Ellipsis button

4. Click the ellipsis button to the right of the cell to start the **Input Mask** wizard and display the first page of the wizard. (If you are prompted to install this feature, click **Yes**.)

5. With **Phone Number** selected in the **Input Mask** list, click **Next**.

   The second page of the wizard displays the input mask and gives you the opportunity to change the placeholder character that will indicate what to type. The exclamation point causes Access to fill the mask from left to right with whatever is typed. The parentheses and hyphen are characters that Access will insert in the specified places. The nines represent optional digits, and the zeros represent required digits. This allows you to enter a telephone number either with or without an area code.

> **Tip** Because Access fills the mask from left to right, you would have to press the Right Arrow key to move the insertion point past the first three placeholders to enter a telephone number without an area code.

6. Change *999* to *000* to require an area code, and then change the placeholder character to #.

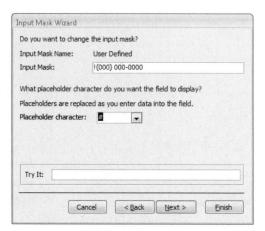

7. Click **Next**.

On the third page of the wizard, you specify whether you want to store the symbols with the data. If you store the symbols, the data will always be displayed in tables, forms, and reports in this format. However, the symbols take up space, meaning that your database will be larger.

8. Accept the default selection—to store data without the symbols—by clicking **Finish**. Access closes the wizard and displays the edited mask as the Input Mask property.

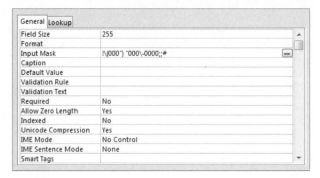

9. Press ⌷Enter⌷ to accept the mask.

   Access changes the format of the mask to *!\(000") "000\-0000;;#*. Notice the two semicolons that separate the mask into its three sections. Because you told Access to store data without the symbols, nothing is displayed in the second section of the mask. Notice also that Access added double quotation marks to ensure that the closing parenthesis and following space are treated as literals.

   > **Tip** When you press Enter, a button appears in front of the Input Mask. This is the Property Update Options button, and if you click it, a list of options is displayed. In this case, the only options are to apply the input mask everywhere fPhone is used, and to provide help. This button disappears when you edit any other property or change to a different field.

10. Save your changes, and then switch to Datasheet view.

11. Press the ⌷↓⌷ key to move to the new record, then press the ⌷Tab⌷ key to move to the **fPhone** field. Type a series of numbers and letters to see how the mask works.

    Access formats the first ten numbers you enter as a telephone number, ignoring any letters or additional digits you type. If you type fewer than ten digits and then press Tab or Enter, Access warns that your entry doesn't match the input mask.

    > **Tip** An input mask can contain more than only placeholders for the data to be entered. If, for example, you type "The number is" in front of the telephone number in the Input Mask property, the default entry for the field is *The number is (###) ###-####*. Then if you place the insertion point at the beginning of the field, the numbers you type replace the # placeholders, not the text. The Field Size setting is not applied to the characters in the mask, so if this setting is *15*, the entry is not truncated even though the number of displayed characters (including spaces) is 28.

12. Switch to Design view, and add a new field below **fBoolean**. Name it LastName. Leave the **Data Type** setting as the default, **Text**.

13. Select the new field, click **Input Mask**, type >L<?????????????????? (18 question marks), and press Enter .

The greater than symbol (>) forces all following text to be uppercase. The *L* requires a letter. The less than symbol ()< forces all following text to be lower-case. Each question mark allows any letter or no letter, and there is one fewer question mark than the maximum number of letters you want to allow in the field (19, including the leading capital letter). The Field Size setting must be greater than this maximum.

14. Save your changes, return to Datasheet view, type smith in the **LastName** field of one of the records, and press Tab . Try entering SMITH, and then McDonald.

Regardless of how you type the name, only its the first letter appears in the record capitalized, This type of mask has its limitations, but it can be useful in many situations.

CLOSE the Field Property Test table and the *Accurate* database.

> **Tip** You can create an input mask manually for text, number, date, or currency fields, or you can apply one of several standard masks for text and date fields by using the Input Mask wizard.

Restricting Data by Using Validation Rules

A *validation rule* is an expression that can precisely define the information that will be accepted in one or several fields in a record. You might use a validation rule in a field containing the date an employee was hired to prevent a date in the future from being entered. Or if you make deliveries to only certain local areas, you could use a validation rule on the phone field or ZIP code field to refuse entries from other areas.

You can type validation rules in by hand, or you can use the *Expression Builder* to create them. At the field level, Access uses the rule to test an entry when you attempt to leave the field. At the table level, Access uses the rule to test the content of several fields when you attempt to leave the record. If an entry doesn't satisfy the rule, Access rejects the entry and displays a message explaining why.

In this exercise, you will create and test several field validation rules and one table validation rule.

> **USE** the *Validate* database. This practice file is located in the *Documents\Microsoft Press\ Access2007SBS\Accuracy* folder.
>
> **OPEN** the *Validate* database. Then display the Field Property Test table in Design view.

1. Select **fPhone**, and then click in the **Validation Rule** box.

    An ellipsis button appears at the end of the Validation Rule box. You can click this button to use the Expression Builder to create an expression, or you can type an expression in the box.

2. Type Like "206*" Or Like "425*" in the **Validation Rule** box, and press Enter.

    > **Troubleshooting** Be sure to include the asterisk after the 206 and 425.

3. In the **Validation Text** box, type Area code must be 206 or 425.

    A rule is set for the first three digits typed in the fPhone field including the text that Access should display if someone attempts to enter an invalid phone number.

4. In the **Caption** box, type Phone Number.

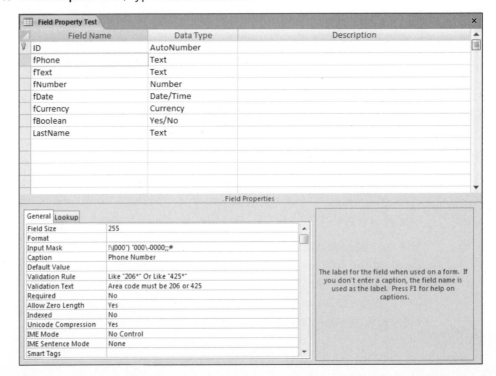

5. Save the table.

Access warns that data integrity rules have changed. The table violates the new rule because it contains blank phone number fields.

6. Click **No** to close the message box without testing the data.

> **Tip** When displaying tables as overlapping windows (rather than tabbed documents), you can test the validation rules in a table at any time by right-clicking the title bar of the table in Design view and then clicking Test Validation Rules. For more information about display options, see "Working in Access 2007" in Chapter 1, "Exploring Access 2007."

7. Return to Datasheet view, where the caption for the first field is now *Phone Number*.

8. Place the insertion point to the left of the first # of any **Phone Number** field, type 3605550109, and then press [Enter].

> **Tip** To select the entire field, move the pointer to the left end of the Phone Number field, and when the pointer changes to a thick cross, click the field. The insertion point is then at the start of the area code when you begin typing.

The Validation Rule setting causes Access to display an alert box, warning you that the area code must be either 206 or 425.

9. Click **OK** to close the alert box, type a new phone number with one of the allowed area codes, and press [Enter].

10. Return to Design view, and add another date field. Type Date2 as the field name, set the data type to **Date/Time**, and drag the new field to just below **fDate**.

11. Right-click in the table window, and then click **Properties**.

Property Sheet		✕
Selection type: Table Properties		
General		
Display Views on SharePoint	Follow Database ⧉▾	
Subdatasheet Expanded	No	
Subdatasheet Height	0"	
Orientation	Left-to-Right	
Description		
Default View	Datasheet	
Validation Rule		
Validation Text		
Filter		
Order By		
Subdatasheet Name	[Auto]	
Link Child Fields		
Link Master Fields		
Filter On Load	No	
Order By On Load	Yes	

> **Tip** The purpose of this Property Sheet is to set properties that apply to more than one field in the table, as opposed to setting properties for a single field in the Field Properties area.

12. Click in the **Validation Rule** box, type [Date2]>[fDate], and press [Enter].

13. In the **Validation Text** box, type Date2 must be later than fDate, and then close the sheet.

A table validation rule is added that ensures that the second date is always later than the first one.

14. Save the table (click **No** to close the data-integrity alert box), and return to Datasheet view.

15. In any record, type 6/1/07 in **fDate** and 5/1/07 in **Date2**, and then click in another record.

Access displays the Validation Text setting from the Table Properties dialog box, reminding you that Date2 must be later than fDate.

16. Click **OK**, change **Date2** to 6/2/2007, and then click in another record.

CLOSE the Field Property Test table and the *Validate* database.

Creating a Simple Lookup List

It is interesting how many different ways people can come up with to enter the same items of information in a database. Asked to enter the name of their home state, for example, residents of the state of Washington will type *Washington*, *Wash*, or *WA*, plus various typographical errors and misspellings. If you ask a dozen sales clerks to enter the name of a specific product, customer, and shipper in an invoice, it is unlikely that all of them will type the same thing. In cases like this, in which the number of correct choices is limited (to actual product name, actual customer, and actual shipper), providing the option to choose the correct answer from a list will improve your database's consistency.

Minor inconsistencies in the way data is entered might not be really important to some-one who later reads the information and makes decisions. For example, *Arizona* and *AZ* refer to the same state. But a computer is very literal, and if you tell it to create a list so that you can send catalogs to everyone living in *AZ*, the computer won't include anyone whose state is listed in the database as *Arizona*.

You can limit the options for entering information in a database in several ways:

- For only two options, you can use a Boolean field represented by a check box. A check in the box indicates one choice, and no check indicates the other choice.

- For several mutually exclusive options on a form, you can use option buttons to gather the required information.

- For more than a few options, a *combo box* is a good way to go. When you click the arrow at the right end of a combo box, a list of choices is displayed. Depending on the properties associated with the combo box, if you don't see the option you want, you might be able to type something else, adding your entry to the list of possible options displayed in the future.

- For a short list of choices that won't change often, you can have the combo box look up the options in a list that you provide. Although you can create a lookup list by hand, it is a lot easier to use the *Lookup wizard*.

In this exercise, you will use the Lookup wizard to create a list of months from which the user can choose.

USE the *SimpleLookup* database. This practice file is located in the *Documents\Microsoft Press\Access2007SBS\Accuracy* folder.

OPEN the *SimpleLookup* database. Then display the Field Property Test table in Design view.

1. Add a new field below **LastName**. Name it **Month1**, and set the data type to **Lookup Wizard**.

   The Lookup wizard starts.

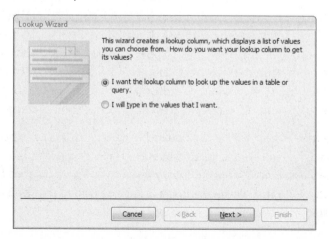

You can use the Lookup wizard to create a combo box that provides the entry for a text field. The combo box list can come from a table or query, or you can type the list in the wizard.

> **Tip** If a field has a lot of potential entries, or if they will change often, you can link them to a table. (You might have to create a table expressly for this purpose.) If a field has only a few possible entries that won't change, typing the list in the wizard is easier.

2. Click **I will type in the values that I want**, and then click **Next**.

3. Leave the number of columns set to *1*, and click in the **Col1** box.

4. Enter the 12 months of the year (January, February, and so on), pressing Tab after each one to move to a new row.

5. Click **Next**, and then click **Finish**.

6. In the **Field Properties** area, click the **Lookup** tab to view the Lookup information for the Month1 field.

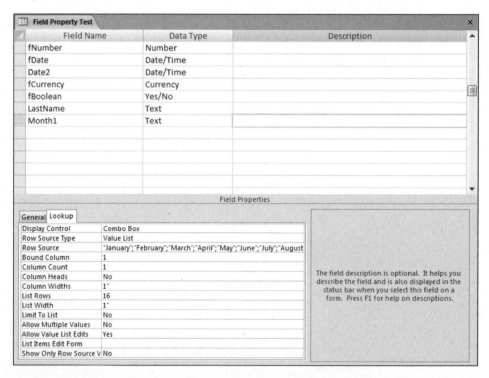

The wizard entered this information, but you can easily figure out what you would have to enter to create a lookup list by hand.

7. Switch to Datasheet view, clicking **Yes** to save your changes.

8. Double-click the vertical bars between the column headers to adjust the column widths so that you can see all the fields.

> **Tip** You can manually resize columns by dragging the vertical bars between the column headers.

9. Click in the **Month1** field of a record, and then click the arrow that appears to display the list of options.

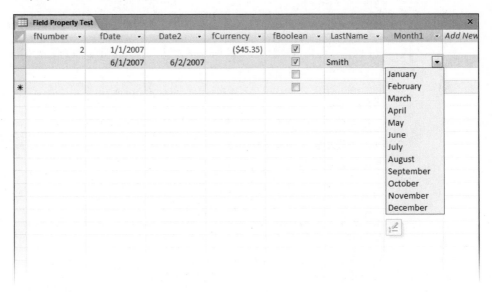

Notice the button below the Month1 options list. Clicking this button opens the Edit List Items dialog box. This feature is new with Access 2007. The database user can open the editor by clicking the button, or by entering text that is not in the list and answering Yes when asked whether she or he wants to edit the list. If you don't want users to be able to edit the list, you can disable this property, as we do later in this exercise.

10. If you opened it, close the **Edit List Items** dialog box and then click **February** to enter it in the field.

11. Click in the next **Month1** field, type Jan, and press [Enter].

As soon as you type the *J*, the combo box displays *January*. If you had typed *Ju*, the combo box would have displayed *June*.

12. In the next **Month1** field, type jly, and press Enter.

    Even though the entry isn't in the list, it is accepted just as you typed it. Although there might be times when you want to allow the entry of information other than the items in the list, this isn't one of those times, so you need to change the field properties to limit what can be entered.

13. Return to Design view.

    The Limit To List property on the Lookup tab for Month1 is currently set to *No*, which allows people to enter information that isn't in the list.

14. Change **Limit To List** to **Yes**.

15. Change **Allow Value List Edits** to **No**.

16. Save the table, return to Datasheet view, type jly in a new **Month1** field, and then press Enter.

    Access informs you that the text you entered is not in the list, and refuses the entry.

17. In the **Microsoft Office Access** message box, click **OK**.

18. In the **Month1** list, click **July**.

    The month of July is displayed in the field.

 CLOSE the *SimpleLookup* database, saving your changes.

Creating a Multi-Column Lookup List

Selecting a month from a list of names is convenient for people, but if your computer has to deal with this information in some mathematical way, a list of the numbers associated with each month is easier for it to use.

In this exercise, you will use the Lookup wizard to create a two-column list of months from which the user can choose.

 USE the *MulticolumnLookup* database. This practice file is located in the *Documents\ Microsoft Press\Access2007SBS\Accuracy* folder.

OPEN the *MulticolumnLookup* database. Then display the Field Property Test table in Design view.

1. Add a new field below **Month1**. Name it Month2, and set the data type to **Lookup Wizard**.

2. Click **I will type in the values that I want**, and then click **Next**.

3. Type 2 to add a second column, and then click in the **Col1** cell.

Access adds a second column, labeled *Col2*.

4. Enter the following numbers and months in the two columns:

Number	Month
1	January
2	February
3	March
4	April
5	May
6	June
7	July
8	August
9	September
10	October
11	November
12	December

It is not necessary to adjust the width of the columns in the Lookup wizard other than to make them visible within the wizard itself.

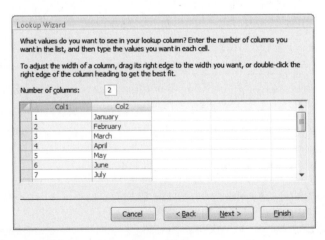

5. Click **Next**, and then click **Finish**.

6. In the **Field Properties** area, click the **Lookup** tab to view the Lookup information for the Month2 field.

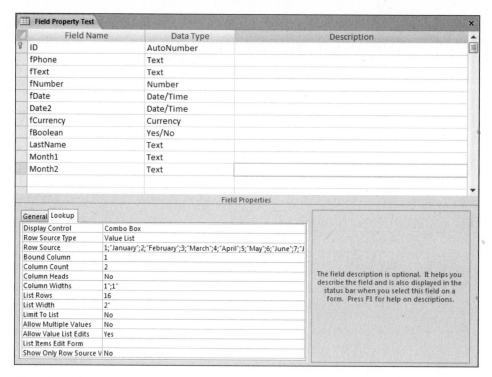

The wizard has inserted your column information into the Row Source box and set the other properties according to your specifications.

7. Change **Limit To List** to **Yes** and **Allow Value List Edits** to **No**.

> **Tip** When a property has two or more possible values, you can quickly cycle through them by double-clicking the value, rather than clicking the arrow to open the list.

8. Save your changes, switch to Datasheet view, and then click the arrow in a **Month2** field to display the list of options.

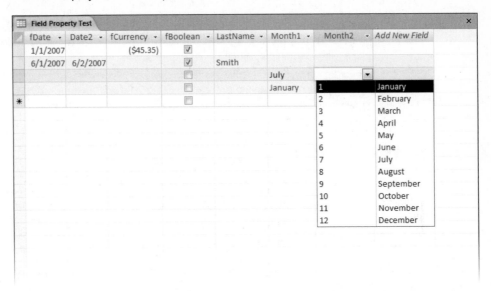

9. In the **Month2** list, click **January**.

Access displays the number *1* in the field, which is useful for the computer. However, people might be confused by the two columns and by seeing something other than what they clicked or typed.

10. Switch back to Design view, and in the **Column Widths** box—which appears as *1";1"*—change the width for the first column to *0* (you don't have to type the symbol for inches) to prevent it from being displayed.

11. Save your changes, return to Datasheet view, and as a test, in the remaining records set **Month2** to **February** in two records and to **March** in one record.

Only the name of the month is now displayed in the list, and when you click a month, that name is displayed in the field. However, Access actually stores the associated number from the list's first column.

12. Right-click any cell in the **Month2** column, point to **Text Filters**, and then click **Equals**.

13. In the **Custom Filter** box, type 2, and then press Enter .

Access now displays only the two records with February in the Month2 field.

14. Click the **Toggle Filter** button, and then repeat Steps 12 and 13, this time typing 3

in the box to display the one record with March in the **Month2** field.

CLOSE the *MulticolumnLookup* database, saving your changes.

Updating Information in a Table

As you use a database and as it grows, you might discover that errors creep in or that some information becomes out of date. You can tediously scroll through the records looking for those that need to be changed, but it is more efficient to use a few of the tools and techniques provided by Access for that purpose.

If you want to find or replace multiple instances of the same word or phrase, you can use the Find and Replace commands on the Edit menu. This command works much like the same commands in Microsoft Office Word or Microsoft Office Excel.

If you want to change information stored in the database only under certain circumstances, you need the power of an *update query*, which is a select query that performs an action on the query's results.

> **Tip** Running an update query makes irreversible changes to the table; therefore, you should always create a backup copy of the table before running a query.
>
> You can quickly create a copy of a table by displaying the Tables list in the Navigation Pane, clicking the table you want to copy pressing Ctrl+C, and then pressing Ctrl+V to paste a copy. In the Paste Table As dialog box, type a name for the new table, and then click OK.

In this exercise, you will create an update query to increase the price of selected items by 10 percent.

> **USE** the *Update* database. This practice file is located in the *Documents\Microsoft Press\ Access2007SBS\Accuracy* folder.
>
> **OPEN** the *Update* database.

Query Wizard

1. On the **Create** tab, in the **Other** group, click the **Query Wizard** button.

2. In the **New Query** dialog box, with **Simple Query Wizard** selected, click **OK**.

3. In the **Tables/Queries** list, click **Table: Categories**.

4. In the **Available Fields** list, double-click **CategoryName** to move it to the **Selected Fields** list.

5. In the **Tables/Queries** list, click **Table: Products**.

6. In the **Available Fields** list, double-click **ProductName** and **UnitPrice** to move them to the **Selected Fields** list.

7. In the **Simple Query Wizard** dialog box, click **Finish** to create the query using the default detail setting and title.

   Access displays the query results in a datasheet. Only the Category Name, Product Name, and Unit Price fields are displayed.

Category Nam ▾	Product Name ▾	Unit Price ▾
Bulbs	Magic Lily	$40.00
Bulbs	Autumn crocus	$18.75
Bulbs	Anemone	$28.00
Bulbs	Lily-of-the-Field	$38.00
Bulbs	Siberian Iris	$12.95
Bulbs	Daffodil	$12.95
Bulbs	Peony	$19.95
Bulbs	Lilies	$10.50
Bulbs	Begonias	$18.95
Bulbs	Bulb planter	$6.95
Cacti	Prickly Pear	$3.00
Ground covers	Crown Vetch	$12.95
Ground covers	English Ivy	$5.95
Ground covers	European Ginger	$6.25
Ground covers	St. John's Wort	$9.75
Ground covers	Fairies Fern	$9.95
Grasses	The Best Bluegrass	$17.95
Grasses	Decorator moss	$15.45
Grasses	Colonial Bentgrass	$15.50
Grasses	Creeping Bentgrass	$12.05
Grasses	Red Fescue	$20.00
Grasses	Perennial Ryegrass	$19.95
Grasses	Redtop	$21.50
Flowers	Lily-of-the-Valley	$33.00

Categories Query1

Record: I◄ ◄ 1 of 189 ► ►I ►⃰ ⫧ No Filter   Search

8. Display the query in Design view.

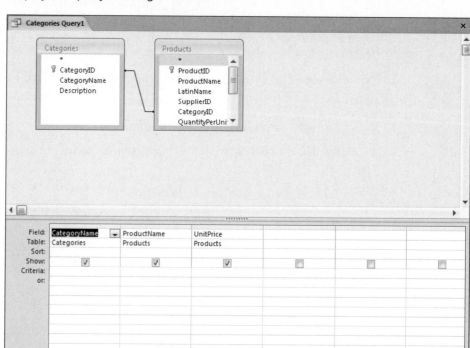

The current query results include the products in all categories. You want to raise the prices of only the products in the *bulbs* and *cacti* categories, so your next task is to change the query to select only those categories.

9. In the **Criteria** row, under **CategoryName**, type bulbs. Then in the **or** row, type cacti.

Run

10. Click the **Run** button to run the query to confirm that only bulbs and cacti are listed, and then return to Design view.

The query now selects only the records you want to change. But to actually make a change to the records, you have to use an update query.

> **Tip** You can't create an action query directly; you must first create a select query and then change the query to one of the action types. With an existing select query open in Design view, you can find the command to convert it to an action query in the Query Type group and on the shortcut menu that appears when you right-click the query window and then point to Query Type.

Update

11. Display the query in Design view. On the **Design** contextual tab, in the **Query Type** group, click the **Update** button.

Access converts the select query to an update query. In the design grid, the Sort and Show rows disappear and an Update To row appears.

12. In the **Update To** row, under **UnitPrice**, type [UnitPrice]*1.1.

> **Tip** Enclosing UnitPrice in brackets indicates that it is an Access object. If you use the Expression Builder to insert this expression, it looks like this: *[Products]![UnitPrice]*1.1*. Because this description of the field includes the table in which it is found, you can also insert this expression in other tables.

13. Display the query in Datasheet view.

In a select query, clicking the View button is the same as clicking the Run button. But in an update query, clicking the View button simply displays a list of the fields that will be updated. In this case, you see a list of unit prices that matches the ones shown earlier in the select query.

14. Switch to Design view. Then on the Query Tools **Design** contextual tab, in the **Results** group, click the **Run** button.

Access displays a warning that you can't undo the changes you are about to make, and asks you to confirm that you want to update the records.

View

15. In the **Microsoft Office Access** message box, click **Yes**. Then click the **View** Datasheet button to display the **UnitPrice** field, where all the prices have been increased by 10 percent.

16. Save and close the query.

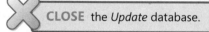
CLOSE the *Update* database.

Deleting Information from a Table

Over time, some of the information stored in a database might become obsolete. The Products table in our sample database, for example, lists all the products the company currently offers for sale or has sold in the past. You can indicate that a product is no longer available for sale by placing a check mark in the Discontinued field. Discontinued products aren't displayed in the catalog or offered for sale, but they are kept in the database for a while in case it becomes practical to sell them again. A similar situation could exist with customers who haven't placed an order in a long time or who have asked to be removed from a mailing list but might still place orders.

To maintain an efficient database, it is a good idea to clean house and discard outdated records from time to time. You could scroll through the tables and delete records manually, but if all the records you want to delete match some pattern, you can use a delete query to quickly get rid of all of them.

> **Important** Keep in mind several things when deleting records from a database. First, you can't recover deleted records. Second, the effects of a delete query can be more far-reaching than you intend. If the table from which you are deleting records is linked to another table, and the Cascade Delete Related Records option for that relationship is selected, records in the second table will also be deleted. Sometimes this is what you want, but sometimes it isn't. For example, you probably don't want to delete records of previous sales at the same time you delete discontinued products.
>
> To safeguard against these problems, it is a good idea to back up your database before deleting the records, or to create a new table (perhaps named *Deleted<file name>*), and then move the records you want to delete to the new table, where you can review them before deleting them permanently.

In this exercise, you will create a delete query to remove all discontinued products from a database table.

USE the *Delete* database. This practice file is located in the *Documents\Microsoft Press\ Access2007SBS\Accuracy* folder.
OPEN the *Delete* database.

Query
Design

1. On the **Create** tab, in the **Other** group, click the **Query Design** button.

   Access opens a new query object and the Show Table dialog box.

2. In the **Show Table** dialog box, double-click **Products** to add that table to the query window list area, and then click **Close**.

3. In the **Products** field list, double-click the asterisk to copy all the fields in the table to the query.

*Products.** appears in the Field row of the first column of the design grid, and *Products* appears in the Table row.

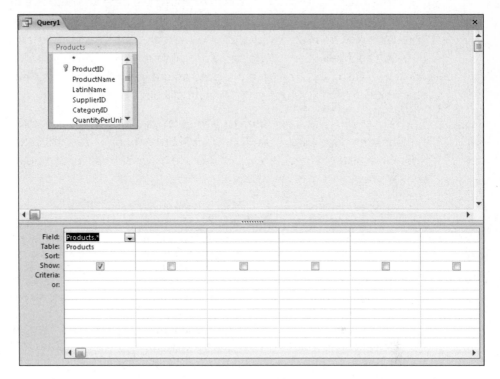

> **Important** Double-clicking the asterisk in the field list is a quick way to move all the fields in a table to the query, without having each field appear in its own column. However, selecting multiple fields in this way prevents you from setting Sort, Show, and Criteria values for individual fields. To set these values, you have to add the specific fields to the design grid, thereby adding them twice. To avoid displaying the fields twice, clear the check mark in the Show row of the duplicate individual fields.

4. In the **Products** field list, double-click **Discontinued** to copy it to the next available column in the design grid.

Delete

5. In the **Query Type** group, click the **Delete** button to convert this select query to a delete query.

A Delete row appears in the design grid, and the Sort and Show rows disappear.

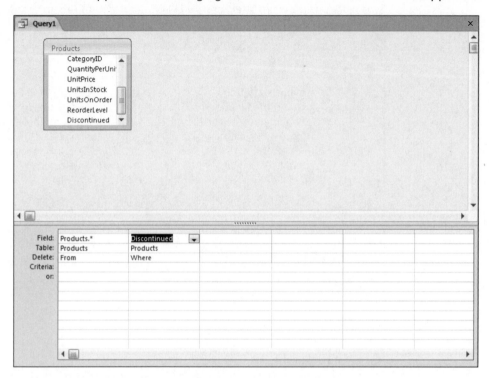

In the first column, which contains the reference to all fields in the Products table, the Delete row contains the word *From*, indicating that this is the table from which records will be deleted. When you add individual fields to the remaining columns, as you did with the Discontinued field, the Delete row displays *Where*, indicating that this field can include deletion criteria.

6. In the **Criteria** row, under **Discontinued**, type **Yes**.

The Discontinued field is set to the Boolean data type, which is represented in the datasheet as a check box that is selected to indicate Yes and cleared to indicate No. To locate all discontinued products, you need to identify records with the Discontinued field set to Yes.

7. To check the accuracy of the query, switch to Database view.

Testing the query results in a list of 18 discontinued products that would be deleted if you ran the query. Scroll to the right to verify that all records display a check mark in the Products.Discontinued field.

Run

8. Switch to Design view. Then on the **Design** contextual tab, in the **Results** group, click the **Run** button to run the delete query.

Access displays a warning to remind you of the permanence of this action.

> **Tip** Before actually deleting records, you might want to display the Relationships window by clicking the Relationships button in the Show/Hide Group on the Database Tools tab. If the table you are deleting data from has a relationship with any table containing information that shouldn't be deleted, right-click the relationship line, click Edit Relationship, and make sure that the Enforce Referential Integrity check box is selected and the Cascade Delete Related Records check box is *not* selected.

9. In the **Microsoft Office Access** message box, click **Yes** to delete the records.

10. Switch to Datasheet view and verify that all the records were deleted.

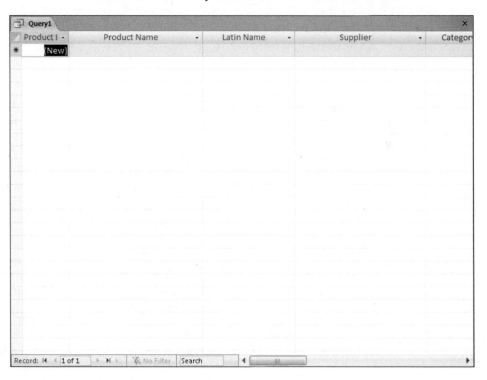

11. If you think you might run the same delete query in the future, save and name the query.

> **Tip** If you are concerned that someone might accidentally run a delete query and destroy records you weren't ready to destroy, change the query back to a select query before saving it. You can then open the select query in Design view and change it to a delete query the next time you want to run it.

 CLOSE the query and the *Delete* database.

Preventing Database Problems

In the day-to-day use of an Access database—adding and deleting records, modifying forms and reports, and so on—various problems can develop. This is especially true if the database is stored on a network share, rather than on a local drive, and is accessed by multiple users. Access monitors the condition of database files as you open and work with them. If a problem develops, Access attempts to fix it. If Access can't fix the problem, it usually provides additional information that might help you to find a solution. But Access doesn't always spot problems before they affect the database; if this happens, you might notice that the database performance seems to slow down or become erratic. Even if no actual errors occur, normal database use causes the internal structure of a database to become fragmented, resulting in a bloated file and inefficient use of disk space.

You don't have to wait for Access to spot a problem. There are various things you can do to help keep your database healthy and running smoothly. Your first line of defense against damage or corruption in any kind of file is the maintenance of backups. Database files rapidly become too large to conveniently back up onto a floppy disk, but you have many other options: you can copy the file to another computer on the network or to removable media such as a USB flash drive, send it as an e-mail attachment to another location, create a tape backup, or burn a CD-ROM.

> **Tip** To back up a database in Access 2007, click the Microsoft Office Button, point to Manage, and then click Back Up Database.

You can use the following Access utilities to keep your database running smoothly:

- **Compact and Repair Database.** This utility first optimizes performance by re-arranging how the file is stored on your hard disk, and then attempts to repair corruption in tables, forms, reports, and modules.

- **Performance Analyzer.** This utility analyzes the objects in your database and offers three types of feedback: ideas, suggestions, and recommendations. You can instruct Access to optimize the file by following through on any of the suggestions or recommendations.

- **Database Documenter.** This tool produces a detailed report containing enough information to rebuild the database structure if that were ever necessary.

- **Analyze Table.** This wizard tests database tables for compliance with standard database design principles, suggests solutions to problems, and implements those solutions at your request.

- **Microsoft Office Diagnostics.** This command attempts to diagnose and repair problems with your Microsoft Office programs.

> **Important** Take care when running the Microsoft Office Diagnostics utility, because it might change files and registry settings that affect all Office programs.

In this exercise, you will back up a database and then run the Compact And Repair Database, Performance Analyzer, and Database Documenter utilities.

USE the *Prevent* database. This practice file is located in the *Documents\Microsoft Press\ Access2007SBS\Accuracy* folder.

OPEN the *Prevent* database. Do not display any of the database tables.

1. Click the **Microsoft Office Button**, point to **Manage**, and then click **Back Up Database**.

2. In the **Save As** dialog box, navigate to the *Documents\Microsoft Press\ Access2007SBS\Accuracy* folder, and then click **Save**.

> **Tip** When you back up a database, Access appends the current date to the database file name in the following format: Prevent_*2007-04-22.accdb*. You can change the file name to suit your needs.

Access creates a compacted copy of the database in the specified folder.

3. Click the **Microsoft Office Button**, point to **Manage**, and then click **Database Properties**.

The Database Properties dialog box opens, displaying information about your database on five tabs.

> **Tip** For more information about setting and changing database properties from the Properties dialog box, click the Help button in the upper-right corner of the dialog box.

4. On the **General** tab, note the size of the database. Then click **OK** to close the dialog box.

5. Click the **Microsoft Office Button**, point to **Manage**, and then click **Compact and Repair Database**. Acknowledge the safety warning if prompted to do so.

The utility takes only a few seconds to run, and you will see no difference in the appearance of the database.

> **Troubleshooting** If you don't have enough space on your hard disk to store a temporary copy of the database, you don't have appropriate permissions, or another user also has the database open, the Compact And Repair Database function will not run.

6. Repeat Steps 3 and 4 to display the database size, and compare it to the original database size.

You can expect a 10 to 25 percent reduction in the size of the database if you have been using it for a while.

> **Tip** It is a good idea to compact and repair a database often. You can have Access do this automatically each time the database is closed. To do so, click the Microsoft Office Button, click the Access Options button, and then on the Current Database page, select the Compact On Close check box, and click OK.

7. On the **Database Tools** tab, in the **Analyze** group, click the **Analyze Performance** button.

The Performance Analyzer dialog box opens.

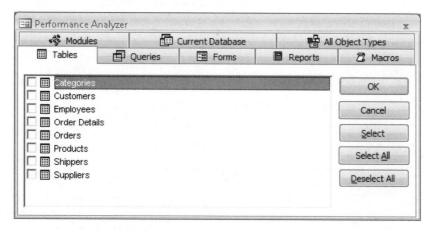

This dialog box contains a tab for each type of object the utility can analyze, and a tab displaying all the existing database objects.

8. On the **All Object Types** tab, click **Select All**, and then click **OK** to start the analyzer.

When it finishes, the Performance Analyzer displays its results. (The results you see might be different from those shown here.)

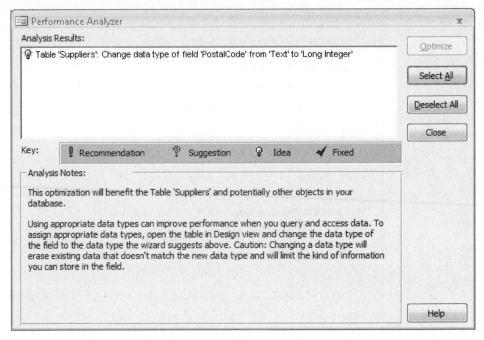

The icons in the left column of the Analysis Results list indicate the category of each entry: *Recommendation*, *Suggestion*, and *Idea*. (After you perform any of the optimizations, *Fixed* entries will also appear in the list.) Clicking an entry displays information about it in the Analysis Notes section.

9. Scroll through the list, clicking each entry in turn, and read all the analysis notes.

   Most of the suggestions are valid, though some, such as the one to change the data type of the PostalCode field to Long Integer, are not appropriate for this database.

10. Close the **Performance Analyzer** dialog box.

11. On the **Database Tools** tab, in the **Analyze** group, click the **Database Documenter** button.

   The Documenter dialog box opens. This dialog box is identical to the Performance Analyzer database. It contains a tab for each type of object the utility can document, and a tab displaying all the existing database objects.

12. On the **Tables** tab, click the **Options** button.

The Print Table Definition dialog box opens.

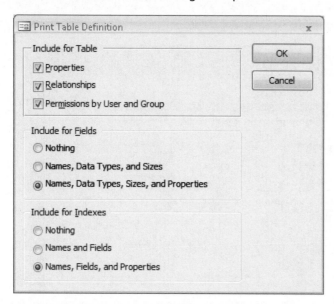

The dialog box offers print options associated with the objects on the selected dialog box tab. The options differ for each tab, but all are similar to these, in that you can use them to specify the documentation to include for each type of object.

13. In the **Print Table Definition** dialog box, click **Cancel**.

14. On the **All Object Types** tab, click **Select All**, and then click **OK** to start the documentation process.

> **Tip** You can't save the report generated by the Documenter utility, but you can export it as a Word RTF file, Access database, text file, XML file, or HTML document. To do so, right-click the report, point to Export, and then click the format you want.

When the process finishes, Access displays a report in Print Preview. This report can run to hundreds of pages, so you probably don't want to print it. However, it is a good idea to create and save a report such as this for your own databases, in case you ever need to reconstruct them.

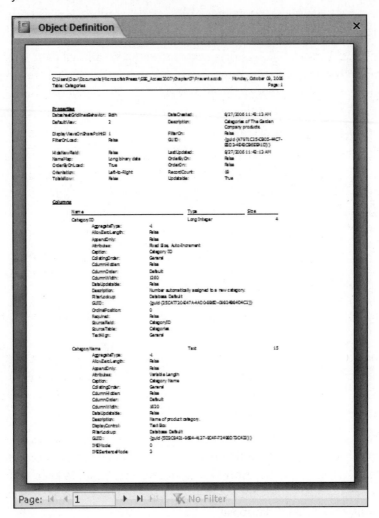

 CLOSE the Object Definition report and the *Prevent* database. If you are not continuing directly on to the next chapter, exit Access.

Key Points

- You can set properties that restrict the type and amount of data that can be entered into an Access database.

- You can replace specific words or phrases by using the Replace command, or quickly enact conditional changes by running an action query.

- The Data Type setting restricts entries to a specific type of data: text, numbers, dates, and so on. The Field Size property for the Text, Number, and AutoNumber data types restricts the number of characters allowed in a text field or the number of digits allowed in a number or AutoNumber field. The Input Mask property controls the format in which data can be entered.

- You can use a validation rule to precisely define the information that will be accepted in one or several fields in a record. At the field level, Access tests each entry against the rule when you attempt to leave a field. At the table level, Access tests the content of several fields against the rule when you attempt to leave a record. In both cases, Access rejects any entry that doesn't comply with the rule.

- For fields with a fixed set of possible entries, you can use a lookup field to ensure that users enter the right information. This helps prevent inconsistencies, thus making it easier to sort and search your data.

- You can use an update query to quickly perform an action, such as replacing the contents of a field, based on the results of a query.

- You can use a delete query to quickly delete records that meet specific criteria. You should always back up your database before running a delete query, and you must exercise caution when deleting records in this way. The effects of a delete query can be far-reaching, and you can't recover deleted records.

- There are several utilities that you can use to keep your database running smoothly—Compact And Repair Database, Performance Analyzer, Database Documenter, and Microsoft Office Diagnostics. You can keep your application healthy by taking advantage of these utilities before Access indicates there is a problem with your database.

Chapter at a Glance

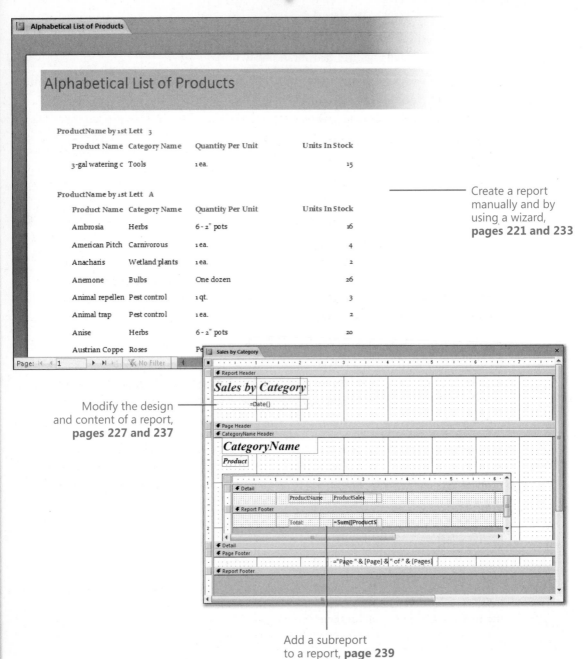

Create a report manually and by using a wizard, **pages 221 and 233**

Modify the design and content of a report, **pages 227 and 237**

Add a subreport to a report, **page 239**

8 Working with Reports

In this chapter, you will learn to:

✔ Create a report manually and by using a wizard.

✔ Modify the design and content of a report.

✔ Add a subreport to a report.

✔ Preview and print a report.

Reports generally represent summaries of larger bodies of information. For example, your database might hold detailed information about thousands of orders. If you want to edit those orders or enter new ones, you can do so directly in the table or through a form. If you want to summarize those orders to illustrate the rate of growth of the company's sales, you generate a report.

Like a book report or an annual report of a company's activities, a report created in Microsoft Office Access 2007 is typically used to summarize and organize information to express a particular point of view to a specific audience. When designing a report, it is important to consider the point you are trying to make, the intended audience, and the level of information they will need.

In this chapter, you will create a report by using a wizard and another by building your own manually. You will learn how to modify the layout and content of a report, and how to embed reports within each other. Finally, you will preview a report as it will appear when printed.

See Also Do you need only a quick refresher on the topics in this chapter? See the Quick Reference section at the beginning of this book.

> **Important** Before you can use the practice files in this chapter, you need to install them from the book's companion CD to their default location. See "Using the Companion CD" at the beginning of this book for more information.

> **Troubleshooting** Graphics and operating system–related instructions in this book reflect the Windows Vista user interface. If your computer is running Windows XP and you experience trouble following the instructions as written, please refer to the "Information for Readers Running Windows XP" section at the beginning of this book.

Forms vs. Reports

In many ways, reports are like forms; for example:

- You can create them by using wizards and modify them in a design environment.
- You can add labels, text boxes, images, and other controls, and set their properties.
- You can display information from one or more records, or from one or more tables or queries.
- You can have multiple sets of headers and footers.

Forms and reports have one purpose in common: to give people easy access to the information stored in a database. The main differences between forms and reports are:

- Forms are used to enter, view, and edit information. Reports are used only to view information.
- Forms are usually displayed on-screen. Reports can be previewed on the screen, but they are usually printed.
- Forms generally provide a detailed look at records and are usually for the people who actually work with the database. Reports are often used to group and summarize data, and are often for people who don't work with the database but who use the information stored in the database for other business tasks.

Forms and reports are sufficiently alike that you can save a form as a report when you want to take advantage of additional report refinement and printing capabilities.

Creating a Report by Using a Wizard

You can divide the content of an Access report into two general categories: information derived from records in one or more tables, and everything else. The *everything else* category includes the title, page headers and footers, introductory and explanatory text, logo, background and graphics, and calculations based on the database content.

See Also For information about performing calculations in reports, see the Access Help system topic "Summing in reports."

You can create a basic report by using the Report wizard, which provides a simple layout, attaches styles, and adds a text box control and its associated label for each field you specify. If the basic report doesn't fit your needs, you can refine it in Design view.

When you include more than one table in a report, the wizard evaluates the relationships between the tables, and offers to group the records in any logical manner available.

> **Important** If relationships between tables aren't already established in the Relationships window, you have to cancel the wizard and establish them before continuing. The necessary relationships have already been defined in the practice files.

See Also For information about creating relationships between tables, see the sidebar "Relationships" in Chapter 5, "Simplifying Data Entry by Using Forms."

You can group the information in a report based on the data in one or more fields. You can, for example, group products by category. When you do this the wizard first sorts the table based on the category, then sorts the products in each category. It then creates a group header each time the category changes. It can also add a footer to each group, in which it summarizes the information in the group.

In this exercise, you will create a simple report that displays an alphabetical list of products.

> **Tip** The Report wizard leads you through a series of questions and then creates a report based on your answers. This exercise guides you through the process of creating a standard report without justifying the data selected, but when you get around to creating your own reports you should first consider the end result you want, and what information you need to include in the report to achieve that result.

USE the *Wizard* database. This practice file is located in the *Documents\Microsoft Press\Access2007SBS\Reports* folder.

BE SURE TO start Access before beginning this exercise.

OPEN the *Wizard* database, and acknowledge the safety warning if prompted to do so.

1. On the **Create** tab, in the **Reports** group, click the **Report Wizard** button.

   The Report wizard starts.

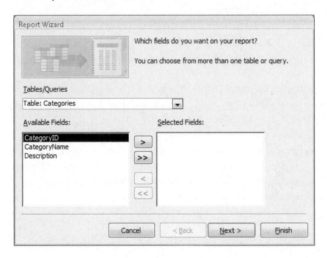

2. On the field selection page, click the **Tables/Queries** arrow, and then in the list, click **Table: Products**.

   Access displays the fields from the Products table.

3. In the **Available Fields** list, double-click **ProductName**, **QuantityPerUnit**, and **UnitsInStock** to move them to the **Selected Fields** list.

   > **Tip** Fields appear in a report in the same order that they appear in the Selected Fields list. You can save yourself the effort of rearranging the fields in the report by entering them in the desired order in the wizard.

4. In the **Tables/Queries** list, click **Table: Categories** to display the fields from the Categories table.

5. In the **Selected Fields** list, click **ProductName**.

   The next field you add will be inserted following the selected field.

6. In the **Available Fields** list, double-click **CategoryName**.

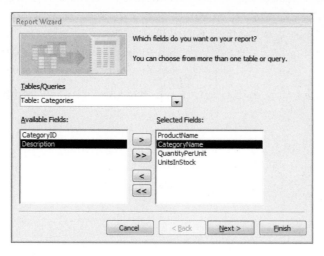

> **Tip** If you are using more than two tables in a form or report, or if you will be using the same combination of tables in several places, you can save time by creating a query based on those tables, and by using the results of that query as the basis for the form or report.

7. On the field selection page, click **Next**.

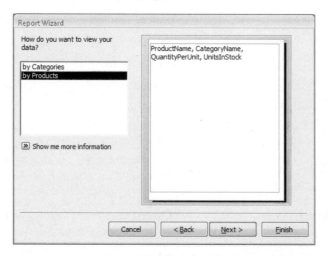

You can view the records in this example by category or by product; clicking either option depicts the arrangement in the right pane.

8. On the grouping page, with **by Products** selected, click **Next**.

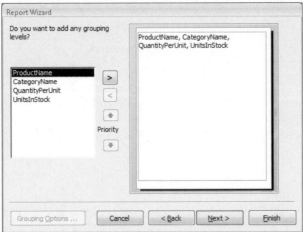

You can specify the fields used to establish *grouping levels*. When you group by a field, the report includes a group header and footer around each group of records that have the same value in that field.

9. On the grouping levels page, double-click **ProductName** to move it to the top of the preview pane. Then click the **Grouping Options** button.

The Grouping Intervals dialog box opens.

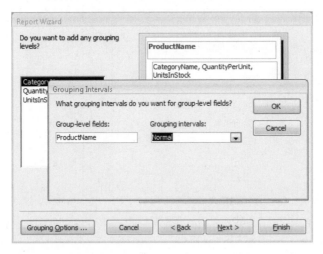

10. In the **Grouping intervals** list, click **1st Letter**. Then click **OK**.

Selecting this option creates a new group header each time the first letter of the category changes.

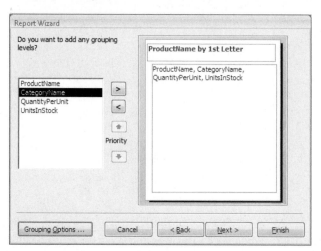

11. On the grouping levels page, click **Next**.

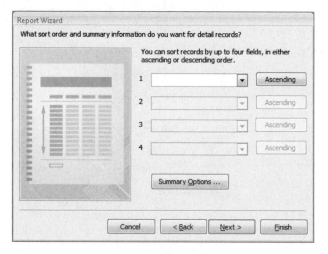

You can sort report information by up to four fields, each in ascending or descending order. When you sort by any field that contains numeric information, the Summary Options button appears at the bottom of the wizard page. In the Summary Options dialog box, you can instruct Access to display the sum, average, minimum, or maximum value for the field in the report.

The only numeric field in this report is UnitsInStock, and there is no need to summarize it.

12. Click the arrow to the right of the first box to display a list of fields, and click **ProductName**. Then click **Next**.

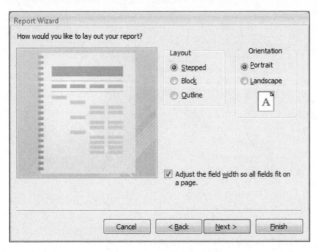

13. In the **Layout** area, select the **Outline** option. With the **Portrait** orientation option and the **Adjust the field width so all fields fit on a page** check box selected, click **Next**.

14. On the style selection page, in the list of styles, click **Flow,** then click **Next** to display the wizard's final page.

15. In the title box, type Alphabetical List of Products, and then with the **Preview the report** option selected, click **Finish**.

Access creates and displays the report.

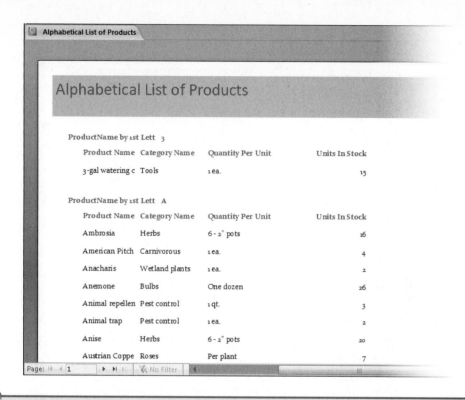

 CLOSE the Alphabetical List Of Products report and the *Wizard* database.

Modifying Report Design

You can use the Report wizard to get a quick start on a report, but you will frequently want to modify the resultant report; you can do this in Design view. Refining a report is an iterative process: you switch back and forth between Design view and Print Preview to evaluate each change and plan the next.

In this exercise, you'll modify the layout and formatting of a report.

 USE the *ModifyDesign* database. This practice file is located in the *Documents\Microsoft Press\Access2007SBS\Reports* folder.
OPEN the *ModifyDesign* database.

1. In the **Navigation Pane**, under **Reports**, right-click the **Alphabetical List of Products** report, and then click **Print Preview**.

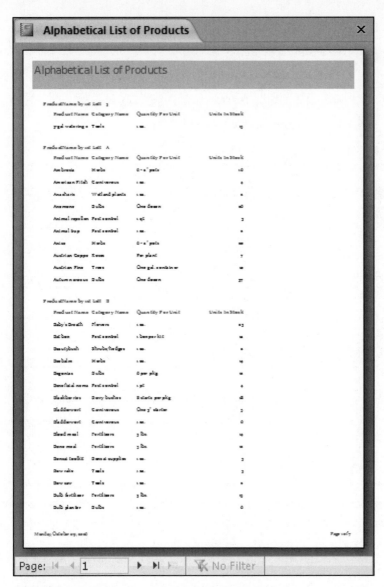

2. Maximize the window if it isn't already, and then point to the previewed report page.

   The pointer changes to a magnifying glass with a plus sign in it to indicate that you can zoom in on the page.

3. Click the previewed page once to zoom in.

> **Tip** You can zoom in and out by dragging the Zoom slider in the lower-right corner of the window. The current zoom level appears to the left of the slider.

Notice that the report has the following design problems:

- ○ There is no date below the title.
- ○ There is some extraneous text.
- ○ Labels need to be rearranged.
- ○ There are a number of general formatting issues.

Design View

4. On the **View** toolbar at the bottom of the screen, click the **Design View** button to switch views, and if the **Field List** pane opens, close it.

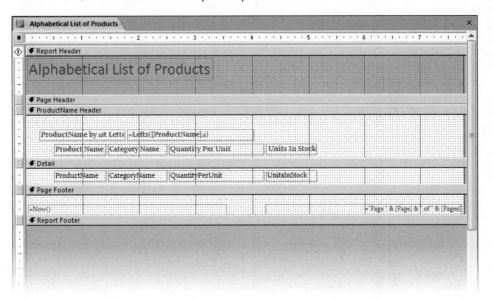

5. Point to the top edge of the **Page Header** selector. When the pointer changes to a two-headed vertical arrow, drag the selector down about a quarter inch to make room for a date.

> **Troubleshooting** Depending on your printer settings, Access might display an error next to the Report Header alerting you that the report is wider than the page. You can ignore this error; it will go away when we change the width property for the report.

> **Tip** The rulers above and to the left of the report form help you judge the size of the printed report. You can toggle the rulers and the grid dots on and off by right-clicking the report and then clicking Ruler or Grid.

Date & Time

6. On the **Design** contextual tab, in the **Controls** group, click the **Date & Time** button. The Date And Time dialog box opens.

7. Select the third date format option, and clear the **Include Time** check box. Then click **OK** to insert the current date in the report.

   The Date text box is inserted in the upper-right corner of the Report Header. You may have to enlarge the report to see it.

8. Drag the **Date** text box until it is just below the title, aligned with its left edge.

Align Text Left

9. With the text box still selected, in the **Font** group, click the **Align Text Left** button to align the date with the left edge of the text box.

Remove

10. Drag through all the controls in the **ProductName Header** and **Detail** sections to select them. Then on the **Arrange** tab, in the **Control Layout** group, click the **Remove** button to remove the Stacked layout.

   Removing the Stacked layout gives you more options for arranging the controls.

11. In the **ProductName Header** section, delete the **Product Name by 1st** label, and then drag the text box to the left edge of the section.

12. In the **Page Footer** section, click the text box containing *=Now()*, and then press [Del].

13. In the **Page Footer** section, click the remaining text box to select it, and press [F4] to open the **Property Sheet**. Change the **Width** property to 2" and the **Left** property to 4.5".

14. In the upper-left corner of the report, click the **Report Selector**. In the **Property Sheet** pane, change the **Width** property to 6.5", and then close the pane.

> **Tip** A square black dot within the Report Selector indicates that the report is currently selected.

If Access displayed the error earlier alerting you that the report width exceeded the page width, setting the Width properties in Steps 13 and 14 causes it to disappear.

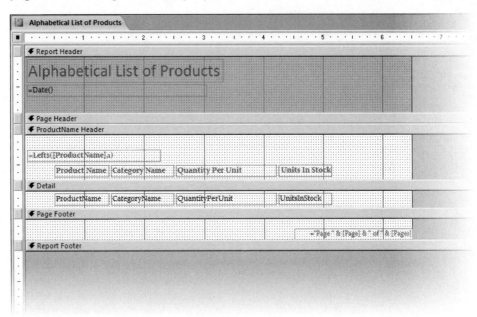

Print Preview

15. Save your changes, and then on the **View** toolbar, click the **Print Preview** button.

Access displays a preview of the report as it will appear when printed.

Next, you will insert a line at the bottom of each group, and prevent the groups from breaking across pages.

16. Switch back to Design view. On the **Design** tab, in the **Grouping & Totals** group, click the **Group & Sort** button.

The Group, Sort, And Total pane appears below the Report window.

You can use this pane, which is a new feature in Access 2007, to quickly add grouping and sorting levels and set related properties.

17. In the **Group, Sort, and Total** pane, in the **Group on ProductName** bar, click **More** to see additional options. Then click the **without a footer section** arrow, and in the list, click **with a footer section**.

    A ProductName Footer section selector appears above the Page Footer section.

18. Click the **do not keep group together on one page** arrow, and then in the list, click **keep whole group together on one page**. Then close the **Group, Sort, and Total** pane by clicking the **Group & Sort** button again.

Line

19. In the **Controls** group, click the **Line** button, and then click near the top of the **ProductName Footer** section to insert a short horizontal line.

20. Press F4 to display the Property Sheet pane, if it is not already visible.

21. On the **Format** tab, change the **Left** setting to 0, the **Width** setting to 6.5". Then in the **Border Color** list, click **Text Black**.

22. Save your changes, and then switch to Print Preview to review them.

    Access displays a preview of the report. You can make changes to the appearance of the report, such as realigning the columns.

23. Switch back to Design view and in the **ProductName Header** and **Detail** sections, drag through the label and text box for **Units In Stock** to select them. Then in the **Property Sheet** pane, change the **Left** setting to 5.5".

    > **Tip** Drag through any portion of the two controls to select them.

24. Select the label and text box for **Quantity Per Unit**. Change the **Left** setting to 4" and the **Width** setting to 1.25".

25. Select the label and text box for **CategoryName**. Change the **Left** setting to 2.25" and the **Width** setting to 1.5".

26. Select the label and text box for **ProductName**, and then change the **Width** setting to 1.5".

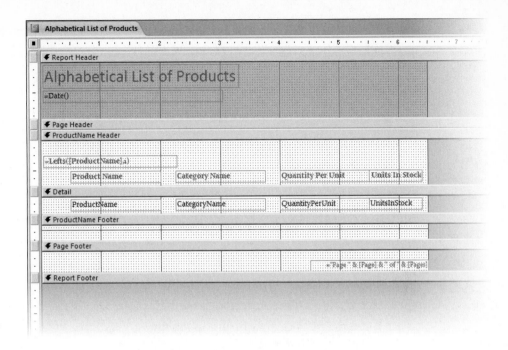

> **Tip** To make changes to two or more controls, select all the controls you want to change, and then drag a handle of any selected control to change all of them the same way.

27. Save your changes, and then switch to Print Preview to see the final result.

 CLOSE the Alphabetical List Of Products report and the *ModifyDesign* database.

Creating a Report Manually

The fastest way to create a report that displays specific field captions and contents from more than one table is by using the Report wizard. Sometimes, however, you might want to create a *main report* that serves as a shell for one or more subreports, but displays little or no information from the underlying tables. It can be easier to create the main report manually in Design view.

In this exercise, you will create a main report based on a query.

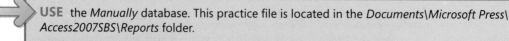

USE the *Manually* database. This practice file is located in the *Documents\Microsoft Press\ Access2007SBS\Reports* folder.

OPEN the *Manually* database.

Report Design

1. On the **Create** tab, in the **Reports** group, click the **Report Design** button.

   Access displays a blank report.

   > **Tip** The Page Header, Detail, and Page Footer sections you see in Design view are the default sections for a new report, but you can add or remove sections to fit your needs.

Add Existing Fields

2. If the **Field List** pane isn't open, click the **Add Existing Fields** button in the **Tools** group.

   > **Troubleshooting** If the Field List pane covers the report, you can make the pane narrower by dragging its left edge to the right.

Report Selector   Field List pane

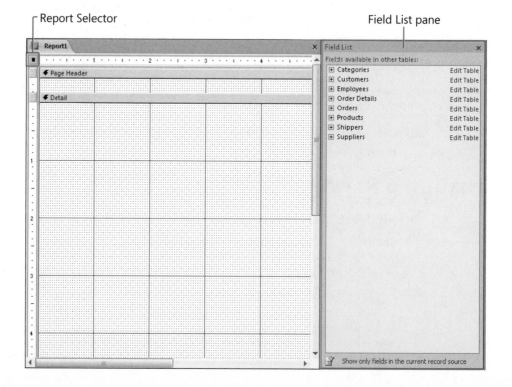

3. Right-click the report, and then click **Report Header/Footer**.

   Report Header and Report Footer sections now enclose the default Page Header, Detail, and Page Footer sections.

   > **Troubleshooting** If the page header and footer disappear from your report, you can restore them by right-clicking the report and then clicking Page Header/Footer to restore them.

4. In the **Field List** pane, expand the **Categories** field list, and then double-click the **CategoryName** field.

   The selected label and text box appear in the Detail section of the report window.

5. Close the **Field List** pane.

6. On the **Design** contextual tab, in the **Grouping & Totals** group, click the **Group & Sort** button.

   The Group, Sort, And Total pane opens below the report.

7. In the **Group, Sort, and Total** pane, click **Add a group**.

   The Group on bar appears, with the select field pane open.

8. In the **select field** pane, click **CategoryName**.

   A CategoryName section header appears in the report.

9. Close the **Group, Sort, and Total** pane.

10. Select the **CategoryName** label and text box, then move the two controls to the grid just below the **CategoryName** header.

Report Selector

11. In the upper-left corner of the report, click the **Report Selector**, and then press ⌊F4⌋ to open the Property Sheet pane.

12. On the **Format** tab, set the **Grid X** and **Grid Y** properties to 10.

    You might find it easier to align controls against this larger grid.

13. Click the **Report Header** section, and then on the **Format** tab in the **Property Sheet** pane, set its **Height** property to 1".

    > **Troubleshooting** Throughout this book we refer to measurements in inches. If your computer is set to display measurements in centimeters, substitute the equivalent metric measurement. As long as you are entering the default units, you don't have to specify the unit type.

14. Repeat step 13 to set the **Height** property for other sections of the report as follows:

Section	Setting
PageHeader	0"
Category/Name Header	2.2"
Detail	0"
Page Footer	0.2"
Report Footer	0"

> **Tip** You can manually set the height of a section by dragging the top edge of the section selector up or down.

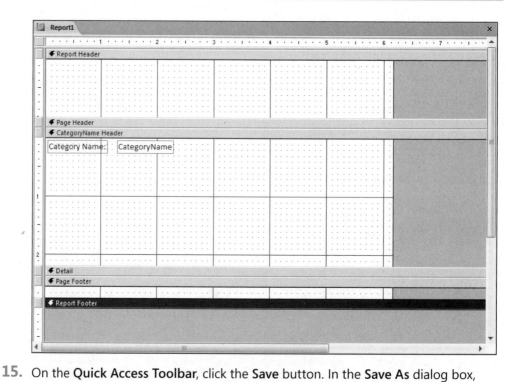

15. On the **Quick Access Toolbar**, click the **Save** button. In the **Save As** dialog box, type Sales by Category in the **Report Name** box, and then click **OK**.

Save

16. On the **View** toolbar, click the **Report View** button to see the results of your work.

Report View

CLOSE the Sales By Category report and the *Manually* database.

Modifying Report Content

Whether you create a report with the Report wizard or manually, you can modify the report later in Design view to add content or change the layout or style of the content.

In this exercise, you'll modify the content of a report by inserting a title, date, and time in the header and page numbers in the footer, inserting and removing labels, and changing the appearance of text.

> **USE** the *ModifyContent* database. This practice file is located in the *Documents\Microsoft Press\Access2007SBS\Reports* folder.
>
> **OPEN** the *ModifyContent* database. Then display the Sales By Category report in Design view.

Title

1. On the **Design** contextual tab, in the **Controls** group, click the **Title** button.

   Access inserts a title (matching the report name) in the Report Header section.

Property Sheet

2. If the Property Sheet pane is not open, press F4 to open it. Then set the font properties as follows:

Property	Setting
Font Name	Times New Roman
Font Size	20
Font Weight	Bold
Font Italic	Yes

   The title text reflects your changes, but no longer fits in its text box.

3. Right-click the title text box, point to **Size**, and then click **To Fit**.

   > **Troubleshooting** If Access displays an error when you navigate away from the label because it isn't associated with a control, click the Smart Tag, and then click Ignore Error.

Date & Time

4. In the **Controls** group, click the **Date & Time** button.

   The Date And Time dialog box opens.

5. With the **Include Date** check box and the first (long) date format options selected, clear the **Include Time** check box, and then click **OK**.

A text box containing *=Date()* appears in the upper-right corner of the Report Header section. When inserting the Date And Time control in a report that doesn't have a Report Header section, the text box appears in the Detail section. You might have to close the Property Sheet pane in order to see the text box.

6. Move the **=Date()** text box below the title and adjust its width to match the title text box.

Center

7. In the **Font** group, click the **Center** button to center the date that will be displayed in this text box.

8. Under the **CategoryName Header**, delete the **Category Name** label that appears to the left of the text box.

9. Select the text box, and set its font properties to the same settings as those used in step 2 for the report title.

10. Right-click the **CategoryName** text box, point to **Size**, and then click **To Fit**.

11. Position the text box with its top against the top of the section and its left edge two gridlines in from the left, and then drag the right edge of the text box to about the 2.4-inch mark.

Aa
Label

12. On the **Design** tab, in the **Controls** group, click the **Label** button. Then click directly below the lower-left corner of the **CategoryName** text box.

13. In the minimized text box that appears, type **Product:** and then press the Enter key.

Because this label is not associated with a control, an error appears.

14. Click the Smart Tag, and then in the list, click **Ignore Error**.

15. Set the font properties for the label as follows:

Property	Setting
Font Name	Times New Roman
Font Size	12
Font Weight	Bold
Font Italic	Yes

16. Right-click the label, point to **Size** on the shortcut menu, and then click **To Fit**.

17. Align the left edges of the label and the **CategoryName** text box.

> **Tip** To precisely align the left edge of one control with that of another, set their Left properties to the same value.

Insert Page
Number

18. In the **Controls** group, click the **Insert Page Number** button.

The Page Numbers dialog box opens.

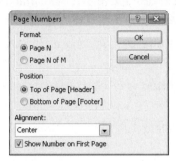

19. In the **Format** area, select the **Page N of M** option. In the **Position** area, select the **Bottom of Page [Footer]** option. Click the **Alignment** arrow, and in the list, click **Center**. Then click **OK**.

Access inserts a text box containing the expression *="Page " & [Page] & " of " & [Pages]* in the center of the Page Footer section.

20. Save the report, and then preview the results.

CLOSE the Sales By Category report and the *ModifyContent* database.

Adding a Subreport to a Report

You can use a wizard to quickly create a report that is bound to the information in one table or in several related tables. However, reports often include multiple sets of information that are related to the topic of the report, but not necessarily related to each other. A report might, for example, include charts, spreadsheets, and other forms of information about several divisions or activities of a company. Or it might include information about production, marketing, sales, compensation, and the company's pension plan. All these topics are related to running the business, but they don't all fit nicely into the structure of an individual Access report.

One solution to this problem is to create separate reports and store them together, for example by printing them and placing them in a binder or by saving them in electronic format in a folder or on an intranet site. An easier and more graceful solution is to use *subreports*. A subreport is a report inserted within another report (usually with others).

You create a subreport as you would any other report, and then use a wizard either to insert it in a main report or to insert a subreport control in the main report. In either case, both the main report and the subreport appear as objects in the Reports pane of the database window.

You might frequently use queries as the basis for reports that require summary calculations or statistics. But you can also enhance the usefulness of both regular reports and subreports by performing calculations in the reports themselves. By inserting unbound controls and then using the Expression Builder to create the expressions that tell Access what to calculate and how, you can make information readily available in one place instead of several.

> **Tip** After establishing the correct relationships, you can quickly insert an existing report as a subreport of another by opening the main report in Design view and then dragging the second report from the Reports pane to the section of the main report where you want to insert it as a subreport.

In this exercise, you will select a record source for a calculated query, and then add a subreport displaying calculated totals to a main report.

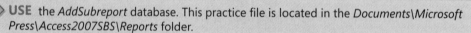

> **USE** the *AddSubreport* database. This practice file is located in the *Documents\Microsoft Press\Access2007SBS\Reports* folder.
>
> **OPEN** the *AddSubreport* database. Display the Sales By Category report in Design view, and then display the Property Sheet pane.

> **Troubleshooting** The database created for this exercise contains additional queries; do not continue with the database from a previous exercise.

1. If the Report Selector in the upper-left corner of the report does not display a black dot to indicate that the report is selected, click it.

2. On the **Data** tab of the **Property Sheet** pane, click the **Record Source** arrow, and in the list, click **Sales by Category**. Then close the **Property Sheet** pane,

Subform/
Subreport

3. On the **Design** contextual tab, in the **Controls** group, click the **Subform/Subreport** button, and then click a point about two gridlines below the left edge of the **Product** label.

Access opens a blank, unbound subreport in the main report and then the SubReport wizard starts.

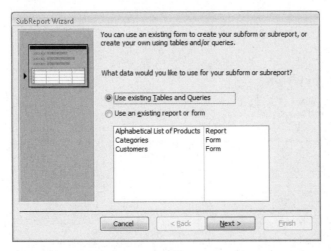

4. With the **Use existing Tables and Queries** option selected, click **Next**.

5. In the **Tables/Queries** list, click **Query: Sales by Category**.

6. In the **Available Fields** list, double-click **CategoryID**, **ProductName**, and **ProductSales** to move them to the **Selected Fields** list, and then click **Next**.

7. With the **Choose from a list** option and **Show Sales by Category for each record in Sales by Category using CategoryID** selected, click **Next**.

8. Click **Finish** to create a subreport with the suggested name, *Sales by Category subreport*.

The Sales By Category subreport takes the place of the unbound subreport in the main report.

9. If the entire subreport isn't selected, click its top edge to select it. If the Property Sheet pane does not open automatically, press F4.

10. On the **Format** tab, set the **Width** property to 6.6" and the **Height** property to 1.5". Then press ⎡Enter⎤.

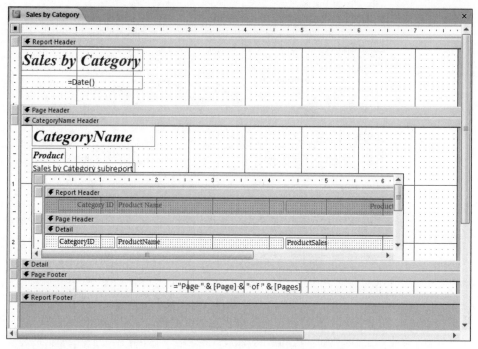

11. In the subreport, click an empty section of the **Report Header** grid, then press ⎡Ctrl⎤+⎡A⎤ to select all the controls.

12. On the **Arrange** tab, in the **Control Layout** group, click the **Remove** button.

Removing the Stacked layout allows you to delete the Report Header without deleting the controls in the Detail section.

13. In the subreport, right-click the **Report Header** section header, and then click **Report Header/Footer** to delete the existing header and footer sections. In the **Microsoft Office Access** message box warning you that any controls in the sections will be deleted, click **Yes**.

14. In the subreport, right-click the **Page Header** section header, and then click **Page Header/Footer** to delete the corresponding header and footer sections.

The subreport now consists of only a Detail section.

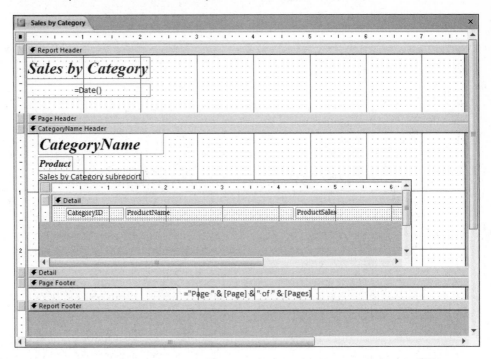

15. In the **Detail** section, click the **CategoryID** text box, and then press the Del key.

16. Click the **ProductName** text box, and in the **Property Sheet** pane, change its **Width** property to 2.125".

17. Click the **ProductSales** text box, and in the **Property Sheet** pane, change its **Left** property to 2.3" and its **Width** property to 1".

The labels overlap.

18. In the main report, delete the partially hidden **Sales by Category** subreport label.

> **Tip** If you accidentally delete a control, press Ctrl+Z or click the Undo button to undo the deletion.

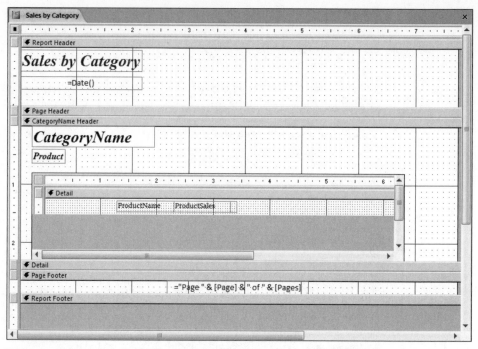

19. Right-click in the grid below the subreport **Detail** section header, and then click **Report Header/Footer** to display those sections.

Text Box

20. Scroll the subreport to display the **Report Footer** section. (You might have to adjust the report window to see the scrollbar.) In the **Controls** group, click the **Text Box** button, and then click in the center of the **Report Footer** section.

    Access inserts an unbound control and its label. You will use this control to perform the calculation.

21. Click the label of the unbound control, and then in the **Property Sheet** pane, set the following properties:

Property	Setting
Caption	Total:
Font Name	Arial
Font Size	9
Font Weight	Bold

Ellipsis

22. Click the unbound text box control, and then in the **Property Sheet** pane, on the **Data** tab, click the ellipsis button in the **Control Source** property to start the **Expression Builder**.

> **Troubleshooting** If you haven't previously used the Expression Builder, Office might install it at this time. The installation process might require you to insert the Office installation CD.

23. In the first column, double-click **Functions**, and then click **Built-In Functions**.

24. In the third column, double-click **Sum**.

Access displays *Sum (<<expr>>)* in the expression box.

25. Click **<<expr>>**. Then click **Sales by Category subreport** in the first column, and double-click **ProductSales** in the second column.

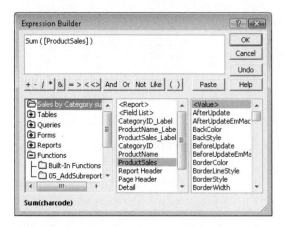

26. Click **OK** to close the **Expression Builder**, and then press Enter to enter the calculation in the unbound text box in the Property Sheet pane.

27. Set the font properties for the unbound text box as you did in step 21.

28. In the Property Sheet pane, on the **Format** tab, click the **Format** arrow, click **Currency**, and then press Enter .

Access will now display the results of the calculation as currency.

29. Set the **Left** and **Width** properties of the calculated control and its label to match the two controls in the Detail section.

Print Preview

30. Save your changes. Then on the **View** toolbar, click the **Print Preview** button to display the results of your work.

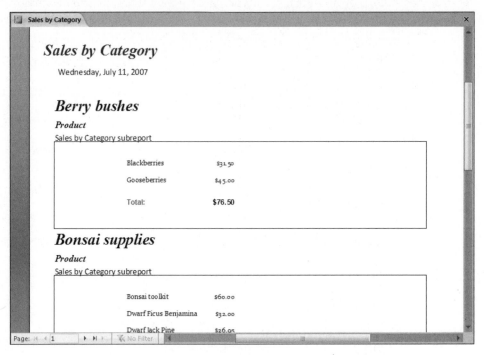

31. On the **View** toolbar, click the **Design View** button to switch views.

> **Tip** Several factors affect the layout of the subreport in the main report when it is displayed in Print Preview. The width of the subreport sets the width of the space available for the display of text. The height of the subreport sets the minimum height of the area where product information is displayed (because the Can Shrink property for the subreport is set to *No*). The maximum height of the product display area is the length of the list (because the Can Grow property is set to *Yes*) plus the space between the bottom of the subreport and the bottom of the Detail section.

32. Click the subreport to select it. In the **Property Sheet** pane, on the **Format** tab, change the **Border Style** property to Transparent.

33. Save your changes, and then preview the report.

 CLOSE the Sales By Category report and the *AddSubreport* database.

Previewing and Printing a Report

Print Preview in Access is very similar to Print Preview in other Microsoft Office System products. If you look at your reports carefully in Print Preview, you won't be in for any major surprises when you print them. But Access also provides a preview option called Layout Preview that displays real data and allows you to refine the layout.

In this exercise, you will preview a report in both Print Preview and Layout Preview, and then review the available printing options.

USE the *Printing* database. This practice file is located in the *Documents\Microsoft Press\Access2007SBS\Reports* folder.

OPEN the *Printing* database, and then display the Alphabetical List Of Products report in Design view.

1. On the **Home** tab, in the **Views** group, click the **View** arrow to display the list of views.

Each of the four choices—Report View, Print Preview, Layout View, and Design View—has an associated icon. The current view is indicated by a border and background. The View button displays the icon of the default view you will see (in this case, Report view) if you click the View button rather than selecting a view from the list. When you are in Design view, Report View, Print Preview, and Layout View are available from the list.

2. In the **View** list, click **Print Preview**.

The preview environment displays an image of how the report will look when it is printed. All tabs other than Print Preview are hidden. If you can't see an entire page in the window, you can maximize the window, or slide the Zoom control to adjust the page magnification.

> **Tip** When the pointer appears as a plus sign, clicking it zooms in on (magnifies) the report. When it appears as a minus sign, clicking it decreases magnification.

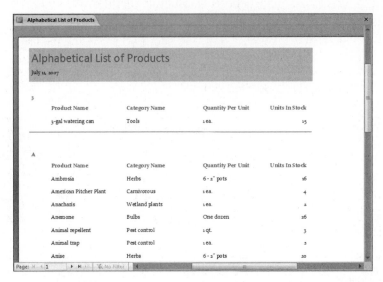

Next Page

3. On the **Navigation** bar, click the **Next Page** button repeatedly to view each page of this report.

4. In the **Close Preview** group, click the **Close Print Preview** button.

Close Print Preview

> **Tip** Automatic error checking identifies common errors in forms and reports and gives you a chance to fix them. For example, Access informs you if a report is wider than the page it will be printed on. To enable error checking, click the Microsoft Office Button, then click Access Options. On the menu, click Object Designers, then scroll to the bottom of the window and select the Enable error checking check box and any other error checking options you want, and then click OK.

5. In the **View** list, click **Layout View**.

Layout View is a cross between Design view and Report view. After you create a report, you can add new fields, adjust the layout, and add grouping and sorting levels in Layout view. (You can't create a report in Layout view, however.) Unlike Design view, Layout view looks very much like the finished report and displays real data from your records in the controls.

6. Scroll through the report to see the results.

7. Click the **Microsoft Office Button**, and then click **Print**.

The Print dialog box opens.

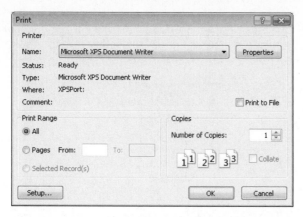

From here, you can click the Setup button to open the Page Setup dialog box, or you can click Properties to open a dialog box in which you can set properties specific to the printer designated in the Name box. You can also specify which pages to print and the number of copies of each. The options you see in this dialog box may vary depending on your individual system.

CLOSE the Print dialog box, the Alphabetical List Of Products report, and the *Printing* database. If you are not continuing directly on to the next chapter, quit Access.

Key Points

- A report created in Access 2007 typically summarizes and organizes information. When designing a report, consider the point you are trying to make, the intended audience, and the level of information they will need.

- You can create a report from scratch or by using a wizard. After creating a report, you can refine it in Design view and view the results of your changes in Print Preview or Layout view.

- You can create a main report and link from it to other reports, referred to as subreports.

- You can add controls to reports and set the properties of those controls. You can display information from one or more records, tables, or queries, and you can add headers and footers specific to the report and to each of its pages.

- You can display summary calculations or statistics in a report and enhance its usefulness by basing it on a query and performing calculations within the report. You describe calculation processes to Access by using the Expression Builder.

Chapter at a Glance

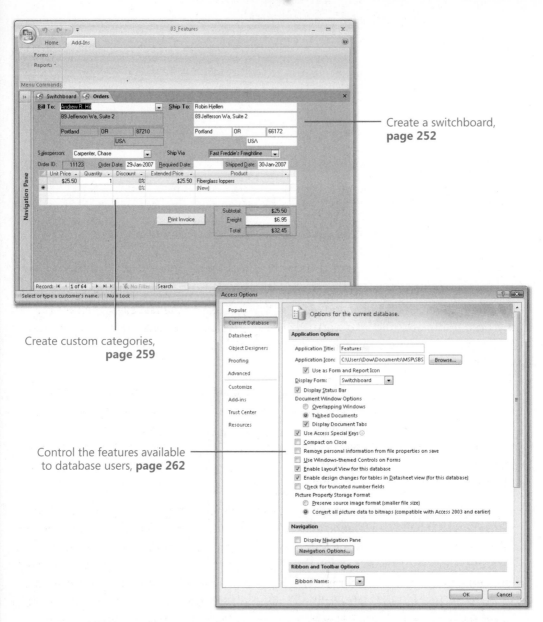

Create a switchboard,
page 252

Create custom categories,
page 259

Control the features available
to database users, **page 262**

9 Making Your Database Easy to Use

In this chapter, you will learn to:

✔ Create a switchboard.

✔ Create custom categories.

✔ Control the features available to database users.

✔ Make favorite Access commands quickly available.

A Microsoft Office Access 2007 database is a complex combination of objects, information, and the tools required to manage and manipulate them. In the first eight chapters of this book, you learned how to work with these components to enter, organize, retrieve, and display information. You can create databases that you, or other people familiar with Access, can use.

However, if information will be entered and retrieved from your database by people who aren't proficient with Access, the information will be safer and the users happier if you take some steps to insulate them from the inner workings of Access. You need to turn your collection of objects and information into an application that organizes related tasks. Then users can focus on the job at hand, rather than on learning to use the program the database is running in.

With a little extra effort on your part, you can make it much easier for other people to access and manipulate your data, and much more difficult to unintentionally change or delete it. In previous versions of Access the most common ways to control access to a database application were through *switchboards* and *startup options*. Access 2007 has reduced support for switchboards and substantially changed the available startup options. Much of the functionality of switchboards is now available in *custom groups*, which are a new feature in Access 2007. However, the Switchboard Manager is still available for creating switchboards in Access 2007, and switchboards created in earlier versions of Access should for the most part still function correctly.

> **Troubleshooting** Some legacy features, such as start-up options and global add-in menus, are available only if you open the database as an Access 2003 MDB file, rather than converting it to the Access 2007 format.

In this chapter, you will learn how to create a simple switchboard, create custom groups, add a custom menu to the ribbon, and set various startup options.

See Also Do you need only a quick refresher on the topics in this chapter? See the Quick Reference section at the beginning of this book.

> **Important** Before you can use the practice files in this chapter, you need to install them from the book's companion CD to their default location. See "Using the Companion CD" at the beginning of this book for more information.

> **Troubleshooting** Graphics and operating system–related instructions in this book reflect the Windows Vista user interface. If your computer is running Windows XP and you experience trouble following the instructions as written, please refer to the "Information for Readers Running Windows XP" section at the beginning of this book.

Creating a Switchboard

A switchboard appears as a hierarchy of pages containing buttons that the user can click to open additional pages, display dialog boxes, present forms for viewing and entering data, preview and print reports, and initiate other activities. For example, a salesperson might use a switchboard to display a form to quickly enter orders or add new customers.

Although switchboards are being phased out, they still work in Access 2007 and are being included in this book for people who want to transition gently to the new format. If you haven't created a switchboard in the past, and want this kind of feature, we suggest you skip this topic and investigate custom groups.

You can create switchboards by hand or with the help of Switchboard Manager. A switchboard created by hand is made up of multiple forms (pages) of your own design that are linked together by macros and Microsoft Visual Basic for Applications (VBA) code. A switchboard created with the help of the Switchboard Manager consists of a Switchboard Items table and one generic form that serves as a template when the program displays your switchboard. You can change the location of buttons and add other visual elements (such as pictures) in Design view. Unlike a switchboard created by hand, you can change the number of active buttons and the action that is performed when each button is clicked only by editing information in the Switchboard Items table.

> **Tip** You don't need to know how switchboards created with Switchboard Manager work to use one, but it helps to know what's going on behind the scenes in case you need to make changes. When the switchboard is opened, Access runs VBA code that reads information stored in the Switchboard Items table and uses it to set form properties that determine the buttons that are visible in the generic form. The code also assigns labels and actions to the visible buttons. If you click a button to go to a second level in the switchboard hierarchy, the code reads the table again and resets the properties for the generic form to create the page for the new level.

In this exercise, you will create a simple switchboard by using Switchboard Manager.

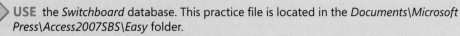

USE the *Switchboard* database. This practice file is located in the *Documents\Microsoft Press\Access2007SBS\Easy* folder.

OPEN the *Switchboard* database.

1. On the **Database Tools** tab, in the **Database Tools** group, click the **Switchboard Manager** button, and then click **Yes** when asked whether you want to create a switchboard.

   The Switchboard Manager window lists any pages created by the Switchboard Manager. Because this database doesn't currently have any switchboard pages, Access lists a default page to get you started.

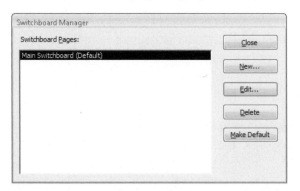

2. With **Main Switchboard (Default)** selected in the **Switchboard Pages** list, click **Edit**.

   The Edit Switchboard Page window opens.

3. In the **Switchboard Name** box, replace *Main Switchboard* with SBS Switchboard. Then click **Close**.

4. In the **Switchboard Manager** window, click **New**.

    The Create New dialog box opens.

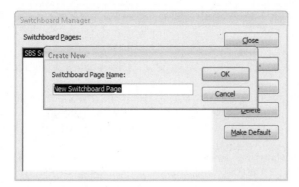

From this dialog box, you can name new pages as you add them to the switchboard.

5. Replace the default new switchboard page name with Forms, and then click **OK**.

6. Repeat Steps 4 and 5 to create a page named Reports.

7. With **SBS Switchboard (Default)** selected in the **Switchboard Pages** list, click **Edit**.

8. In the **Edit Switchboard Page** window, click **New**.

   The Edit Switchboard Item dialog box opens. From this dialog box, you can assign properties to the buttons on the generic switchboard page.

9. In the **Text** box, type Forms.

   This text will become a button label for the command specified in the Command box.

10. Click the **Command** arrow to display the list of commands you can choose. Then click the original selection, **Go to Switchboard**.

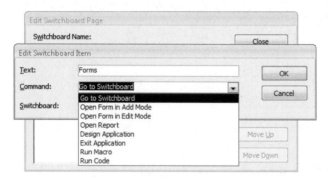

With the current settings in the Edit Switchboard Item dialog box, when a user clicks the Forms button on the SBS Switchboard page, Access will display the switchboard page you specify in the Switchboard box.

11. Click the **Switchboard** arrow, and then in the list, click **Forms**.

    The Switchboard list items reflect the options for the currently selected command.

12. In the **Edit Switchboard Item** dialog box, click **OK**.

13. Repeat Steps 8 through 12, using the following information to create three more buttons on the SBS Switchboard page:

Text	Command	Switchboard or Macro
Reports	Go to Switchboard	Reports
Close Switchboard	Run Macro	Switchboard.closeSB
Close Database	Exit Application	(none)

When a user clicks the Close Switchboard button on the SBS Switchboard page, Access will open the Switchboard macro group, and start running the macro at the *closeSB* line.

> **Tip** The Switchboard.closeSB macro does not come with Access; it is a simple macro written specifically for this exercise. You can review the macros included with the database, by clicking Macros on the Objects bar and then opening the macro you want in Design view.

The Edit Switchboard Page window lists the four items you've just created.

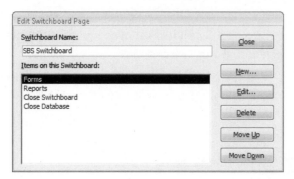

14. In the **Edit Switchboard Page** window, click **Close** to return to Switchboard Manager.

15. In the **Switchboard Pages** list, click **Forms**, and then click **Edit**.

16. Repeat Steps 8 through 12, using the following information to create five buttons on the Forms switchboard page:

Text	Command	Form or Switchboard
Edit/Enter Categories	Open Form in Edit Mode	Categories
Edit/Enter Orders	Open Form in Edit Mode	Orders
Edit/Enter Products	Open Form in Edit Mode	Products
Edit/Enter Suppliers	Open Form in Edit Mode	Suppliers
Return	Go to Switchboard	SBS Switchboard

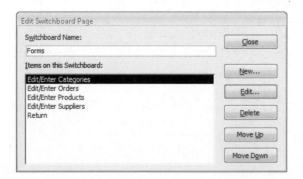

17. Close the **Edit Switchboard Page** window to return to Switchboard Manager. In the **Switchboard Pages** list, click **Reports**, and then click **Edit**.

18. Use the following information to create five buttons on the Reports switchboard page:

Text	Command	Report or Switchboard
Preview/Print Catalog	Open Report	Catalog
Preview/Print Customer Labels	Open Report	Customer Labels
Preview/Print Invoices	Open Report	Invoice
Preview/Print Products	Open Report	Open Report
Return	Go to Switchboard	SBS Switchboard

19. Close the **Edit Switchboard Page** dialog box and **Switchboard Manager**.

20. On the **Navigation Pane**, under **Forms**, double-click **Switchboard**.

Your new switchboard opens in Form view.

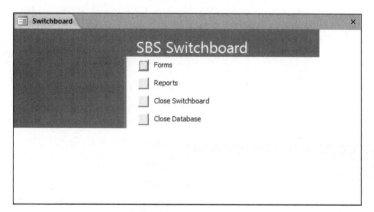

21. On the **SBS Switchboard** page, click the **Forms** button, and then on the **Forms** switchboard, click the **Edit/Enter Categories** button to display the Categories form.

22. Close the **Categories** form, and then on the **Forms** switchboard, click the **Return** button to return to the central switchboard.

23. Switch to Design view.

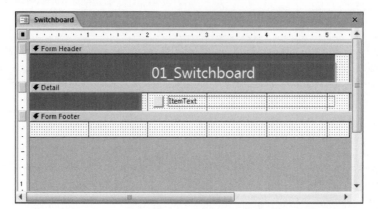

The form, which currently has only one button and its default label text, is essentially a template for your switchboard. The Switchboard table created by the Switchboard Manager contains the information needed to add the buttons and labels.

Each event is associated with a variable in the Switchboard Items table. This variable is in turn associated with the command and parameters (if any) you specified. When you click a button in Form view, Access refers to the On Click property, looks up the variable in the Switchboard Items table, and carries out the associated command.

24. Click the button or label, and press F4 to open the Properties dialog box.

25. Click the **Event** tab of the **Properties** dialog box to display the On Click event for the buttons and labels.

The event that is fired when the user clicks a button is in an embedded macro. Embedded macros are a new feature in Access 2007. They are stored with a form or report, rather than in the Macros group on the Navigation Pane, and offer a higher level of security than do normal macros. To view or edit the embedded macros you would click the ellipsis (...) button.

> **Tip** You can reopen Switchboard Manager to add more pages or commands, and
> you can open the Switchboard form in Design view to add graphics or other objects.
>
> Everything needed to produce the working switchboard is contained in the Switchboard
> form and its Switchboard Items table. You can create a similar switchboard by copying or
> importing the form and the table to any other database, and modifying them as needed
> with Switchboard Manager.

 CLOSE the Property sheet, save and close the Switchboard form, and then close the
Switchboard database.

Creating Custom Categories

Although you can use a switchboard to provide users with easy access to selected objects,
when you're working in Access 2007 it is a lot easier to do so by using a custom category.

As described in Chapter 1, "Exploring Access 2007," the large bar at the top of the
Navigation Pane is a category heading. Each of the smaller bars beneath it is a group
heading. A number of built-in categories are available, and you can filter the groups listed
under a category in various ways.

You can also create up to ten custom categories, each of which can contain multiple
custom groups. You can drag and drop any valid Access object into a custom group to
create a shortcut to the object; the object itself remains in its original group. This combination of categories, groups, and object shortcuts can easily replace the most common
aspects of switchboard pages, items, and commands. For example, if the accounting
department runs a set of reports on the last day of each month, you could create an
Accounting category containing a Month End Reports group, and add the reports to that
group. Or if the Marketing department routinely works with several forms, queries, and
reports, you could create a Marketing category for them. This category could contain one
group holding shortcuts to all the objects, or a group for each object type—there are no
restrictions in the mix of objects placed in one group.

In this exercise, you will create a custom category, and then add groups to it.

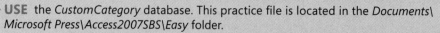

USE the *CustomCategory* database. This practice file is located in the *Documents\Microsoft Press\Access2007SBS\Easy* folder.

OPEN the *CustomCategory* database.

1. At the top of the **Navigation Pane**, right-click the **All Access Objects** category, and then click **Navigation Options**.

    The Navigation Options dialog box opens.

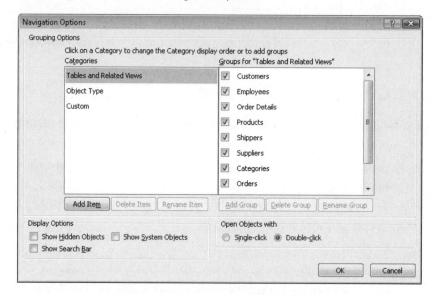

2. In the **Grouping Options** area, click the **Add Item** button.

    A new category appears in the Categories list. The category name is selected.

3. Replace *Custom Category 1* with SBS Category, and then press Enter .

    The heading above the right pane changes to reflect the selected category name.

4. Click the **Add Group** button, and then in the **Groups** list, replace *Custom Group 1* with Forms.

    > **Tip** Every category contains a default group named Unassigned Objects. This group contains a list of all objects in the database, and is the source for the shortcuts you create in your custom groups.

5. Repeat step 4 to add a group named Reports. Then in the **Navigation Options** dialog box, click **OK**.

Although you can't see it now, your new category has been added to the Navigation Pane.

6. Click the category header at the top of the **Navigation Pane** to display a list of categories, and then click your new category, **SBS Category**.

The Forms group that you created for your category appears in the upper section of the menu, followed by the Reports group and the Unassigned Objects group.

7. In the **Unassigned Objects** group, click the **Categories** form (not the table—you can distinguish between the items by their icons), hold down the [Ctrl] key, and click the **Orders**, **Products**, and **Suppliers** forms. Release the [Ctrl] key, scroll the list back to the top, and then drag **Categories** on top of the **Forms** group header.

> **Tip** The icon to the left of the object name identifies the object type.

Access moves the shortcuts for the selected forms from Unassigned Objects to the Forms group.

8. In the **Unassigned Objects** group, click the **Alphabetical List of Products** report, hold down the [Ctrl] key, and click the **Catalog**, **Customer Labels** and **Invoice** reports. Then right-click any selected object, point to **Add to group**, and click **Reports**.

Access moves the shortcuts for the selected reports from Unassigned Objects to the Reports group.

> **Tip** You can leave the Unassigned Objects group visible in the Navigation Pane, or you can hide it. To hide it, right-click the Unassigned Objects title bar and then click Hide. To restore the group, display the Navigation Options dialog box, click SBS Category, select the Unassigned Objects check box, and then click OK.

9. To test the new shortcuts, open each form and report.

 CLOSE the *CustomCategory* database.

There were 25 complex steps in the Switchboard exercise and 9 simple ones in this exercise. Not only is creating categories much faster than creating switchboards, you can have different categories for different people or purposes, and you can add and remove objects easily.

Controlling the Features Available to Database Users

If your database will be used by people with little or no experience with Access, you might want to control which features are available when a database opens. There are several ways to do this. If you want users to be able to open only one database, you can add one or more options to the Access desktop shortcut and Start menu link. These options can open a specific database, run macros, and perform other tasks. For more information about the available options, search Microsoft Office Access Help for *Command-line switches*.

A more common way to control the user's environment is to set startup options in each database. You can use startup options to control the menus and Ribbon tabs available to the user, the initial form displayed (such as a switchboard), and other features. The startup form can include macros and VBA procedures that run automatically to set other conditions.

In this exercise, you will set startup options that tie together a switchboard and some custom menus to create a version of the database that is appropriate for inexperienced users. You will experiment with these options, and then bypass them.

> **Tip** This exercise uses custom menus that were created specially for the sample database. For more information about how to create menus such as these, search for *AddMenu* in the Access Help system.
>
> The Orders form in this exercise uses several custom macros. You can review these macros by clicking Macros on the Objects bar and then opening orderForm in Design view.

 USE the *Features* database and the *Icon* icon. These practice files are located in the *Documents\Microsoft Press\Access2007SBS\Easy* folder.
OPEN the *Features* database.

1. Click the **Microsoft Office Button**, and in the lower-right corner of the menu, click **Access Options**.

2. In the left pane of the **Access Options** window, click **Current Database**.

   Access displays the options for the current database.

3. In the **Application Options** area, type Features in the **Application Title** box, and then press the ⇥ key.

   Access displays the text you entered in the database title bar, in place of the usual *Microsoft Access* title.

4. Click the **Browse** button to the right of the **Application Icon** box. In the **Icon Browser** dialog box, navigate to the *Documents\Microsoft Press\Access2007SBS\ Easy* folder, and then double-click the *Icon* icon.

5. Below the **Application Icon** box, click **Use as Form and Report Icon**.

   The selected icon will appear at the left end of form and report title bars, or on their tabs, depending on the navigation properties you have set.

6. Click the **Display Form** arrow, and then in the list, click **Switchboard**.

   This switchboard will be displayed each time the database is opened.

> **Tip** With the Use Access Special keys check box selected, the following special key combinations are available to database users.
>
> F11 shows and hides the Navigation Pane.
>
> Ctrl+G shows the Immediate window in the Visual Basic Editor.
>
> Alt+F11 switches to the Visual Basic Editor.
>
> Ctrl+Break stops Access from retrieving records from the server.
>
> It is useful to have these options available while developing a database, but you might want to disable them before you make the database available to other users.

7. Clear the **Display Navigation Pane** check box.

This prevents the Navigation Pane from initially being displayed. If you disable the use of Access Special keys, the user won't be able to display the Navigation Pane at all.

8. In the **Ribbon and Toolbar Options** area, clear the **Allow Full Menus** and **Allow Default Shortcut Menus** check boxes.

By disabling these options, you prevent the user from having access to these tools, which helps prevent inappropriate changes to the database. All they will see is the Home tab and any Add-In menus you create.

> **Tip** With the default Shortcut Menu Bar selected in the Ribbon And Toolbar area, the standard shortcut menu appears when a user right-clicks a form. You can also create a custom shortcut menu and specify it in this window or in the form's properties, to provide just the necessary commands.

9. In the **Access Options** window, click **OK**.

   Most startup options don't go into effect until you close and reopen the database. The only changes you should see now are the name in the Access window's title bar and the icon in the forms and reports.

10. Close and reopen the *Features* database.

    Access displays the selected startup options: you see the new title bar, the Home tab, and the Switchboard. From the first exercise in this chapter you are familiar with the process of using the Switchboard to work with forms and reports. You can still do this in the current database, but we have also created an Add-In menu and attached it to the Switchboard form, so when that form is active, the Add-In menu is displayed.

11. Press F11.

    This Access Special Key displays or hides the Navigation Pane—if you don't want database users to have this ability, you will probably wnt to disable the Access Special Keys.

12. On the **Add-Ins** tab, in the **Menu Commands** group, click **Forms**, and then in the list, click **Edit/Enter Categories**.

    The form appears on a new document tab. Note that the Add-Ins menu tab has disappeared. This menu is visible only while the object to which it is attached is active.

13. Close the **Categories** form.

    Note that the Switchboard is again active, and the Add-Ins menu is again visible.

14. In the **Menu Commands** group, on the **Forms** list, click **Edit/Enter Orders**.

    The Orders form is displayed, but this time the Add-Ins menu remains visible. This is because it is attached to both the Switchboard form and the Orders form. There is no way for you to see how this is done in the current database, as most advanced functionality has been disabled by your settings in the Access Options.

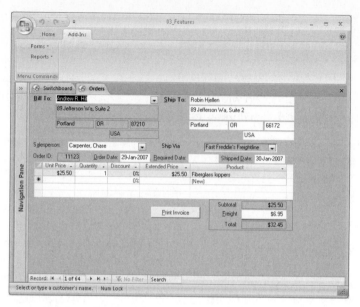

15. Close the *Features* database.

16. While holding down the ⇧ shift key, open the *Features* database. If a safety warning appears, continue to hold the ⇧ shift key down while you acknowledge the warning.

    Holding down the Shift key while you open the database bypasses all the startup options, so the database starts the same way it did before you set those options.

    > **Tip** The only way to prevent a user from bypassing your startup options is to write and run a VBA procedure that creates the AllowByPassKey property and sets it to *False*. There is no way to set this property through Access. For information about how to do this, search for *AllowByPassKey* in the Visual Basic Editor Help file.

17. Open the **Orders** form in Design view, and then display its **Property Sheet** pane. Click the **Other** tab, and note the setting for **Menu Bar**. It should be set to *sbMenu*.

    You attach a menu to a form or report by setting the Menu Bar property to the name of a macro. That macro (sbMenu in this case) lists the names of the menus to add to the menu Command group on the Add-Ins tab. It also points to other macros (TG1 and TG2 in this case) for information about the commands to display on each menu and the actions to take when they are clicked.

You can open sbMenu, TG1, and TG2 in design view to see what they contain. If you want to learn more about this, or create your own menus, search for *addmenu* in the Access Help system.

You could create different menus for every form and report in your database, and use them in conjunction with custom groups or a switchboard to provide a great deal of control over what your users can do in the database.

 CLOSE the *Features* database.

Making Favorite Access Commands Quickly Available

The commands you use to control Access are available from menus and toolbars within the program window. The basic command structure hasn't changed substantially from that in previous versions of Access: Buttons representing common commands are located on the Standard and Advanced toolbars, and other commands that you probably use less frequently can be found on the File, Edit, View, Go, Tools, Actions, and Help menus. You can also invoke many commands by using *keyboard shortcuts*.

> **Tip** To see a list of the available keyboard shortcuts, click the Microsoft Office Access Help button, type keyboard shortcuts in the Search box, and press Enter. Then click the Keyboard Shortcuts For Access topic.

As we first discussed in "Introducing Microsoft Office Access 2007" at the beginning of this book, big changes have been made to the way commands are presented within the Access object windows (tables, forms, reports, and so on). Buttons representing commonly used commands are grouped on *tabs* to make them easily accessible in the specific context in which you're working. This new design makes most of the commands you need at any given time available with only one click. However, you might find that the buttons you use most frequently are scattered on different tabs, or that certain commands you used in previous versions of Access are not available from the Ribbon. To give you more control over the way you work in the 2007 Microsoft Office system, Microsoft has provided the *Quick Access Toolbar*, the Office equivalent of the Quick Launch bar available in Windows XP and Windows Vista. The Quick Access

Toolbar is located to the right of the Microsoft Office Button in Access object windows, as well as in the Microsoft Office Word 2007, Microsoft Office Excel 2007, Microsoft Office PowerPoint 2007 program windows, and Microsoft Office Outlook 2007 item windows. You can add a button for any command to the Quick Access Toolbar so that it is always available no matter which tab is currently active.

In this exercise, you will add a button to the Quick Access Toolbar. There are no practice files for this exercise.

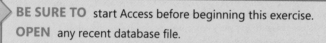

BE SURE TO start Access before beginning this exercise.

OPEN any recent database file.

Customize Quick
Access Toolbar

1. At the right end of the **Quick Access Toolbar**, click the **Customize Quick Access Toolbar** button.

   The Customize Quick Access Toolbar menu opens, displaying a short list of common commands that you can click to add to the toolbar.

2. Near the bottom of the menu, click **More Commands**.

   The Access Options window opens, displaying the Customize The Quick Access Toolbar page. The commands currently appearing on the Quick Access Toolbar are listed (in order of appearance) in the right pane.

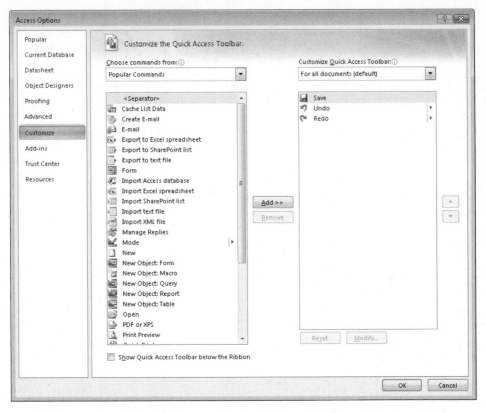

3. Click the **Choose commands from** arrow, and then in the list, click **Create Tab**.

   The list displays all the commands available from the Create tab.

> **Tip** You can display an alphabetical list of all Access commands by clicking All Commands in the Choose Commands From list. In some cases, multiple instances of a command appear in the list—these correspond to the locations in which the command appears within the program. Pointing to a command displays the command location in a ScreenTip. Commands that appear on contextual tabs and commands that don't appear on any tab are also available from this list.

4. In the **Create Tab** list, point to the first command, **Advanced**.

   A ScreenTip displays the tab and group where you can locate this command. Point to a few other commands to view their ScreenTips and gain a better understanding of how commands are grouped and where you can find them.

5. In the **Create Tab** list, click **Table**. Then between the two command lists, click **Add**.

Access adds the Table command to the end of the list of commands available from the Quick Access Toolbar.

Move Up

6. In the right pane, click **Table**, and then click the **Move Up** button two times to move the selected command to the second position in the list.

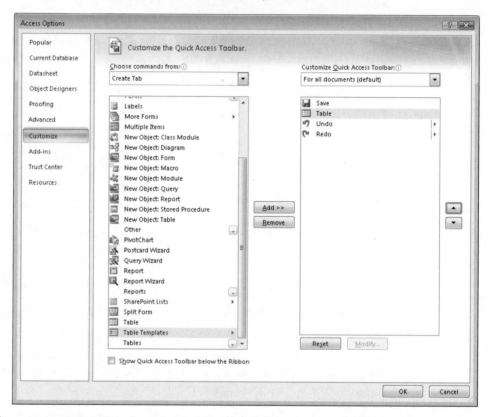

7. At the bottom of the **Customize** page, click **OK**.

The Table command button now appears on the Quick Access Toolbar so that you can conveniently create a new table from anywhere in Access.

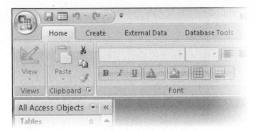

You can remove the button from the Quick Access Toolbar by repeating Steps 1 and 2, selecting the command in the right pane, and then clicking Remove and OK.

> **Tip** You can add any command to the end of the Quick Access Toolbar by right-clicking the command on the Ribbon, and then clicking Add To Quick Access Toolbar. Similarly, you can delete any command from the Quick Access Toolbar by right-clicking the command on the toolbar, and clicking Remove From Quick Access Toolbar.

 BE SURE TO remove the command from the Quick Access Toolbar if you don't want to keep it there.

Key Points

- You can create a switchboard and set startup options to make it easier for others to access and manipulate your data, and more difficult to unintentionally change or delete data.

- You can use custom categories and groups to organize commonly-used forms, reports, and other objects for easy access, and to limit access to objects. This replaces the basic functionality of the switchboard.

- You can place any command on the Quick Access Toolbar common to all databases, or on a custom toolbar specific to one database.

Chapter at a Glance

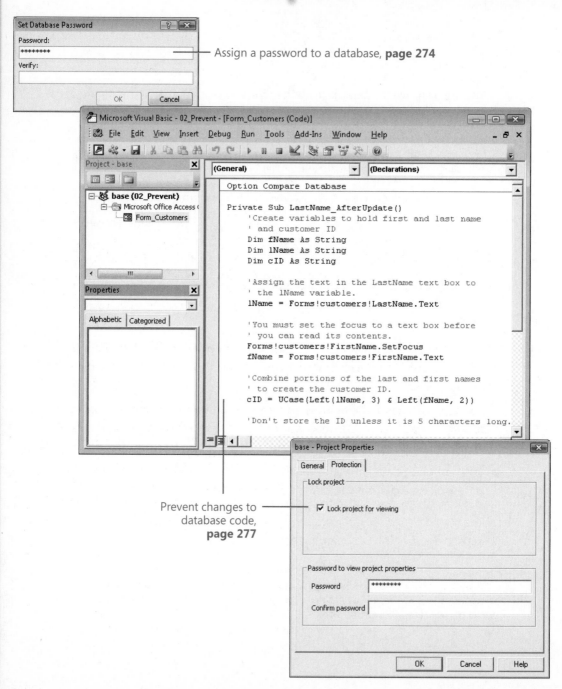

Assign a password to a database, **page 274**

Prevent changes to database code, **page 277**

10 Securing and Sharing Information

In this chapter, you will learn to:

✔ Assign a password to a database.

✔ Prevent changes to database code.

✔ Secure a database for distribution.

The need for *database security* is an unfortunate fact of life. As with your house, car, office, or briefcase, the level of security required for your database depends on the value of what you have and whether you are trying to protect it from curious eyes, accidental damage, malicious destruction, or theft.

The security of a company's business information can be critical to its survival. For example, you might not be too concerned if a person gained unauthorized access to your products list, but you would be very concerned if a competitor managed to see—or worse, steal—your customer list. And it would be a disaster if someone destroyed your critical order information.

Your goal as a database developer is to provide adequate protection without imposing unnecessary restrictions on the people who should have access to your database. The type of security required to protect a database depends to a large extent on how many people are using it and where it is stored. If your database will never be opened by more than one person at a time, you don't have to worry about the potential for corruption caused by several people trying to update the same information at the same time. If your database is sold outside of your organization as part of an application, you will want to take steps to prevent it from being misused in any way.

> **Tip** In previous versions of Access you could set up *workgroups* and assign *permissions* to restrict the information available to members of each group and the actions they can perform. Access 2007 doesn't offer this feature.

Another way to protect a database is by securing the distribution channel; for example, by making it available from a password-protected Web site.

In this chapter, you will explore ways to protect data from accidental or intentional corruption, and ways to make it difficult for unauthorized people to gain access to private information. Then you will learn about ways of sharing databases among team members and backing up a shared database.

See Also Do you need only a quick refresher on the topics in this chapter? See the Quick Reference section at the beginning of this book.

Important Before you can use the practice files in this chapter, you need to install them from the book's companion CD to their default location. See "Using the Companion CD" at the beginning of this book for more information.

Troubleshooting Graphics and operating system–related instructions in this book reflect the Windows Vista user interface. If your computer is running Windows XP and you experience trouble following the instructions as written, please refer to the "Information for Readers Running Windows XP" section at the beginning of this book.

Assigning a Password to a Database

You can prevent unauthorized users from opening a database by assigning it a *password*. Access will prompt anyone attempting to open the database to enter the password. The database will open only if the correct password is entered.

Creating a Secure Password

You can use any word or phrase as a password, but to create a *secure password*, keep the following in mind:

- Passwords are case-sensitive.
- You can include letters, accented characters, numbers, spaces, and most punctuation.

A good password includes uppercase letters, lowercase letters, and symbols or numbers, and isn't a word found in a dictionary. For more information about strong passwords, visit

www.microsoft.com/athome/security/privacy/password.mspx

A secondary benefit of assigning a password is that your database will automatically be encrypted each time you close it, and decrypted when you open it and provide the correct password.

> **Tip** In previous versions of Access, encrypting and decrypting a database was a separate function from assigning a password to it. If you open a database created in Access 2002 or Access 2003 from Access 2007, you will still have the option of encoding or decoding it, which is what the process was called in those versions.

It is easy to assign a database password, and certainly better than providing no protection at all, in that it keeps most honest people out of the database. However, many inexpensive password recovery utilities are available, theoretically to help people recover a lost password. Anyone can buy one of these utilities and "recover" the password to your database. Also, because the same password works for all users (and nothing prevents one person from giving the password to many other people), simple password protection is most appropriate for a single-user database.

To assign a password to or remove a password from a database, you must first open the database for *exclusive use*, meaning that no one else can have the database open. This will not be a problem for the database used in the following exercise, but if you want to set or remove a password for a real database that is located on a network share, you will need to make sure nobody else is using it.

Database Encrypting

A database created in Microsoft Office Access 2007 is a *binary file*; if you open it in a word processor or a text editor, its content is mostly unreadable. However, if you look closely enough at the file, you can discover quite a bit of information. It is unlikely that enough information will be exposed to allow someone to steal anything valuable. But if you are concerned that someone might scan your database file with a utility that looks for key words that will lead them to restricted information, you can *encrypt* the file to make it really unreadable.

In previous versions of Access, the process of encoding (encrypting) a database and assigning a password were separate. In Access 2007, they have been combined as one command.

Encrypting a file prevents people who don't have a copy of Access from being able to read and perhaps make sense of the data in your file.

In this exercise, you will assign a password to a database.

> **USE** the *Password* database. This practice file is located in the *Documents\Microsoft Press\Access2007SBS\Securing* folder.
>
> **BE SURE TO** start Access before beginning this exercise, but don't open the *Password* database yet.

Microsoft Office
Button

1. Click the **Microsoft Office Button**, and then on the menu, click **Open**.

2. In the **Open** dialog box, navigate to the *Documents\Microsoft Press\Access2007SBS\ Reports* folder, and click (don't double-click) the *Password* database. Then click the **Open** arrow, and in the list, click **Open Exclusive**.

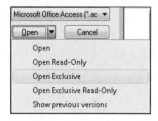

Access opens the database for your exclusive use—no one else can open the database until you close it.

3. On the **Database Tools** tab, in the **Database Tools** group, click the **Encrypt with Password** button.

The Set Database Password dialog box opens.

> **Tip** Access 2007 includes many database-management tools. Familiarize yourself with the commands available from the Database Tools tab. From this tab you can, for example, display an object's dependencies, document the entire database, and update the linked tables.

4. In the **Password** box, type 2007!SbS, and then press the ⎾Tab⏋ key.

Access disguises the characters of the password as asterisks as you type them, to protect against other people seeing your password.

5. In the **Verify** box, type 2007!SbS. Then click **OK**.

6. Close and reopen the database.

   The Password Required dialog box opens.

7. In the **Enter database password** box, type 2007_SBS, and then click **OK**.

   Access warns you that the password is not valid.

8. In the **Microsoft Office Access** message box warning you that the password you entered is not valid, click **OK**.

9. In the **Password Required** dialog box, type the correct password (2007!SbS), and then click **OK**.

   The database opens.

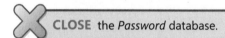 **CLOSE** the *Password* database.

> **Tip** To remove a password from a database, open the database exclusively, entering the password when prompted to do so. On the Database Tools tab, in the Database Tools group, click the Decrypt Database button. Enter the password, and then click OK. Access removes the password, allowing anyone to open the database.

Preventing Changes to Database Code

If you have added Microsoft Visual Basic for Applications (VBA) procedures to a database, you certainly don't want users who aren't qualified or authorized to make changes to your code. You can prevent unauthorized access in two ways: by protecting your VBA code with a password, or by saving the database as a Microsoft Database Executable (ACCDE) file. If you set a password for the code, it remains available for editing by anyone who knows the password. If you save the database as an ACCDE file, people using the database application can run your code, but they can't view or edit it.

See Also For information about saving a database as an executable file, see "Securing a Database for Distribution" later in this chapter.

In this exercise, you will secure the VBA code in a database by assigning a password to it.

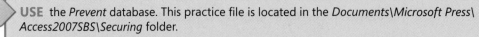

USE the *Prevent* database. This practice file is located in the *Documents\Microsoft Press\ Access2007SBS\Securing* folder.

BE SURE TO start Access before beginning this exercise.

OPEN the *Prevent* database.

Visual
Basic

1. On the **Database Tools** tab, in the **Macro** group, click the **Visual Basic** button.

The Visual Basic Editor starts.

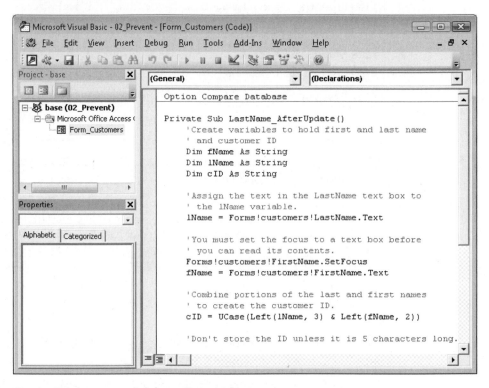

2. On the **Tools** menu, click **base Properties**.

The Project Properties dialog box opens.

3. On the **Protection** tab, select the **Lock project for viewing** check box.

4. In the **Password** box, type 2007!VbA, and then press the [Tab] key.

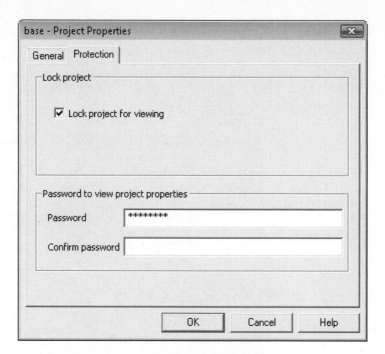

Access disguises the characters of the password as asterisks as you type them, to protect against other people seeing your password.

> **Tip** The Lock and Password settings operate independently. Selecting the Lock Project For Viewing check box requires the user to enter the password to view the project. If a password has been set and the Lock Project For Viewing check box is not selected, the user can view the project code but has to enter the password to open the Project Properties dialog box.

5. In the **Confirm Password** box, type 2007!VbA, and then click **OK**.

   The password is set, but you won't have to enter it again until the next time you open the database and attempt to edit the VBA code.

6. Close the Visual Basic Editor, and then close the database.

7. Reopen the database, and then on the **Database Tools** tab, in the **Macro** group, click the **Visual Basic** button (or press [Alt]+[F11]).

   The Visual Basic Editor opens, displaying only the name of the project, and not the Code window.

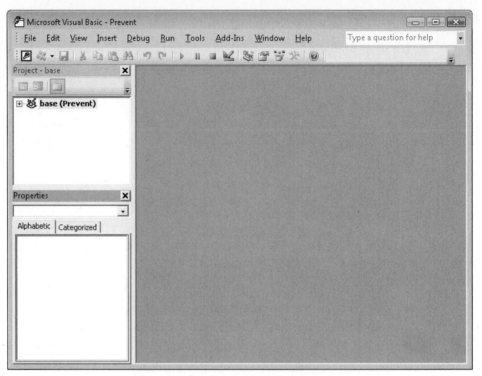

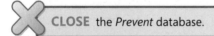
Expand

8. Click the **Expand** button to the left of the *Prevent* database project.

   The Password dialog box opens.

9. In the **Password** dialog box, type 2007!VbA, and then click **OK**.

   The project expands to display its components.

> **Tip** You need to enter the password only once per database session. In other words, you won't have to enter it again unless you close and reopen the database.

CLOSE the *Prevent* database.

> **Tip** To remove the password, on the Visual Basic Editor Tools menu, click Base Properties. On the Protection tab, clear the Lock Project For Viewing check box, delete the asterisks from the two password boxes, and then click OK.

Securing a Database for Distribution

When a database is used locally, on a local area network (LAN), or on a wide area network (WAN), you have considerable control over who has access to it. But if you send the database out into the world, on its own or as part of a larger application, you lose that control. There is no way you can know who is using the database or what tools they might have available to hack into it. If this is of concern to you, consider distributing your database as an Access Database Executable (ACCDE) file.

> **Tip** In previous versions of Access this was called a *Microsoft Database Executable (MDE)* file. The functionality and creation process are the same. If you open an older (Access 2002 or Access 2003) MDB file in Access 2007, a Make MDE command appears in the Database Tools group on the Database Tools tab in place of the Make ACCDE command that appears when you're working in an Access 2007 database.

Suppose you want to make a database available for use by several organizations in the area, but the organizations don't want their members to be able to change the database objects and perhaps "break" things. Saving a database as an ACCDE file compiles all modules, removes all editable source code, and compacts the destination database. Users of the ACCDE file can view forms and reports, update information, and run queries, macros, and VBA code. They *cannot* do the following:

- View, edit, or create forms, reports, or modules in Design view.
- Add, delete, or change references to other objects or databases.
- Modify VBA code.
- Import or export forms, reports, or modules.

Access can save a database as an ACCDE file only if it is in Access 2007 format. Access 2002 and Access 2003 databases can be saved as MDE files.

You can't convert a database from ACCDE format to the source ACCDB format, so after saving a database as an ACCDE file, retain the original ACCDB file in a safe place. If you need to make changes to forms, reports, or VBA code, you will have to make them in the original database and then save it as an ACCDE again.

Splitting a Database for Distribution

To help database performance and reliability in a shared implementation, such as when multiple people will access a database over a network at the same time, you can split the database into two parts: A back-end database containing the tables and a front-end database containing the forms, queries, and reports. To split a database:

1. Make a copy of the database on your computer, and then open it.

2. On the **Database Tools** tab, in the **Move Data** group, click the **Access Database** button. Then in the Database Splitter wizard, click **Split Database**.

3. In the **Create Back-end Database** dialog box, specify a name and storage location for the back-end database, click **Split**, and then click **OK** in the message box telling you that the split was successful.

   Distribute the front-end file (the one you started with) to the database users. It will automatically connect to the back-end file (stored in the location you specified in step 3).

In this exercise, you will secure a database by saving it as a distributable ACCDE file.

USE the *Distribute* database. This practice file is located in the *Documents\Microsoft Press\Access2007SBS\Securing* folder.

OPEN the *Distribute* database.

Make ACCDE

1. On the **Database Tools** tab, in the **Database Tools** group, click the **Make ACCDE** button.

2. In the **Save As** dialog box, navigate to the *Documents\Microsoft Press\Access2007SBS\Securing* folder, and then click **Save**.

   The process takes only a moment; no message alerts you when it is completed.

Microsoft Office Button

3. Click the **Microsoft Office Button**, and then click **Open**.

4. In the **Open** dialog box, navigate to the *Securing* folder.

   Access has created a database executable file named *Distribute.accde*. The file icon displays a blue lock over the standard Access icon.

> **Tip** The *Distribute.laccdb* file indicates that your database is locked, because it is currently open. When you close the database, the *.laccdb* file will disappear.

5. Double-click the *Distribute* database executable file, and if the **Microsoft Office Access Security Notice** message box appears, click **Open**.

6. In the **Navigation Pane**, right-click one object of each type (table, query, and so on), and note whether the **Design View** button on the shortcut menu is active.

    The Design View button is available for tables, queries, and macros, but unavailable for all other object types. This prevents you or another user from making any design changes to forms or reports, or changing any VBA code associated with the database.

CLOSE the *Distribute* database.

Important When creating an ACCDE file from a database with multiple users, first make sure that all other users close the database. You will know that someone else has the database open if you locate it in Windows Explorer and see a file of the same name, with an *.laccdb* (locked Access database) extension. If you open the database anyway, when you attempt to create the accde file you will be warned that the database is already opened by someone else (the username and machine name are provided) and told to try again later.

Collaborating Through SharePoint

If your organization has a Microsoft Office SharePoint Server 2007 collaboration site, you can manage data collection and distribution through that site, by making your Access database available online, in one of these ways:

- Migrate a database to a collaboration site. The Move To SharePoint Site wizard creates SharePoint lists linked to your database. The linked data can be accessed and managed from the collaboration site or from Access.

- Publish a database to a collaboration site. You can publish your database to a SharePoint library, and provide forms, queries, and reports through which other people can update or extract information.

After you make the database available to collaboration site users, they can work with the information as they would with any other SharePoint list content—online or offline—but they can also view the content as it would appear in Access, without first starting the program.

One benefit of sharing a database in this way is that permissions are regulated by SharePoint rather than set for the individual database. Another is that you can track changes made to the data by site users and recover previous versions of information, thus safeguarding against lost data in a way that you can't with Access alone.

Conversely, you can create a database from existing SharePoint lists, and integrate workflow processes with a database.

Key Points

- Your goal as a database developer is to adequately protect your database and the information it contains, without imposing unnecessary restrictions on the people who use it. The type of security required to protect a database depends on how many people are using it and where it is stored.

- You can encrypt a database, which does not prevent it from being opened and viewed in Access, but does keep people who don't have a copy of Access from reading or making sense of the data.

- You can assign a password to your database to prevent unauthorized users from opening it. The database is automatically encrypted when you assign it a password.

- If your database contains VBA procedures, you can protect your VBA code by assigning it a password, or by saving the database as an Access Database Executable (ACCDE) file. If you set a password for the code, it remains available for editing by anyone who knows the password. If you save the database as an ACCDE file, people using the file can run your code, but they can't view or edit it.

- Other members of your organization can input and extract data through a SharePoint collaboration site. By making database information available through SharePoint, you can regulate permissions, track changes, and manage versioning in ways that you can't within Access.

Glossary

Access Database Executable (ACCDE) A compiled version of a database. Saving a database as an ACCDE file compiles all modules, removes all editable source code, and compacts the destination database.

action query A type of query that quickly updates information or deletes selected records from a table. See also *crosstab query*, *select query*, and *parameter query*.

aggregate function A function, such as Sum, Avg, or Count, that groups fields and performs calculations on the field values.

append query A query that adds, or appends, records from one or more tables to the end of one or more tables.

arithmetic operator An operator that is used with numerals: + (addition), - (subtraction), * (multiplication), or / (division).

binary file A file composed of data that appears as gibberish in a word processing application and can be read only by a computer.

bound Linked, as when a text box is linked to a specific field in a table. See also *unbound*.

combo box A control that displays a list of choices when you click the arrow on its right side. It might also allow you to enter a different choice from those available on the list.

comma-delimited text file A text file in which each field is separated from the next by a comma.

command button A control that appears as a button, which performs an action when clicked.

comparison operator An operator that compares values: < (less than), > (greater than), and = (equal to). These operators can also be combined, as in <= (less than or equal to), >= (greater than or equal to), and <> (not equal to).

constant A part of an expression that represents a constant value.

control An object such as a label, text box, option button, or check box in a form or report that either displays information to people or allows people to enter information.

control property A setting, accessible through the Properties dialog box, that determines a control's appearance, and what kind of data it can display.

control source The Access object, such as a field, table, or query, to which a control is bound. See also *record source*.

crosstab query A query that calculates a sum, average, count, or other type of total for data that is grouped by two types of information. See also *action query, parameter query*, and *select query*.

custom group A user-created group containing a combination of categories, groups, and object shortcuts.

database application A database that is made easier to use by the inclusion of queries, forms, reports, a switchboard, custom categories and groups, and various other tools.

database program An application for creating databases, ranging from simple programs that can store one table per file (referred to as *flat databases*) to more complex programs that can store information in multiple related tables (referred to as *relational databases*).

database security Protecting data from accidental or intentional corruption, and making it difficult for unauthorized people to gain access to private information, through the use of passwords, encryption, ACCDE files, and other security measures.

database window The window in which all database objects are displayed.

Datasheet view The view in which you can see and modify information in a table or query. Along with Design view, one of the two most common views for tables. See also *view*.

delete query A query that deletes records that match a specified pattern from one or more tables.

delimited text file A text file in which each record and each field is separated from the next by a comma or other special character called a *delimiter*.

delimiter A character, such as a comma (,), semicolon (;), or backslash (\), that is used to separate records and fields in a delimited text file.

deselect Clicking away from selected data or controls to release the selection.

design grid In Design view, the grid in which you can manually work with advanced filters and queries.

Design view The view in which you can see and modify the structure of a table or query. Along with Datasheet view, one of the two most common views for tables. See also *view*.

Dialog Box Launcher A button that launches a dialog box containing options for refining a command.

digital signature A security mechanism used on the Internet that relies on two keys, one public and one private, which are used to encrypt messages before transmission and to decrypt them on receipt.

docking Dragging a toolbar, task pane, or similar item so it connects to one edge of the program window.

duplicate query A type of select query that finds records containing identical information in one or more specified fields.

empty string An Access field that has two quotation marks with nothing in between. Access is able to differentiate between an empty string and a Null (blank) field.

encrypting "Scrambling" data and applying a password for security reasons.

event An action, including Click, Double Click, Mouse Down, Mouse Move, and Mouse Up, to which code can be attached. The events recognized by an object are listed on the Event tab in the object's Property Sheet pane.

exclusive use A setting that permits only one person to have a database open, generally used when setting or removing a database password.

exporting The process of converting an Access table or database into a format that can be used by other programs. See also *importing*.

expression A combination of functions, field values, constants, and operators that can be used to assign properties to tables or forms, to determine values in fields or reports, as a part of a query, and in many other places. Also known as a *formula*.

Expression Builder A tool with which you can quickly create expressions (formulas) in queries, forms, and reports.

Extensible Markup Language (XML) Plain text files that indicate formatting within tags, similar to HTML tags, that specify the structure of the elements in a document.

field A specific category of information. Represented in Access as a column in a database table. See also *record*.

field property A property that controls what can be put into a field and how it can be placed there.

filtering A way to organize information so that some combination of characters is displayed or excluded from the display.

firing event The phrase used to describe when objects signal events in a form.

fixed-width text file A common text file format that is often used to transfer data from older applications. The same field in every record contains the same number of characters. If the actual data doesn't fill a field, the field is padded with spaces so that the starting point of the data in the next field is the same number of characters from the beginning of every record.

flat database A simple database program that can store information in only one table. See also *relational database*.

form An organized and formatted view of some or all of the fields from one or more tables or queries. Forms work interactively with the tables in a database.

function A named procedure or routine in a program, often used for mathematical or financial calculations.

group One of four elements—the other three being object, permission, and user—on which the Access user-level security model is based.

groups An organization of buttons on a tab.

grouping level The level by which records are grouped in a report. When you group on a field, the report will add a group header and and footer around each group of records that have the same value in that field.

HTML See *Hypertext Markup Language*.

HTML tag An HTML command that determines the display of tagged information in Web documents.

Hypertext Markup Language (HTML) An authoring language with which you mark up documents with tags for publication to the Web.

importing The process of converting outside data into a format that can be used by Access. See also *exporting*.

intranet A local network used for sharing data exclusively within a company or group.

label control A form control containing text as it will appear on the form.

LAN See *local area network (LAN)*.

linking The process of connecting to data in other applications so that you can view and edit it in both programs.

local area network (LAN) A network of computers, printers, and other hardware that covers a small area, such as a home or an office.

Lookup wizard An Access wizard with which you can easily create a lookup list.

macro A simple program that can perform multiple actions. A macro can respond to events such as opening forms, updating records, and clicking buttons.

main form A form that contains other embedded forms. See also *subform*.

main report A simple report that serves as a shell for one or more subreports, but displays little or no information from the underlying tables. See also *subreport*.

make-table query A query that combines all or part of the data from one or more tables into a new table.

many-to-many relationship Two one-to-many relationships tied together through a third table. See also *one-to-many relationship*; *one-to-one relationship*.

mapped network drive A network drive to which you have assigned a drive letter so that it can be accessed as a hard drive on your local computer. See also *universal naming convention (UNC) path*.

mask A property that controls the appearance, format, and type of data in a field.

Microsoft Database Executable (MDE) See *Access Database Executable (ACCDE)*.

Microsoft Office Button A button that gives access to a menu with commands that manage Word and Word documents as a whole (rather than document content).

module A Microsoft Visual Basic for Applications (VBA) program.

named range A group of cells in an Excel spreadsheet that you can import into an Access table.

object One of the components of an Access database, such as a table, query, form, report, page, macro, or module.

one-to-many relationship A relationship in which each record in one table is linked to multiple records in another table. See also *many-to-many relationship*; *one-to-one relationship*.

one-to-one relationship A relationship in which each record in one table has one and only one associated record in the other table. See also *many-to-many relationship*; *one-to-many relationship*.

operator See *arithmetic operator*; *comparison operator*.

option button A form control with which users can choose preselected settings.

parameter query A query that prompts for the information to be used in the query, such as a range of dates. This type of query is useful when used as the basis for a report that is run periodically. See also *action query, crosstab query*, and *select query*.

parsing The process of analyzing an imported document, such as an HTML document, and identifying anything that looks like structured data.

password An access code needed to open a secured database.

permission An attribute that specifies how a user can access data or objects in a database.

populate To add data to a table or other object.

primary key One or more fields (columns) whose values uniquely identify each record in a table. A primary key cannot allow Null values and must always have a unique index. A primary key is used to relate a table to foreign keys in other tables.

property A setting applied to an object that can determine its content, such as the Required and Input Mask properties, and appearance, such as the Font and Alignment properties.

publisher The person or entity who digitally signs a database or other file, thereby guaranteeing its source.

query A database object that locates specific information stored in a table and allows you to view and manipulate the results. The results of a query can be used as the basis for forms, reports, and data access pages.

Quick Access Toolbar A toolbar that displays the Save, Undo, Repeat, and Print buttons by default, but can be customized to show other commands.

record All the items of information (fields) in a table that are related to one particular entity, such as a customer, employee, or project. Represented in Access as a row in a database table. See also *field*.

record selector The gray bar along the left edge of a table or form. You can select an entire record by clicking the record selector next to it.

record source The source from which the data in a bound record originates. See also *control source*.

relational database A complex type of database in which data is stored in multiple related tables, allowing the tables to be treated as a single storage area. See also *flat database*.

relationship An association between common fields in two or more tables.

report A database object used to display table information in a formatted, easily accessible manner, either on the screen or on paper. It can include items from multiple tables and queries, values calculated from information in the database, and formatting elements such as headers, footers, titles, and headings.

result In an Access formula, the *result* equals the outcome of the equation.

Ribbon A group of tabs that appears across the top of the program window, replacing the layers of menus and toolbars in earlier versions of Access.

schema The structure of an XML file, contained in an *.xsd* file.

ScreenTip A small pop-up window containing information that appears when you hover the pointer over a command or control.

secure password A password that includes uppercase letters, lowercase letters, and symbols or numbers, and is not a word found in a dictionary. Also called a *strong password*.

security warning A warning that appears when a database that contains one or more macros is opened.

select query A query that retrieves, or selects, data matching specified criteria from one or more tables and displays the results in a datasheet. See also *action query, crosstab query*, and *parameter query*.

selector A small box attached to an object that you click to select the object, and drag to resize it.

signing The act of guaranteeing the source and content of a file by attaching a digital signature.

sorting Arranging information so that it's based on any field or combination of fields.

startup options Features available to users when a database is opened.

subdatasheet A datasheet that is contained within another datasheet.

subform A form contained within another form. See also *main form*.

subreport A report contained within another report. See also *main report*.

switchboard A hierarchy of pages containing buttons that the user can click to open additional pages, display dialog boxes, present forms for viewing and entering data, preview and print reports, and initiate other activities.

syntax The required format in which expressions must be entered.

tab An area on the Ribbon that contains commands organized in groups, which are related to working with document content.

tabbed documents The default display of objects in an Access window, in which the objects are displayed on tabbed datasheets, one behind the other.

table Information arranged in columns (records) and rows (fields).

tags Codes in HTML or XML that give instructions for formatting or defining the structure of a document, or other actions.

template A ready-made database application or table that users can adapt to meet their personal requirements.

text box control A control on a form or report in which text can be entered or edited.

title bar An area at the top of a document that displays the name of the active database object and contains the Maximize, Minimize/Restore Down, and Close buttons.

transaction record A record of transactions.

transform A type of template used to convert XML data to other formats.

unbound A control that is not linked to a field, as when it is being used to calculate values from multiple fields. See also *bound*.

undocking Dragging a toolbar, task pane, or similar item so it floats in the program window.

universal naming convention (UNC) path A path format that includes the computer name, drive letter, and nested folder names. It is the preferred format for linking to local area network (LAN) files. See also *mapped network drive*.

unmatched query A select query that locates records in one table without any related records in another table.

update query A select query that performs an action on the query's results in some way, such as by changing a field.

validation rule A field property that ensures entries contain only the correct types of information.

view The display of information from a specific perspective. Each Access object has two or more views, such as Datasheet view and Design view.

wildcard character A placeholder, such as an asterisk (*) or question mark (?) representing an unknown character or characters in search criteria.

workgroup A group of users in a multiuser environment who share data and the same workgroup information file. When you install Access, the setup program creates a default workgroup and sets up two groups, Admins and Users, within that workgroup.

worksheet A page in a Microsoft Office Excel spreadsheet, which can be imported into an Access table.

XML See *Extensible Markup Language (XML)*.

Index

A

.accdb file extension, 9, 40
ACCDE (Access Database Executable) files
  defined, 277, 285
  distributing databases as, 281
  saving databases as, lxv
Access
  closing, 14
  Help button, xxxiii–xxxiv
  integration with other Office programs, 10
  objects. See Access objects
  portability of skills, 9
  size restrictions, viewing, 14
  specifications, viewing, 14
  starting, 13
  starting, on Windows XP, xvi
  versions of, outdated, updating databases from, 57
Access button (Import group), 55
Access Database Executable (ACCDE) files
  defined, 277, 285
  distributing databases as, 281
  saving databases as, lxv
Access objects
  defined, 124, 288
  displaying all instances of, 14
  events recognized by, 124
  export formats available for, viewing, 80
  exporting, 79
  importing (see importing)
  forms. See forms; AutoForms
  macros. See macros
  modules. See modules
  queries. See queries; action queries; append
    queries; crosstab queries; delete queries;
    make-table queries; select queries; update
    queries
  reports (see reports)
  shortcuts, creating with custom groups (see
    custom groups)
  tables (see tables)
  uses for, 9
  views (see views)

Access Options window, 269
action queries. See also append queries; crosstab
    queries; delete queries; make-table queries;
    queries; select queries; update queries
  converting select queries to, 204
  creating, lvii, 204
  defined, 179, 285
  types of, 161
actions
  basic, 124
  defined, 286
  for objects, displaying list of, 125
Add Existing Fields button, 234
Add Group button, 260
add-ins for exporting to PDF/XPS files, 89
Add Item button, 260
address books (Outlook), importing from, 74
Advanced Filter Options button, 154, 157
Advanced Filter/Sort command, liv
aggregate functions, 174, 285
Align Left button, 230
Align Text Left button, 230
aligning
  form controls, l, 113
  report columns, lix
  report text, lix, 230
Allow Zero Length field property, 180
Analyze Table wizard, 211
analyzing performance, 211, 213
And operator, 152
append queries, 161, 285. See also action queries;
    crosstab queries; delete queries; make-table
    queries; queries; select queries; update queries
applications, database
  defined, 285
  macros in, 40
  specialized commands in, 40
  templates for (see templates)
  when appropriate, 37
Apply Filter button, liv
arithmetic operators, 285
  + (add), 152
  & (concatenate), 152
  / (divide), 152

E

F

S

What do you think of this book?

We want to hear from you!

Your feedback will help us continually improve our books and learning resources for you. To participate in a brief online survey, please visit:

microsoft.com/learning/booksurvey

...and enter this book's ISBN-10 or ISBN-13 number (appears above barcode on back cover). As a thank-you to survey participants in the U.S. and Canada, each month we'll randomly select five respondents to win one of five $100 gift certificates from a leading online merchant. At the conclusion of the survey, you can enter the drawing by providing your e-mail address, which will be used for prize notification only.*

Thank you in advance for your input!

Where to find the ISBN on back cover

Example only. Each book has unique ISBN.

Stay in touch!

To subscribe to the *Microsoft Press* Book Connection Newsletter—for news on upcoming books, events, and special offers—please visit:

microsoft.com/learning/books/newsletter